J o h B

Maintaining Focus, Energy, and Options Over the Career

A volume in
Research in Careers

Series Editors:
S. Gayle Baugh, *University of West Florida*
Sherry E. Sullivan, *Bowling Green State University*

Research in Careers

S. Gayle Baugh and Sherry E. Sullivan, Series Editors

Maintaining Focus, Energy, and Options Over the Career (2009)
edited by S. Gayle Baugh and Sherry E. Sullivan

Maintaining Focus, Energy, and Options Over the Career

S. Gayle Baugh
University of West Florida

and

Sherry E. Sullivan
Bowling Green State University

Information Age Publishing, Inc.
Charlotte, North Carolina • www.infoagepub.com

Library of Congress Cataloging-in-Publication Data

Maintaining focus, energy, and options over the career / edited by S. Gayle Baugh
and Sherry E. Sullivan.
    p. cm. — (Research in careers; v. 1)
  Includes bibliographical references.
  ISBN 978-1-59311-957-7 (pbk.) — ISBN 978-1-59311-958-4 (hbk.)
1. Career development. 2. Career changes. 3. Quality of work life.
I. Baugh, S. Gayle. II. Sullivan, Sherry E., 1961-
  HF5381.M2785 2009
  650.1—dc22

                                          2009014747

Printed in the United States of America

Dedication

This volume is dedicated to two special colleagues, Ellen Fagenson-Eland and Saroj Parasuraman, who left us much too soon. They both contributed greatly to enhance the scholarship in the careers field as well as to enrich the lives of those around them. We miss you dearly.

For Ellen:
Your energy and intellect proved to be quite an inspiration.
—Gayle

For Saroj:
Thank you for your wonderful spirit, courage, and wisdom.
—Sherry

CONTENTS

INTRODUCTION TO THE *RESEARCH IN CAREERS* SERIES

Welcome to the first volume of *Research in Careers*! This series is designed in five volumes to provide scholars a unique forum to examine career issues in today's changing, global workplace. What makes this series unique is that the volumes are connected by the use of Mainiero and Sullivan's (2006) Kaleidoscope Career Model (KCM) as the organizing framework and the theme underlying the volumes.

To understand how this series is organized requires a brief overview of the KCM (Mainiero & Sullivan, 2006). Just as rotating the tube of a kaleidoscope produces changing patterns when its glass chips fall into new arrangements, individuals change the patterns of their career by rotating the varied aspects of their life in order to arrange their relationships and roles in new ways. Individuals evaluate the choices and options available through the lens of the kaleidoscope to determine the best fit among work opportunities, constraints, and demands as well as relationships and personal values and interests. It is a dynamic model; each decision an individual makes will affect his or her kaleidoscope career pattern.

Like a kaleidoscope, which uses three mirrors to create infinite patterns, individuals focus on three key parameters when making decisions, thus creating the kaleidoscope pattern of their career. These key parameters are (a) *authenticity*, whereby the individual's internal values are aligned

Maintaining Focus, Energy, and Options Over the Career
pp. ix–xi
Copyright © 2009 by Information Age Publishing

with his or her external behaviors; (b) *balance,* such that the individual strives to reach an equilibrium between personal investments in work and nonwork pursuits; and (c) *challenge,* which is an individual's need for stimulating work (e.g., responsibility, autonomy) as well as career advancement. Over the course of the life span, as a person searches for the fit that best matches the character and context of his or her life, the kaleidoscope's parameters shift in response, with one parameter moving to the foreground and taking priority at that time. The other two parameters lessen in intensity and recede to the background, but are still present and active, as all three parameters are necessary to create the current pattern of an individual's life/career.

The KCM is based on the results of five different studies (interviews, focus groups, and three surveys) of over 3,000 U.S. professionals (Mainiero & Sullivan, 2006). Other independent studies have also supported the basic tenets of the KCM (Cabrera, 2007, in press; Godshalk, Nobel, & Line, 2007; Segers, Inceoglu, Vloeberghs, Bartram, & Henderickx, 2008).

Using the KCM as the foundation, we have organized the five volumes in this series to recognize the key points of the theory. The first volume, *Maintaining Focus, Energy, and Options Over the Career,* centers on how individuals enact their career and keep their career vital over the course of their life. The respective authors in this volume have examined current theories and research within the context of change over the life span, while acknowledging potential obstacles to career growth, transitions to new career phases, and renewal.

The second volume, *Searching for Authenticity,* focuses on a person's quest for authenticity, defined as an individual's need to be genuine to himself or herself and to do meaningful work. Within the context of an organization, authenticity includes the need for one's values to match the values of the employing firm. In volume 2, we will examine the intrinsic enjoyment of one's career, alternative career paths (especially those that are pursued for "love not money"), and career changes and transitions that are made in order to pursue something more important than or beyond money.

In volume 3, *Striving for Balance,* we will consider how individuals seek a healthy alignment between work and nonwork. In addition to building upon the established literature on work/family conflict, in this volume we will also examine the reciprocal positive influences between work and nonwork, considering such issues as balancing work with commitments to others, including spouse/partner, children, elderly relatives, friends, and the community.

In the fourth volume we will focus on *Seeking Challenge,* looking at why individuals need simulating work, what work and nonwork factors influence challenge, and the role played by others (e.g., leaders, mentors), who may contribute to an individual's career success. We will also explore how employer and individual needs can be matched so as to produce both personal challenge and organizational profitability.

In the fifth volume of the series we will examine *Threats and Opportunities*. The great opportunities offered by new career patterns as well as the possible losses and problems associated with nontraditional careers will be discussed. In this volume we will also look at how organizations are managing in this new work era and how nontraditional careers can be both a boon and a bane to them.

In sum, each volume represents an in-depth examination of a major theme within the field of careers. As such, each is independent of the others, providing the reader with original and varying perspectives on that volume's theme. Additionally, each volume will provide the novice and the established scholar alike with numerous ideas for future research. The five volume series, considered in its entirety, should provide the reader with a deeper understanding of the changing nature of careers as well as the factors that influence how individuals enact their career within and outside of the context of organizations. By organizing the series using the framework of the Kaleidoscope Career Model, we hope to provide a detailed and realistic examination of the increasing complex nature of careers in the twenty-first century.

REFERENCES

Cabrera, E. F. (2007). Opting out and opting in: Understanding the complexities of women's career transitions. *Career Development International, 12*, 218-237.

Cabrera, E. F. (in press). Protean organizations: Reshaping work and careers to retain female talent. *Career Development International.*

Godshalk, V. M., Noble, A. M., & Line, C. (2007, August). *High achieving women: An exploratory study of the differences between kaleidoscope career types.* Paper presented at the annual meeting of the Academy of Management, Philadelphia, PA.

Mainiero, L. A., & Sullivan, S. E. (2006). *The opt-out revolt: How people are creating kaleidoscope careers outside of companies.* New York: Davies-Black.

Segers, J., Inceoglu, I., Vloeberghs, D., Bartram, D., & Henderickx, E. (2008). Protean and boundaryless careers: A study on potential motivators. *Journal of Vocational Behavior, 73*, 212-230.

INTRODUCTION
TO THE VOLUME

This volume contains eight chapters that examine the theme of sustaining focus, energy, and career options over the life span derived from the Kaleidoscope Career Model (KCM; Mainiero & Sullivan, 2005; see *Introduction to the* Research in Careers *Series*). Emerging trends and issues are covered, including (a) the impact of changes in person-environment fit on careers over the life span, (b) the evolving nature of mentoring and other developmental relationships over the career, (c) generational differences in career development and learning, (d) the process of midcareer renewal, (e) the effect of aging upon career plateaus, (f) retirement and bridge employment, (g) gender differences in career enactment, and (h) women's use of self-initiated expatriation as a means of career development. Each chapter reflects the dynamic nature of contemporary careers and how careers change as individuals change in response to aging, learning, experience, and contextual changes.

In chapter 1, the dynamic nature of careers is clearly evident in Daniel Feldman and Ryan Vogel's analysis of person-environment (P-E) fit. While the changing nature of work environments has garnered a great deal of scholarly attention, the study of the changes in the "person" side of P-E fit has received scant empirical attention. Feldman and Vogel address this lack of research by providing a detailed examination of how aging impacts the level of P-E fit over time. As organizations and individuals

Maintaining Focus, Energy, and Options Over the Career
pp. xiii–xvii
Copyright © 2009 by Information Age Publishing
All rights of reproduction in any form reserved.

change, P-E fit may be lost and may require some effort for reestablishment. Based on a dynamic model of P-E fit, the authors offer specific propositions as well as avenues for future theory development and research.

While the dynamics of P-E fit are examined in the first chapter, in chapter 2 the evolution of developmental relationships over the life span is explored. Gayle Baugh and Sherry Sullivan suggest that as an individual's needs for authenticity, balance, and challenge change over the life span, the individual requires the assistance of multiple mentors or developers to meet these shifting needs. By integrating the research on multiple mentoring (Baugh & Scandura, 1999) and the KCM, the authors provide a new lens to study the career motives underlying the initiation, maintenance, adjustment, or termination of developmental relationships over the course of one's career.

Whereas in chapters 1 and 2 changes are considered in P-E fit and developmental relationships, respectively, as the individual ages, in chapter 3 age cohorts and generational differences are examined. The potential for conflict among employees of different generations has gained increasing attention in the popular press, fueled by anecdotal reports of the collision of workplace attitudes based on generational differences. The topic of generational differences in career attitudes, however, has been subject to little academic research. In their pioneering study, William Gentry, Tracy Griggs, Jennifer Deal, and Scott Mondore empirically test whether generational differences influence attitudes about learning and development. Despite the suggestions in recent literature that younger generations, due to their more protean career orientation and the necessity for taking responsibility for their own career, should hold stronger beliefs about the importance of continuous learning, Gentry and associates find few generational differences in beliefs about learning and development. Along the same lines, plans for developmental activities and preferences for learning techniques are also quite similar across generations. The authors offer interesting directions for future research based on their unexpected results.

Like Gentry and associates' study of generational differences in learning, in chapter 4 Dianne Bown-Wilson and Emma Parry investigate why some workers, particularly those in midlife, engage in continuous learning while others plateau. Most of the previous research on plateauing was completed during the downsizing era of the 1980s. Bown-Wilson and Parry offer a refreshingly new perspective on career plateaus. They offer a contemporary model of career plateaus based on a consideration of career attributes, career decisions, and career motivators, and conclude that career plateaus are not necessarily a negative phenomenon for either the individual or the organization.

Following Bown-Wilson's and Parry's investigation of midlife plateau-ing, in chapter 5 factors that influence midcareer renewal are examined. Using the lens of career counseling and vocational psychology, Sally Power provides novel insights on midcareer renewal. Although scholars from many disciplines (e.g., social work, psychotherapy, education, adult development, and management) have studied renewal over the last 50 years, the literature is fragmented, with no consensus even on the defini-tion of career renewal. Based on a review and critical analysis of theories and research on renewal, Power offers an integrative definition of midca-reer renewal and a framework to guide future research on this neglected area of study.

Moving from midcareer to later career, in chapter 6, Mo Wang, Gary Adams, Terry Beehr, and Kenneth Shultz direct their attention to the changing relationship between workforce participation and retirement. Traditionally, the transition to retirement has been viewed as the end of an individual's career, representing a permanent exit from the workplace. Wang and associates challenge the traditional notion of retirement, offer-ing instead a dynamic model that suggests retirement can be a period of growth, change, and continued career development. In this chapter, they explain why individuals may cycle in and out of the workplace between retirement and various forms of bridge employment (e.g., full-time and part-time work as well as self-employment) and the outcomes of these multiple exits and entries over time.

Chapter 7 and 8 round out the volume by providing in-depth analyses of gender differences in the enactment of careers. In chapter 7, Theresa Smith-Ruig presents her qualitative findings testing the popular bound-aryless career concept (Sullivan & Arthur, 2006) and the KCM. Despite the common belief that the traditional, organizational career is dead, Smith-Ruig suggests that professional context may influence whether an individual has a more traditional or boundaryless career. Half of the Aus-tralian accountants she studied enacted traditional organizational careers—hardly the sea change in career systems that is implied in much of the literature on careers. In addition, she found gender differences in career patterns consistent with predictions of the KCM. She offers a num-ber of intriguing questions for future research with regard to the influence of context on career development.

In chapter 8, Phyllis Tharenou examines how the increasingly global-ized workplace has created opportunities for careers that cross national borders. She explores the growing trend of self-initiated expatriates—professionals who initiate and finance their own expatriation in order to take advantage of profitable and personally rewarding work prospects abroad. Unlike participation in company-assigned expatriation, where participation among women lags behind that of men, women engage in self-initiated expatriation as much as men do. Tharenou analyzes why women are using self-initiated expatriation as a new option for career development and asks the provocative question. Are the same factors that constrain career advancement for women in the domestic workplace going to affect women's advancement in the global workplace? Drawing from the literatures on expatriation, gender differences, and career development, Tharenou establishes an ambitious research agenda for scholars.

In addition to thanking the authors included in this volume for contributing their excellent scholarship, there are a number of other individuals who should also be recognized for their contributions to this work. First, we owe a large debt of gratitude to our reviewers who offered thoughtful comments and shaped the development of the chapters. Each chapter was blind-reviewed by at least two independent reviewers. The chapters, all strong contributions to begin with, benefited from the insights offered by these outstanding reviewers. The reviewers for this volume were Susan Adams (Bentley University), Gary Blau (Temple University), Jon Briscoe (Northern Illinois University), Shawn Carraher (Cameron University), Madeline Crocitto (State University of New York at Old Westbury), Deborah Ettington (Pennsylvania State University), Monica Forret (St. Ambrose University), Martin Greller (The New School), Hugh Gunz (University of Toronto), Linda Hite (Indiana University-Purdue University), Maria Kraimer (University of Iowa), Lisa Mainiero (Fairfield University), Deborah O'Neil (Bowling Green University), Matt Quigley (Reed Center for Diversity and Careers), Barbara Ribbens (Western Illinois University), Denise Rotondo (Meredith College), Terri Scandura (University of Miami), Siri Terjesen (Indiana University), Howard Tu (University of Memphis), and Susan Vinnicombe (Cranfield University).

Second, we each want to extend our gratitude to our department chair and dean for their support for producing this volume. Gayle Baugh appreciates the good humor and constant support of Arup Mukherjee, department chair, and Ed Ranelli, dean, in the College of Business at the University of West Florida. Sherry Sullivan sincerely thanks her department chair, Janet Hartley, and her dean, Rodney Rogers, in the College of Business Administration at Bowling Green State University for their support.

Third, we thank Evelyn Grosse, proof-reader extraordinaire. Evelyn has patiently read every word of this volume, keeping authors and editors alike aware of the rules of grammar and of the American Psychological Association style guide. Her attention to detail is very much appreciated. We are responsible, of course, for any remaining errors in the volume.

Fourth, the most important individual in the development of this series is our wonderful publisher, George Johnson of Information Age Publishing. We are deeply grateful to him for understanding the importance of research on careers and encouraging us to take on this series. He has provided support and guidance throughout the project and we are very happy to be working with him.

And finally, we thank you, the reader, for your interest in this volume and series. We hope the chapters provide you not only with expert knowledge and insights, but inform and inspire your own research in careers.

REFERENCES

Baugh, S., & Scandura, T. A. (1999). The effect of multiple mentors on protégé attitudes toward the work setting. *Journal of Social Behavior and Personality, 14*, 503-522.

Mainiero, L. A., & Sullivan, S. E. (2005). Kaleidoscope careers: An alternative explanation for the opt-out generation. *Academy of Management Executive, 19*(1), 106-123.

Sullivan, S. E., & Arthur, M. B. (2006). The evolution of the boundaryless career concept: Examining physical and psychological mobility. *Journal of Vocational Behavior, 69*, 19-29.

CHAPTER 1

THE AGING PROCESS AND PERSON-ENVIRONMENT FIT

Daniel C. Feldman and Ryan M. Vogel

The construct of "fit" is arguably the first construct to have emerged within the field of organizational behavior. Researchers and practitioners alike have acknowledged the importance of achieving congruence between individuals' abilities and organizations' demands, particularly since the publication of Chris Argyris's *Integrating the Individual and the Organization* (1964). While scholarship in this area has been performed across different disciplines and under different labels, what is now known as "person-environment fit" (P-E fit) has important implications for workers' attitudes and behaviors as well as for organizational outcomes and effectiveness (Kristof, 1996; Tinsley, 2000).

As Ostroff, Shin, and Feinberg (2002) note, most P-E research focuses on "static fit," that is, it examines relatively stable aspects of the person (e.g., "Big 5" personality traits) and relatively stable aspects of the environment (e.g., organizational values) at one point in time. However, as both Tinsley (2000) and Schneider (1987) point out, achieving P-E fit is a dynamic process. Jobs, organizations, and occupations change over time; individuals change over time. Moreover, changes in work environments create changes in individuals (e.g., mass layoffs lead to more job insecu-

Maintaining Focus, Energy, and Options Over the Career
pp. 1–26
Copyright © 2009 by Information Age Publishing
All rights of reproduction in any form reserved.

rity in individuals), while changes in individuals create changes in work environments (e.g., more working parents wanting and receiving parental leaves from organizations). Individuals can maintain focus, energy, and options across the life span only by re-establishing fit as they age and organizations change.

When Argyris (1964) was writing about congruence over 40 years ago, the vast majority of workers were employed in the same occupation and/or organization for most of their careers. Today, though, careers are more "boundaryless" (Arthur, 1994), with individuals experiencing much more mobility across both occupations and organizations. Part of that increased mobility is due to changes in organizational contexts, such as widespread restructuring, which make the "environment" side of the fit equation a moving target (Feldman & Ng, 2007).

However, while dynamic work environments have received a great deal of attention from researchers, changes in the "person" side of the equation have received far less. There are several reasons for this research imbalance. First, much of the research on the person side of the equation has been cross-sectional in nature, and so intra-individual changes that might affect fit over time are infrequently examined. A second reason is that much of the research on the person side of the equation has been on individual differences (particularly personality traits), which almost by definition do not change dramatically over time (cf. Bradley, Brief, & George, 2002). Third, at least historically, the vocational psychology literature has largely focused on early career as the stage at which P-E fit is achieved. Consequently, much of what we know about P-E fit comes from studies of young adults just beginning their career and finding their first jobs and employers (Osipow, 1990).

To address this imbalance, the present chapter focuses primarily on the person side of the fit equation and how intra-individual changes impact the level of P-E fit over time. More specifically, the chapter examines the role that aging plays in the achievement, maintenance, and decline of person-environment fit across the life span. The aging process contributes to major changes in individuals' cognitive abilities, physical capabilities, emotions, values, and goals (Kanfer & Ackerman, 2004). Taken together, these age-related changes not only have direct effects on P-E fit but also strengthen (or weaken) the relationships between P-E fit and important outcome variables (e.g., core job performance and citizenship behavior).

In the first section of this chapter, then, we review the P-E fit literature, especially the different types of fit and their impact on work outcomes. In the second section, we examine the multitude of changes that occur with aging and how those changes might affect different components of P-E fit. In the third section, we present specific propositions regarding the effects of aging on fit, while in the fourth section we look at how aging might strengthen or attenuate the relationships of P-E fit with employees' attitudes and behaviors. Finally, in the last section, we discuss avenues for future theory development and research methodology.

THE NATURE OF PERSON-ENVIRONMENT FIT

The ways in which P-E fit has been conceptualized and operationalized have varied widely over the years. Some of the most frequently used distinctions in the person-environment fit literature—and their likely impact on outcome variables—are briefly discussed below.

Abilities-Demands Versus Needs-Supplies Fit

These two types of P-E fit were made distinct in early work by Dawis, Lofquist, and Weiss (1968) and Caplan, Cobb, French, Harrison, and Pinneau (1975). Abilities-demands fit refers to the extent to which an individual's physical abilities, cognitive skills, education, and work experience match the demands of the work environment. In contrast, needs-supplies fit refers to the extent to which an organization fulfills an individual's needs, goals, and desires (for example, through providing high salaries or promotions). Abilities-demands fit has been most frequently linked to high core task performance and tenure in the occupation, while needs-supplies fit has been more frequently linked to discretionary citizenship behaviors and job satisfaction (Tinsley, 2000).

Supplementary Versus Complementary Fit

When an individual's skills, abilities, and needs are similar to those of others in the organization, P-E fit is said to be supplementary (Ostroff et al., 2002). That is, the individual possesses many of the same skills and interests as other employees in the organization. In contrast, when an individual's skills and interests are dissimilar to those of other employees in the organization, P-E fit is said to be complementary (Muchinsky & Monahan, 1987). In this case, the individual brings new or different abilities and perspectives to the group.

As might be expected, the outcomes of supplementary and complementary P-E fit parallel those associated with relational demography. Because individuals with supplementary fit find others who are very similar to themselves, they tend to experience higher job satisfaction and are rated more highly on their job performance by supervisors. Workers with complementary fit might help the group perform more effectively as a unit, but individuals with complementary fit might feel more isolated and less integrated into the group (Chatman, 1991; Kristof-Brown, Zimmerman, & Johnson, 2005; Ostroff et al., 2002).

Levels of Fit

Several researchers have disaggregated the construct of environment into more specific components and have examined these different "levels of fit" separately. Each of these levels describes a distinctive part of an individual's work environment and can add unique variance in explaining the impact of P-E fit on employees' attitudes and behaviors (O'Reilly, Chatman, & Caldwell, 1991).

Person-vocation fit. At the broadest level, fit may be achieved between an individual and his/her chosen profession. Person-vocation fit (P-V) refers to the alignment of an individual's skills, interests, and needs to the requirements and rewards of an occupation. Thus, person-vocation fit combines both abilities-fit and needs-fit on the person-side of the equation and both vocational demands and supplies on the environment side of the equation.

Historically, P-V fit has been of particular concern to scholars interested in early career issues, since initial P-V fit is of critical importance to subsequent career success (Feldman & Ng, 2007; Holland, 1985). However, skills, interests, and values change over time, often making it necessary for individuals to renegotiate P-V fit along the way (Assouline & Meir, 1987; Spokane, 1985; Tranberg, Slane, & Ekeberg, 1993). Further, in an era of "boundaryless careers," the demands and supplies offered by vocations change over time as well (Bird, 1994). In sum, then, while it is theoretically possible to achieve fit at the organization, job, or group level without achieving P-V fit first, in practice it would be very hard to do so.

Person-organization fit. Person-organization fit (P-O) refers to the congruence between individuals and the organizations for which they work (Kristof et al., 2005). Most commonly, measures of P-O fit have tapped value congruence, since individuals frequently exert more effort when they work in environments which support their personal beliefs and values (Verquer, Beehr, & Wagner, 2003). P-O fit is also the type of fit that has been most frequently studied in the literature. By and large, P-O fit has shown strong positive relationships with a wide range of employee attitudes, job behaviors, and indicators of performance (Vancouver & Schmitt, 1991).

Person-job fit. Person-job fit (P-J) refers to the degree of congruence between the individual and his/her job (Edwards, 1991). It can be achieved when the individual's skills and abilities match the specific tasks of a job (abilities-demands fit) (Bretz, 1993) and/or when the needs of the worker are met by the rewards provided by the job (needs-supplies fit) (Rynes, Bretz, & Gerhart, 1991).

Like P-O fit, person-job fit has been linked to a variety of positive outcomes (Chatman, 1991; Kristof-Brown, 2000). However, as the literature on job embeddedness suggests, it is often hard to disentangle the *job* environment from the *organization* environment in practice. For example, it is sometimes hard to distinguish whether pay is a supply associated with the organization or with the job, particularly where both P-J fit and P-O fit are defined in part by skill fit (Feldman & Ng, 2007).

Person-group fit. Person-group fit (P-G) refers to the interpersonal compatibility of an individual with other members of the work group (Jackson, Brett, Sessa, Cooper, Julin, & Peyronnin, 1991; Judge & Ferris, 1992). Previous research suggests that individuals seek out environments in which they share the goals and values of coworkers (Chatman, 1991; Harrison, Price, & Bell, 1998), while the attraction-similarity-attrition (ASA) model suggests that individuals who do not achieve fit on this dimension are more likely to leave their organization (Byrne, 1971; Schneider, 1987).

By and large, person-vocation fit and person-job fit have been most closely tied to skill-related outcomes, such as core task performance and tenure in position. In contrast, person-group fit has been tied more consistently to overall job satisfaction and discretionary extra-role behaviors (Feldman, 2007). Having strong bonds with coworkers seems to elevate job attitudes and energize individuals to go above and beyond the call of duty to help others.

Static Versus Dynamic Fit

The final distinction we consider in the fit literature is the difference between static and dynamic fit. Static fit refers to the degree of P-E fit at any one point in time, while dynamic fit refers to changes in the degree of P-E fit over time (Ostroff et al., 2002). While the research difficulties associated with collecting longitudinal data on P-E fit are substantial, several scholars have noted that measuring static fit at one particular moment does not provide an accurate sense of how individuals and environments mesh in the long run (Tinsley, 2000). Rather, achieving fit should be viewed as a dynamic process, with changes in individuals requiring changes in environments and changes in environments requiring changes in individuals.

Consider, for example, the role of information technology in the achievement of P-E fit. As technology improves and new practices are adopted by organizations, the skills required to perform jobs satisfactorily can change substantially. Individuals cannot sustain high P-J fit without considerable retraining or without transferring to a job requiring less information technology (IT). At the same time, the widespread adoption of IT by organizations has forced many individuals to acquire or upgrade their skills in IT, whether or not those skills are really their true interest.

AGE-RELATED CHANGES IN INDIVIDUALS

Aging is the most powerful intra-individual force for change in P-E fit (Avolio & Waldman, 1994; Levinson, 1979). Aging affects virtually every aspect of an individual's capabilities and interests in work, including his or her cognitive skills, physical abilities, values, life goals, and emotions. The changes that accompany aging, singly or in combination, can substantially alter the degree of fit individuals experience with their vocation, organization, job, and work group.

Many conceptualizations of age exist in the organizational sciences literature. Shore and Goldberg (2005) point out that age can be thought of in terms other than *chronological* age. For example, they highlight the importance of *normative* age (the age at which people typically hold certain positions), *subjective* age (how old people feel), and *relative* age (how old people are relative to others in their work group), all of which may be considered important when discussing age.

Nonetheless, even Shore and Goldberg (2005) acknowledge that chronological age is the most reliably measured and widely used definition of age. Because many of the effects of aging are most highly associated with chronological age, our discussion of age largely focuses on this conceptualization, but we do consider these other types of age later in the chapter.

Cognitive Abilities

While there is not complete consistency across studies in the literature (cf. Ng & Feldman, 2008a), the weight of the evidence suggests that cognitive abilities decline somewhat with age, with the declines more noticeable after middle age (Park, 2000; Willis & Schaie, 1999). Reaction time (Ratcliff, Thapar, & McKoon, 2001), working memory capacity (Spencer & Raz, 1995), inhibition function (Hasher & Zacks, 1988), dual-task performance (Verhaeghen, Steitz, Sliwinski, & Cerella, 2003), spatial and reasoning abilities (Salthouse, Mitchell, Skovronek, & Babcock, 1989), and verbal memory span (Bopp & Verhaeghen, 2005) all decline with age. This "slowing" phenomenon has been observed across diverse sets of tasks and jobs (Cerella, 1994; Cerella, Poon, & Williams, 1980; Faust, Balota, Spieler, & Ferraro, 1999).

While overall cognitive abilities may decline with age, there may not be commensurate drops in core task performance (Ng & Feldman, 2008a). Two explanations have been offered for why performance may remain stable even after cognitive abilities decline somewhat. Kanfer and Ackerman (2004) make a distinction between "fluid intelligence" (cognitive processes used to process new information) and "crystallized intelligence" (knowledge and experience accumulated over time). Thus, one explanation is that these increases in crystallized intelligence can counteract declines in fluid intelligence that occur with aging (Warr, 2001). A second explanation is that, as individuals age, they become more aware of this *slowing* phenomenon and compensate by increasing their work effort (Bunce & Sisa, 2002) or becoming more conscientious about their job (Farr & Ringseis, 2002).

As cognitive abilities decline with age, there may be changes in the degree of person-environment fit. Particularly in vocations and jobs where fluid intelligence (e.g., quick information processing, multi-tasking, and memory) are important ingredients of job success, P-V fit and P-J fit are likely to decline. The declines in P-O fit and P-G fit directly attributable to declines in cognitive ability may not be especially large, however, since cognitive ability is a less dominant factor in achieving or maintaining these types of P-E fit.

Physical Abilities

Work-related physical abilities are unlikely to decline noticeably until late middle age (Fielding & Meydani, 1997). Moreover, the jobs of many workers do not require much physical ability (in terms of strength, endurance, and speed) at all. For those workers whose jobs do require physical abilities, however, age-related declines in those abilities do hinder job performance over the life span. In general, declines in physical abilities are most likely to affect P-V fit and P-J fit, but have little direct or independent effects on P-O and P-G fit.

As people age, muscle strength declines, the rebuilding of muscles takes longer (Khalil & Merhi, 2000; McArdle, Vasilaki, & Jackson, 2002), bone loss begins to occur (Currey, Brear, & Zioupos, 1996), and the metabolism slows down (Sterns & Miklos, 1995). On the positive side, older employees tend to work more slowly and, as a result, tend to incur fewer work-related injuries (Sterns, Barrett, & Alexander, 1985). On the negative side, when older adults have work-related accidents, those incidents tend to be more severe and require longer recovery time (Sterns et al., 1985; Warr, 1994). Along the same lines, older workers are more conscientious and are less likely to take unnecessary "sick days" (Farr & Ringseis, 2002), but the length of time associated with each illness absence increases with age (Thomson, Griffiths, & Davison, 2000).

Values

Unlike the cases of cognitive and physical abilities, the issue surrounding values is not whether values decline, per se. Values are sets of enduring beliefs individuals use to set standards of acceptable behavior both for themselves and for others (Rokeach, 1973; Ros, Schwartz, & Surkiss, 1999; Schwartz, 1992). As such, values cannot be hierarchically ranked; rather, the issue here is whether individuals' values change as they age and how those changes affect the degree of P-E fit.

Previous research suggests that, as individuals grow older, they place different priorities on extrinsic and intrinsic rewards (Borg, 1990; van der Velde, Feij, & van Emmerik, 1998). That is, as individuals get older, they place less value on the extrinsic rewards of a job (e.g., pay and advancement opportunities) and more value on passing along their knowledge to the next generation (Levinson, 1979; Mor-Barak, 1995). Another key finding has been that, as individuals age, they direct more energy toward organizationally-valued outcomes and less time to their own personal career advancement (Bégat, Ellefsen, & Severinsson, 2005; Feldman, Doerpinghaus, & Turnley, 1995). Furthermore, as individuals grow older their values regarding social interactions change, too (Kacmar & Ferris, 1989). Younger people tend to focus on broadening their social circles and business networks, while older people want to spend more time with close friends and family and reduce the amount of energy they invest in peripheral relationships (Carstensen, Pasupathi, Mayr, & Nesselroade, 2000; Wright & Hamilton, 1978).

Changes in values are most likely to impact P-O and P-G fit because needs-supplies congruence is a key component of these two types of fit. On the other hand, value changes which occur with aging are less likely to impact P-V fit and P-J fit because these two types of fit are more concerned with abilities-demands congruence.

Life Goals

Consistent with the earlier discussion of values, researchers have also found that individuals' life goals change with age. More specifically, young adults are largely concerned with goals that revolve around themselves (most notably, their own education and career development), while middle-aged and older workers are more likely to emphasize contributing to the well-being of their children, families, and friends (Nurmi, 1992). Individuals at different life stages also utilize different strategies for selecting life goals (Baltes, 1997; Baltes & Baltes, 1990; Freund & Baltes, 2002). Compared to young adults, older adults set fewer goals because they have more limited resources (in terms of time and energy) available to achieve them (Lachman, 2004).

To date, there has been little research which has directly examined how shifting life goals affect different types of P-E fit. Extrapolating from what we do know, older workers' increased focus on their families and friends seems likely to take away energy previously devoted to achieving P-E fit at work.

Emotions

Finally, socioemotional selectivity theory (Carstensen, 1995; Carstensen, Isaacowitz, & Charles, 1999) suggests that as individuals get older, they perceive time is running out and may start pursuing some other activities they find emotionally gratifying, as well. In particular, older adults display less "negativity bias" than young adults (Charles, Mather, & Carstensen, 2003). That is, when young adults evaluate situations, they tend to focus more attention on the negative aspects. In contrast, older adults attend more closely to the positive aspects of their environments. Researchers have noted that these changes in emotions are not driven by increases in trait positive affect, which remains fairly stable with age; rather, there are observable decreases in trait negative affect that occur with aging (Ryff, 1989). In addition, older adults are much more likely than younger ones to use positive emotions to deal with personal and work-related problems (Folkman, Lazarus, Pimley, & Novacek, 1987).

As with the case of life goals, there is little research which directly examines the impact of age-related changes in emotions on person-environment fit. Our expectation would be that these changes in emotions would lead older workers to put more time and energy into sustaining P-G fit because the work group can be a source of immediate gratification and affirmation. In contrast, older adults might put less energy into achieving P-O fit because the organization is a more distal and abstract referent.

THE EFFECTS OF AGING ON P-E FIT

The age-related changes we identified above may have significant consequences for individuals' abilities to achieve and maintain person-environment fit. Below we consider the effects of aging on different levels of P-E fit.

Person-Vocation Fit

P-V fit is initially achieved at the beginning of workers' careers when individuals have made their first serious assessments of their interests, skills, and needs. Certainly, young adults are taking longer to decide upon their vocation than they used to, as norms about "keeping options open" and "finding oneself" have become stronger (Feldman, 2002, 2007). However, even if there have been delays in choosing a vocation, the search for good P-V fit is especially strong when individuals are young adults.

The attraction-selection-attrition (ASA) model (Schneider, 1987) helps us understand how vocational fit might decline with age. Individuals who share common interests or have similar personalities are attracted to the same types of vocations. Consequently, young adults are simultaneously attracted to both the kinds of work and the kinds of people associated with a given career. However, as the context, tasks, and colleagues in a career change over time, individuals may experience corresponding declines in P-V fit. For instance, many young doctors who eagerly entered medicine in the 1970s now find themselves, in late middle age, in a career they barely recognize.

Moreover, declines in cognitive abilities and physical abilities that co-occur with aging may accentuate those declines in P-V fit (Farr & Ringseis, 2002). Older workers who are unable or unwilling to change skills and interests will find themselves increasingly out of sync with others in their profession. In addition, because individuals' motivation to seek out new work environments also declines with age (Farr & Ringseis, 2002), older workers may be less inclined to look for new vocations as P-V fit worsens. Thus, we predict:

P1:   Age is inversely related to P-V fit.

Person-Organization Fit

P-O fit is also likely to be high at the beginning of a career. Organizational socialization processes tend to be most powerful in early career, as companies try to inculcate organizational values and norms into relatively young and malleable new hires (Chatman, 1991; Davis, 1965; Holland, 1976; Johnson, 2001). As workers age, though, person-organization fit with employers may decline (Mishel, Bernstein, & Schmitt, 2001). At the environmental level, there may be changes in corporate values and priorities that make the present employer less attractive to older employees. Equally important, intra-individual changes in values, life goals, and emotions may make P-O fit decline over time, even if the organizational context does not change at all (Meglino & Ravlin, 1998).

Moreover, older workers may have more difficulty in finding alternative employers where P-O fit might be higher. First, older individuals are more selective about the types of environments in which they are willing to work (Farr & Ringseis, 2002); they are less willing to settle for marginal fit. Second, older adults are more likely to be subjected to age discrimination in the workplace (Ng & Feldman, 2008a). Unfortunately, older workers are frequently stereotyped as poorer performers and as more difficult to train (Lyon & Pollard, 1997; Vrugt, 1996; Wang, Adams, Beehr, & Shultz, this volume). For both these reasons, then, we predict:

P2:   Age is inversely related to P-O fit.

Person-Job Fit

In early career, individuals are more motivated to find jobs which match their interests than their abilities (Feldman, 2002). Fortunately, organizations spend much of their training budgets on young new hires just starting their career, so initial lack of skill fit can be mitigated. However, as job demands increase over time, older workers without good initial skill fit find themselves having to exert more and more effort just to keep up.

Further, as the embeddedness literature suggests, it is very hard to change jobs without changing organizations, too (Feldman & Ng, 2007). Consequently, the age discrimination barriers that prevent older workers from changing organizations also inhibit older workers from changing jobs (Shore & Goldberg, 2005). In addition, as a group, older workers tend to have lower self-esteem than their younger colleagues (Robins, Trzesniewski, Tracy, Gosling, & Potter, 2002) and are reluctant to put their self-concept on the line in risky situations (Ng & Feldman, 2008b). For this reason, too, older workers tend to find job hunting quite aversive.

Another issue regarding the effects of aging on person-job fit warrants attention. As noted previously, much of the research in this area has focused on declines in abilities and resulting declines in job performance and marketability. However, equally problematic is the "underemployment" older workers experience as they stay in their job long periods of time (Feldman, 2007). That is, performance of older workers may drop off not because abilities decline but because their motivation does. Thus, low P-J fit can also occur because older workers now find their job monotonous and unfulfilling (Maurer, 2001). More training on the current job, even if offered, would not fix the problem of low intrinsic motivation (Kubeck, Delp, Haslett, & McDaniel, 1996; Warr, 1993). Thus, we predict:

P3:   Age is inversely related to P-J fit.

Person-Group Fit

In contrast, we expect that P-G fit will increase with age. As noted above, older individuals tend to derive more satisfaction from their social relationships than their younger counterparts do. In addition, as a group, older workers have higher social needs than achievement needs (Kacmar & Ferris, 1989; van der Velde et al., 1998). Consequently, these higher social needs are likely to drive older workers to develop stronger personal relationships within the workplace and, as a result, we anticipate that older workers will experience greater levels of P-G fit.

The ASA model (Schneider, 1987) predicts that individuals who are similar in demographic background and personal style are more attracted to (and are more likely to be selected to) work with each other. Furthermore, homogeneity of interests evokes interpersonal liking among coworkers and decreases the likelihood of affective conflict (Jehn, 1995). Over time, those individuals who are unhappy with the group are more likely to leave, while individuals who are happy with their colleagues are likely to develop even stronger affective bonds (Mishel et al., 2001). This model, too, would predict that P-G fit would be stronger for older workers than for younger workers.

There are some scenarios, though, in which P-G fit might decline as individuals age. First, a job that once had good P-G fit might become one with poor P-G fit as members of the original work group start retiring. In addition, individuals who have supplementary fit might experience greater declines in P-G fit than individuals who have complementary fit. While the original work group might have been willing to tolerate a very different perspective or a very different work style, the tolerance of the group as a whole may decline as original team members leave and new ones come on board. In general, however, we believe that P-G fit is more likely to increase than decrease with age.

P4:   Age is positively related to P-G fit.

THE MODERATING EFFECTS OF AGE

In the preceding section, we examined the ways in which age directly affects person-environment fit. In this section, we examine the ways in which age can also strengthen (or attenuate) the relationships between P-E fit and important outcome variables, depending upon which type of P-E fit and which dependent variable we consider.

Below, we briefly introduce the employee attitudes and behaviors most frequently associated with P-E fit, including core task performance, citizenship behaviors, turnover behavior, and career success (Bretz & Judge, 1994; Kristof-Brown et al., 2005). Then, we consider how age might moderate the relationships between different types of P-E fit and different outcome variables. While we cannot consider every potential moderating relationship, we do address what we believe are the most important and informative relationships in the following sections.

Outcome Variables

In-role performance. Not surprisingly, individuals who have achieved P-E fit (particularly in terms of abilities-demands fit) are likely to perform better on core job tasks (Edwards, 1991). There is some evidence that poor P-E fit (in terms of needs-supplies fit) contributes to poor job performance, too, since employees who are psychologically disengaged from their work may grow bored and careless on their jobs (Humphrys & O'Brien, 1986).

Citizenship behaviors. Organizational citizenship behaviors (OCBs) are voluntary behaviors engaged in by employees, outside the scope of the formal reward system, that are directed toward helping coworkers or the organization as a whole (Podsakoff, MacKenzie, Paine, & Bachrach, 2000). A distinction is often made between two categories of OCBs on the basis of the "target" of assistance, with one set referred to as OCB-others (e.g., helping others who have been absent or adjusting one's work schedule to accommodate others' requests for time off) and the other set referred to as OCB-organization (e.g., adhering to informal workplace rules or offering ideas to improve the functioning of the organization) (Organ, 1997). Previous research suggests that when individuals identify highly with an organization and view their own future as tied to it, they are more likely to go above and beyond their formal job requirements (O'Reilly & Chatman, 1986).

Turnover. The weight of the evidence suggests that individuals with high P-E fit are less likely to think about leaving their employer (Edwards, 1991; Griffeth, Hom, & Gaertner, 2000; Kristof-Brown et al., 2005).

Workers with good skill fit, for example, are more likely to receive greater extrinsic rewards (e.g., pay and promotions), which make leaving less attractive. Similarly, individuals who are compatible with their coworkers are more likely to feel bound to their employer, since individuals with close social ties feel *embedded* or *entrenched* where they are (Carson et al., 1995; Feldman & Ng, 2007). The ASA model, too, suggests that individuals with high P-E fit would have lower rates of attrition over time (Schneider, 1987).

This general observation, however, is tempered by the level of investment individuals have made in their initial vocation and by the impermeability of labor markets. Individuals who have made great financial investments in their initial occupation (in terms of direct costs of education or foregone earnings to obtain training) face significant economic barriers to starting over even when they realize P-E fit is poor (Feldman, 2007). Some occupations are difficult to enter after a certain age because of the length of training required (e.g., medicine) or because critical skills decline (e.g., professional sports). In addition, individuals not only have financial commitments to vocations, but also emotional investments as well. Moreover, for some older workers, the anticipated emotional costs of searching for a new career and concerns about the limited options available may make these workers more likely to stay put despite low satisfaction (Carson, Carson, & Bedeian, 1995).

Career success. The final outcome variable we will consider here is career success. Researchers have typically made a distinction between "objective" and "subjective" career success. Objective career success refers to tangible indicators of career advancement, such as salary level, frequency of promotions, or current position in the organizational hierarchy. Person-vocation (P-V) fit and person-job (P-J) fit have typically been linked to objective career success through their connection to abilities-demands (skills) fit.

In contrast, subjective career success refers to individuals' favorable perceptions of, and satisfaction with, their career. Indicators of subjective career success include life satisfaction and professional commitment (Feldman & Ng, 2007; Judge, Cable, Boudreau, & Bretz, 1995). P-O fit and P-G fit have typically been linked to subjective career success because they enhance needs-supplies (needs) fit in particular (Assouline & Meir, 1987; Tsabari, Tziner, & Meir, 2005).

Moderating Relationships

P-J fit and in-role performance. Our first moderator proposition is that the relationship between P-J fit and in-role performance will be stronger for younger workers than for older workers. As noted previously, individuals' skills decay with age (Cerella, 1994; Sterns & Miklos, 1995), making it more difficult for older workers to perform their job effectively. Undoubtedly, there will be variance in the degree of the decline, depending upon the demands of the job and the rate of decay of the specific skills involved (e.g., crystallized versus fluid intelligence). In general, though, there will be some skill decline over time and the impact of that decline will be more noticeable in the in-role performance of older workers.

Further, because older workers face greater barriers to getting a new job elsewhere, they are more likely to stay in a job with poor P-J fit rather than simply leave for different opportunities. As a result, older workers with poor P-J fit might experience even greater and faster declines in job performance over time. Thus, we predict:

> *P5:* The positive relationship between P-J fit and in-role performance is moderated by age, such that the relationship is stronger for younger workers than for older workers.

P-G fit and organizational citizenship behaviors. As people get older, the emotional components of their lives, such as their values and life goals, become more salient to them (Carstensen et al., 1999; Carstensen et al., 2000). It is likely, then, that the positive relationship between P-G fit and organizational citizenship behavior will be stronger for older workers than for younger workers because older workers care more deeply about having close emotional attachments with others and derive more satisfaction from them. Older workers are also more focused on helping others than on building their own career. Consequently, older workers are more likely to provide assistance to colleagues and to view the costs of doing so to be low (Carstensen et al., 2000).

In addition, the moderating effects of age will be especially strong when we consider OCBs directed at others (rather than at the organization as a whole). Because older workers prefer to focus on a few deep relationships and to drop more peripheral relationships, we expect that older workers' motivation to engage in OCBs will be especially high when the targets of their OCBs are personal friends rather than a more abstract or distal "organization." Thus, we predict:

> *P6:* The positive relationship between P-G fit and other-directed organizational citizenship behavior is moderated by age, such that the relationship is stronger for older workers than for younger workers.

P-O fit and turnover. We expect that the negative relationship of P-O fit and voluntary turnover will be stronger for younger workers than for older workers. There are two reasons for this prediction.

First, due to age discrimination in the marketplace, it will be harder for older workers with low P-O fit to find a new employer in the outside market (Shore & Goldberg, 2005). Older workers may be more inclined to wait out poor P-O fit until they can retire. In contrast, younger workers do not relish having to spend 40 more years laboring for the "wrong" organization. Rather, they will be much more motivated to locate and accept attractive alternatives elsewhere. Second, older workers are especially reluctant to put their self-concept at risk (Ng & Feldman, 2008b), and job hunting is certainly an activity that can evoke frequent negative feedback. By contrast, younger workers may be more used to job hunting and therefore do not take job rejections so personally (Bretz & Judge, 1994). In either event, it appears young workers are less willing to ride out poor P-O fit for long periods of time and are more willing to take the initiative to find suitable alternative employers (Finegold, Mohrman, & Spreitzer, 2002). Thus, we predict:

P7: The negative relationship between P-O fit and voluntary turnover is moderated by age, such that the relationship is stronger for younger workers than for older workers.

P-V fit and career success. In the case of the relationship between P-V fit and career success, we propose that the moderating effects of age will differ depending upon whether we are considering subjective or objective career success (Tsabari et al., 2005). We expect that the positive relationship between P-V fit and subjective career success will be stronger for older workers than for younger workers. As noted earlier, older adults tend to focus less on negative information and more on positive information (Charles et al., 2003). This decrease in negativity bias (Charles et al., 2003) is likely to strengthen the relationship between P-V fit and subjective career success for older workers, since they will be less likely to pick up or obsess about negative cues in the environment (Meir, 1999).

In contrast, we expect that the positive relationship between P-V fit and objective career success will be stronger for younger workers than for older workers. Young adults are typically given more opportunities for training and development to prepare them for promotions (Maurer, 2001). However, companies often neglect training for older workers because firms assume they will have more trouble learning and will have fewer years of employment remaining to justify those training costs (Shore, Cleveland, & Goldberg, 2003). Younger adults are also more likely to see a direct link between their person-vocation fit and objective rewards. In part, this is due to the fact that new entrants into the labor force get "market wages" and have not suffered yet from wage compression. In part, this may be due to organizations being more responsive to outside offers that younger workers generate and less concerned about voluntary turnover of older workers. Thus, we predict:

P8a: The positive relationship between P-V fit and subjective career success is moderated by age, such that the relationship is stronger for older workers than for younger workers.

P8b: The positive relationship between P-V fit and objective career success is moderated by age, such that the relationship is stronger for younger workers than for older workers.

FUTURE DIRECTIONS AND RECOMMENDATIONS

Much work remains to be done on how P-E fit is achieved, maintained, and/or lost across the life span. In this final section, we highlight some of the most important ideas for future research.

Conceptualizations of Fit

In this chapter, we largely concentrated on chronological aging, both in terms of its direct impact on P-E fit and in terms of its moderating effects on relationships between P-E fit and outcome variables. As research in this area proceeds, though, more attention will have to be paid to the overlapping and counteracting effects of related constructs, such as career stage, organizational tenure, and job tenure.

For instance, ordinarily we would expect that older workers with low person-vocation (P-V) fit would be less likely to experience objective career success because they would have poorer skills and/or poorer job attitudes. However, the relationship between age and P-V fit might be more positive when older workers are new to their job and are therefore coming in at higher market wages. Along the same lines, organizational tenure might temper the relationships between P-E fit and outcome variables. For example, two older workers of the same chronological age may exhibit very different behaviors and attitudes, depending upon whether they have spent their entire careers with one organization or have moved around repeatedly. In general, we might expect higher levels of enthusiasm about the work from more mobile workers, but lower levels of P-G fit. The inter-relationships among career stage, organizational tenure, and job tenure and how they affect fit, then, clearly warrant more research attention.

Conceptualizations of Age

As noted earlier, most of the research on age and fit has used chronological age as its main operationalization. While chronological age has many advantages as a construct on the face of it, there are still numerous issues surrounding its use in organizational research. When researchers look at group differences between older and younger workers, how "old" is defined depends upon the age distribution of the specific samples utilized, with "older workers" defined as young as 35 and as old as 60 depending upon the specific population investigated (Feldman, 2007). Thus, while some of the effects of chronological age can often be objectively and reliably recorded, other consequences are strongly filtered by the context in which chronological age is measured, particularly when group-level differences are being addressed.

When subjective age, normative age, and relative age are used as alternative operationalizations, some of the relationships we predicted here might be altered. For example, while ordinarily we might expect P-G fit to increase with chronological age, P-G fit might be lower if individuals are a great deal older than the rest of their colleagues (relative age). In addition, we predicted that chronological age would moderate the relationship between P-E fit and voluntary turnover, with the relationship being stronger for younger workers than for older workers. It is also possible, though, that older workers who "feel older" (subjective age) will leave more frequently than their chronological age alone would suggest. Incorporating more insights from the relational demography literature might be particularly helpful in future research on aging (O'Reilly et al., 1991).

The Role of Person-Vocation Fit

As Feldman and Ng (2007) suggest, most of the research in organizational behavior on P-E fit has focused on P-O and P-J fit, with substantially less research examining person-vocation fit. However, initial person-vocation fit might put a ceiling on how much subsequent P-O and P-J fit could ever be achieved. In some cases, poor P-V fit might have occurred because of inadequate job search activity by the individual or cognitive biases in his or her decision making. In other cases, poor P-V fit might have occurred because of misleading advertising, selection procedures with low validity or reliability, or simply random error or bad luck. Whatever the reason for poor P-V fit, though, individuals who do not have the right skills to succeed in an occupation will find it hard—if not impossible—to achieve P-O and P-J fit over the long haul. Thus, why poor P-V fit occurs initially—and how it affects other types of fit over time—is a critical item on the research agenda in this area (Ostroff et al., 2002).

Both in the P-V fit literature and in the research on other types of P-E fit, there is a considerable gap in our knowledge about the distinction between supplementary and complementary fit. There has been little empirical research on complementary fit in particular (Muchinsky & Monahan, 1987; Ostroff et al., 2002). More research in this area would help us better understand the tradeoffs between achieving P-E fit at the individual level of analysis and facilitating diversity of perspectives and skills at the group and organizational levels of analysis.

Research Methodology

In terms of methodology, there has been considerable progress made in constructing appropriate measures of P-E fit and in identifying the tradeoffs among them (Edwards, 1991; Kristof-Brown et al., 2005; Tsabari et al., 2005). What is needed now is more longitudinal research on P-E fit because, without it, the effects of age, career stages, and life stages on fit cannot be determined with confidence (Anderson, Herriot, & Hodgkinson, 2001; Ng & Feldman, 2008a). For example, one potential alternative explanation for research results from cross-sectional studies of fit is that group differences between older and younger workers may be due to generational differences rather than to intra-individual aging (Feldman, 2002; see Gentry, Griggs, Deal, & Mondore, this volume, for a discussion of generational differences). Without more longitudinal research, this legitimate concern cannot be addressed.

Researchers have important decisions to make concerning fit methodologies. For instance, objective measures of fit tend to correlate highly with work behaviors, while subjective, self-report measures of fit tend to be related more closely to work attitudes. It is possible, then, that perceptual P-E measures may not tap fit as much as they reflect individuals' affect toward their work environment in general (Edwards, Cable, Williamson, Lambert, & Shipp, 2006). Furthermore, the manner in which fit is measured is being heavily debated. For instance, polynomial regression and response surface methodologies may be more valid ways of assessing fit than traditional difference scores (Edwards, 2001). Certainly, recent methodological advances must also be incorporated into future empirical analyses of P-E fit data.

CONCLUSION

As the workforce continues to age (U.S. Census Bureau, 2005), it will become even more important to study the ways in which older adults achieve fit with their vocation, organization, job, and work group. With greater economic uncertainty and volatility in the stock market, older workers may be forced to stay in their job longer than they had planned and the long-expected grand exodus of Baby Boomers from the workforce may not unfold as expected (see Wang et. al., this volume, for a discussion of retirement and bridge employment).

It is suggested in this chapter that (a) P-E fit may not be achieved once and for all at the time of hiring, (b) P-E fit for older worker may look quite different from P-E fit for younger workers, and (c) the consequences of achieving P-E fit may vary over time (Craft, Doctors, Shkop, & Benecki, 1979; Kogan & Shelton, 1960; Lyon & Pollard, 1997; Vrugt, 1996). Thus, the ability of older workers to maintain energy, focus, and job options across the life span will continue to be an increasingly important issue not only for older workers themselves, but for their colleagues and supervisors as well.

REFERENCES

Anderson, N., Herriot, P., & Hodgkinson, G. P. (2001). The practitioner-researcher divide in Industrial, Work and Organizational (IWO) psychology: Where are we now, and where do we go from here? *Journal of Occupational and Organizational Psychology, 74*, 391-411.

Argyris, C. (1964). *Integrating the individual and the organization*. New York: John Wiley.

Arthur, M. B. (1994). The boundaryless career: A new perspective for organizational inquiry. *Journal of Organizational Behavior, 15*, 295-306.

Assouline, M., & Meir, E. I. (1987). Meta-analysis of the relationship between congruence and well-being measures. *Journal of Vocational Behavior, 31*, 319-332.

Avolio, B. J., & Waldman, D. A. (1994). Variations in cognitive, perceptual, and psychomotor abilities across the working lifespan: Examining the effects of race, sex, experience, education, and occupational type. *Psychology and Aging, 9*, 430-442.

Baltes, P. B. (1997). On the incomplete architecture of human ontogeny: Selection, optimization, and compensation as foundation of developmental theory. *American Psychologist, 52*, 366-380.

Baltes, P. B., & Baltes, M. M. (1990). *Successful aging: Perspectives from the behavioral sciences*. Cambridge, England: Cambridge University Press.

Bégat, I., Ellefsen, B., & Severinsson, E. (2005). Nurses' satisfaction with their work environment and the outcomes of clinical nursing supervision on nurses' experiences of well-being—a Norwegian study. *Journal of Nursing Management, 13,* 221-230.

Bird, A. (1994). Careers as repositories of knowledge: A new perspective on boundaryless careers. *Journal of Organizational Behavior, 15,* 325-344.

Bopp, K. L., & Verhaeghen, P. (2005). Aging and verbal memory span: A meta-analysis. *The Journals of Gerontology: Psychological Sciences and Social Sciences, 60,* 223-233.

Borg, I. (1990). Multiple facetisations of work values. *Applied Psychology: An International Review, 39,* 401-412.

Bradley, J. C., Brief, A. P., & George, J. M. (2002). More than the Big Five: Personality and careers. In D. C. Feldman (Ed.), *Work careers: A developmental perspective* (pp. 27-62). San Francisco: Jossey Bass.

Bretz, R. (1993). Recruiter perceptions of applicant fit: Implications for individual career preparation and job search behavior. *Journal of Vocational Behavior, 43,* 310-327.

Bretz, R. D., & Judge, T. A. (1994). Person-organization fit and the theory of work adjustment: Implications for satisfaction, tenure, and career success. *Journal of Vocational Behavior, 44,* 32-54.

Bunce, D., & Sisa, L. (2002). Age differences in perceived workload across a short vigil. *Ergonomics, 45,* 949-960.

Byrne, D. (1971). *The attraction paradigm.* New York: Academic Press.

Caplan, R. D., Cobb, S., French, J. R. P., Harrison, R. V., & Pinneau, S. R. (1975). *Job demands and worker health* (HEW Publication No.NIOSH-75-160). Washington, DC: National Institute of Occupational Safety and Health.

Carson, K. D., Carson, P. P., & Bedeian, A. G. (1995). Development and construct validation of a career entrenchment measure. *Journal of Occupational and Organizational Psychology, 68,* 301-320.

Carstensen, L. L. (1995). Evidence for a life-span theory of socioemotional selectivity. *Current Directions in Psychological Science, 4,* 151-156.

Carstensen, L. L., Isaacowitz, D. M., & Charles, S. T. (1999). Taking time seriously. A theory of socioemotional selectivity. *American Psychologist, 54,* 165-181.

Carstensen, L. L., Pasupathi, M., Mayr, U., & Nesselroade, J. R. (2000). Emotional experience in everyday life across the adult life span. *Journal of Personality and Social Psychology, 79,* 644-655.

Cerella, J. (1994). Generalized slowing in Brinley plots. *Journal of Gerontology, 49*(2), 65-71.

Cerella, J., Poon, L. W., & Williams, D. M. (1980). Age and the complexity hypothesis. In L. W. Poon (Ed.), *Aging in the 1980s* (pp. 332-340). Washington, DC: American Psychological Association.

Charles, S. T., Mather, M., & Carstensen, L. L. (2003). Aging and emotional memory: The forgettable nature of negative images for older adults. *Journal of Experimental Psychology: General, 132,* 310-324.

Chatman, J. A. (1991). Matching people and organizations: Selection and socialization in public accounting firms. *Administrative Science Quarterly, 36,* 459-484.

Craft, J. A., Doctors, S. I., Shkop, Y. M., & Benecki, T. J. (1979). Simulated management perceptions, hiring decisions and age. *Aging and Work, 2,* 95-100.

Currey, J. D., Brear, K., & Zioupos, P. (1996). The effects of ageing and changes in mineral content in degrading the toughness of human femora. *Journal of Biomechanics, 29*, 257-260.

Davis, J. A. (1965). *Undergraduate career decisions: Correlates of occupational choice.* Chicago: Aldine.

Dawis, R. V., Lofquist, L. H., & Weiss, D. J. (1968). *A theory of work adjustment (A revision).* (Minnesota Studies in Vocational Rehabilitation No. 23.) Minneapolis: University of Minnesota Press.

Edwards, J. R. (1991). Person-job fit: A conceptual integration, literature review, and methodological critique. In *International review of industrial and organizational psychology* (Vol. 6, pp. 283-357). Oxford, England: John Wiley & Sons.

Edwards, J. R. (2001). Alternatives to differences scores: Polynomial regression analysis and response surface methodology. In F. Drasgow & N. Schmitt (Eds.), *Measuring and analyzing behavior in organizations: Advances in measurement and data analysis* (pp. 350-400). San Francisco: Jossey-Bass.

Edwards, J. R., Cable, D. M., Williamson, I. O., Lambert, L. S., & Shipp, A. J. (2006). The phenomenology of fit: Linking the person and environment to the subjective experience of person-environment fit. *Journal of Applied Psychology, 91*, 802-827.

Farr, J. L., & Ringseis, E. L. (2002). The older worker in organizational context: Beyond the individual. In *International review of industrial and organizational psychology* (Vol. 17, pp. 31-75). Chichester, England: Wiley.

Faust, M. E., Balota, D. A., Spieler, D. H., & Ferraro, F. R. (1999). Individual differences in information-processing rate and amount: Implications for group differences in response latency. *Psychology Bulletin, 125*, 777-799.

Feldman, D. C. (Ed.). (2002). When you come to a fork in the road, take it: Career indecision and vocational choices of teenagers and young adults. In *Work careers: A developmental perspective* (pp. 93-125). San Francisco: Jossey-Bass.

Feldman, D. C. (2007). Career mobility and career stability among older workers. In K. S. Shultz & G. A. Adams (Eds.), *Aging and work in the 21st century* (pp. 179-197). Mahwah, NJ: Erlbaum.

Feldman, D. C., Doerpinghaus, H. I., & Turnley, W. H. (1995). Employee reactions to temporary jobs. *Journal of Managerial Issues, 7*, 127-141.

Feldman, D. C., & Ng, T. W. H. (2007). Careers: Mobility, embeddedness, and success. *Journal of Management, 33*, 350-377.

Fielding, R. A., & Meydani, M. (1997). Exercise, free radical generation, and aging. *Aging, 9*, 12-18.

Finegold, D., Mohrman, S., & Spreitzer, G. M. (2002). Age effects on the predictors of technical workers' commitment and willingness to turnover. *Journal of Organizational Behavior, 23*, 655-674.

Folkman, S., Lazarus, R. S., Pimley, S., & Novacek, J. (1987). Age differences in stress and coping processes. *Psychology and Aging, 2*, 171-184.

Freund, A. M., & Baltes, P. B. (2002). Life-management strategies of selection, optimization, and compensation: Measurement by self-report and construct validity. *Journal of Personality and Social Psychology, 82*, 642-662.

Gentry, W. A., Griggs, T. L., Deal, J. J., & Mondore, S. P. (2009). Generational differences in attitudes, beliefs, and preferences about development and learning at work. In S. G. Baugh & S. E. Sullivan (Eds.), *Research in careers: Vol. 1. Maintaining focus, energy, and options over the career* (pp. 51-74). Charlotte, NC: Information Age.

Griffeth, R. W., Hom, P. W., & Gaertner, S. (2000). A meta-analysis of antecedents and correlates of employee turnover: Update, moderator tests, and research implications for the next millennium. *Journal of Management, 26*, 463-488.

Harrison, D. A., Price, K. H., & Bell, M. P. (1998). Beyond relational demography: Time and the effects of surface- and deep-level diversity on work group cohesion. *Academy of Management Journal, 41*, 96-107.

Hasher, L., & Zacks, R. T. (1988). Working memory, comprehension, and aging: A review and a new view. In G. H. Bower (Ed.), *The psychology of learning and motivation* (Vol. 22, pp. 193-225). San Diego, CA: Academic Press.

Holland, J. L. (1976). Vocational preferences. In M. Dunnette (Ed.), *Handbook of industrial and organizational psychology* (pp. 521-570). Chicago: Rand McNally.

Holland, J. L. (1985). *Making vocational choices: A theory of vocational personalities and work environments*. Englewood Cliffs, NJ: Prentice Hall.

Humphrys, P., & O'Brien, G. E. (1986). The relationship between skill utilization, professional orientation, and job satisfaction for pharmacists. *Journal of Occupational Psychology, 59*, 315-326.

Jackson, S. E., Brett, J. F., Sessa, V. I., Cooper, D. M., Julin, J. A., & Peyronnin, K. (1991). Some differences make a difference: Individual dissimilarity and group heterogeneity as correlates of recruitment, promotions, and turnover. *Journal of Applied Psychology, 76*, 675-689.

Jehn, K. A. (1995). A multimethod examination of the benefits and detriments of intragroup conflict. *Administrative Science Quarterly, 40*, 256-282.

Johnson, M. K. (2001). Change in job values during the transition to adulthood. *Work and Occupations, 28*, 315-345.

Judge, T. A., Cable, D. M., Boudreau, J. W., & Bretz, R. D. (1995). An empirical investigation of the predictors of executive career success. *Personnel Psychology, 48*, 485-519.

Judge, T. A., & Ferris, G. R. (1992). The elusive criterion of fit in human resources staffing decisions. *Human Resource Planning, 15*(4), 47-67.

Kacmar, K. M., & Ferris, G. R. (1989). Theoretical and methodological considerations in the age-job satisfaction relationship. *Journal of Applied Psychology, 74*, 201-207.

Kanfer, R., & Ackerman, P. L. (2004). Aging, adult development, and work motivation. *Academy of Management Review, 29*, 440-458.

Khalil, Z., & Merhi, M. (2000). Effects of aging on neurogenic vasodilator responses evoked by transcutaneous electrical nerve stimulation: Relevance to wound healing. *The Journals of Gerontology: Biological and Medical Sciences, 55*, 257-263.

Kogan, N., & Shelton, F. C. (1960). Differential cue value of age and occupation in impression formation. *Psychological Reports, 7*, 203-216.

Kristof, A. L. (1996). Person-organization fit: An integrative review of its conceptualizations, measurement, and implications. *Personnel Psychology, 49*, 1-49.

Kristof-Brown, A. L. (2000). Perceived applicant fit: Distinguishing between recruiters' perceptions of person–job and person–organization fit. *Personnel Psychology, 53*, 643-671.

Kristof-Brown, A. L., Zimmerman, R. D., & Johnson, E. C. (2005). Consequences of individuals' fit at work: A meta-analysis of person-job, person-organization, person-group, and person-supervisor fit. *Personnel Psychology, 58*, 281-342.

Kubeck, J. E., Delp, N. D., Haslett, T. K., & McDaniel, M. A. (1996). Does job-related training performance decline with age? *Psychology and Aging, 11*, 92-107.

Lachman, M. E. (2004). Development in midlife. *Annual Review of Psychology, 55*, 305-331.

Levinson, D. J. (1979). *The seasons of a man's life*. New York: Ballantine Books.

Lyon, P., & Pollard, D. (1997). Perceptions of the older employee: Is anything really changing? *Personnel Review, 26*, 245-257.

Maurer, T. J. (2001). Career-relevant learning and development, worker age, and beliefs about self-efficacy for development. *Journal of Management, 27*, 123-140.

McArdle, A., Vasilaki, A., & Jackson, M. (2002). Exercise and skeletal muscle ageing: Cellular and molecular mechanisms. *Ageing Research Reviews, 1*, 79-93.

Meglino, B. M., & Ravlin, E. C. (1998). Individual values in organizations: Concepts, controversies, and research. *Journal of Management, 24*, 351-389.

Meir, E. I. (1999). Congruence studies: Right and wrong conclusions. *Man and Work, 9*, 108-114.

Mishel, L., Bernstein, J., & Schmitt, J. (2001). *The state of working America: 2000-2001*. Ithaca, NY: Cornell University Press.

Mor-Barak, M. E. (1995). The meaning of work for older adults seeking employment: The generativity factor. *International Journal of Aging & Human Development, 41*, 325-344.

Muchinsky, P. M., & Monahan, C. J. (1987). What is person-environment congruence? Supplementary versus complementary models of fit. *Journal of Vocational Behavior, 31*, 268-277.

Ng, T. W. H., & Feldman, D. C. (2008a). The relationship of age to ten dimensions of job performance. *Journal of Applied Psychology, 93*, 392-423.

Ng, T. W. H., & Feldman, D.C. (2008b). Can you get a better deal elsewhere? The effects of psychological contract replicability on organizational commitment over time. *Journal of Vocational Behavior, 73*, 268-277.

Nurmi, J. E. (1992). Age differences in adult life goals, concerns, and their temporal extension: A life course approach to future-oriented motivation. *International Journal of Behavioral Development, 15*, 487-508.

O'Reilly, C., & Chatman, J. (1986). Organizational commitment and psychological attachment: The effects of compliance, identification, and internalization on prosocial behavior. *Journal of Applied Psychology, 71*, 492-499.

O'Reilly, C., Chatman, J., & Caldwell, D. F. (1991). People and organizational culture: A profile comparison approach to assessing person-organization fit. *Academy of Management Journal, 34*, 487-516.

Organ, D. W. (1997). Organizational citizenship behavior: It's construct clean-up time. *Human Performance, 10*, 85-97.

Osipow, S. H. (1990). Convergence in theories of career choice and development: Review and prospect. *Journal of Vocational Behavior, 36,* 122-131.

Ostroff, C., Shin, Y., & Feinberg, B. (2002). Skill acquisition and person-environment fit. In D. C. Feldman (Ed.), *Work careers: A developmental perspective* (pp. 63-90). San Francisco: Jossey-Bass.

Park, D. C. (2000). The basic mechanisms accounting for age-related decline in cognitive function. In D. C. Park & N. Schwarz (Eds.), *Cognitive aging: A primer* (pp. 3-21). Philadelphia: Psychology Press.

Podsakoff, P. M., MacKenzie, S. B., Paine, J. B., & Bachrach, D. G. (2000). Organizational citizenship behaviors: A critical review of the theoretical and empirical literature and suggestions for future research. *Journal of Management, 26,* 513-562.

Ratcliff, R., Thapar, A., & McKoon, G. (2001). The effects of aging on reaction time in a signal detection task. *Psychology and Aging, 16,* 323-341.

Robins, R. W., Trzesniewski, K. H., Tracy, J. L., Gosling, S. D., & Potter, J. (2002). Global self-esteem across the life span. *Psychology and Aging, 17,* 423-434.

Rokeach, M. (1973). *The nature of human values.* New York: Free Press.

Ros, M., Schwartz, S. H., & Surkiss, S. (1999). Basic individual values, work values, and the meaning of work. *Applied Psychology: An International Review, 48,* 49-71.

Ryff, C. D. (1989). In the eye of the beholder: Views of psychological well-being among middle-aged and older adults. *Psychology and Aging, 4,* 195–210.

Rynes, S. L., Bretz, R. D., & Gerhart, B. (1991). The importance of recruitment in job choice: A different way of looking. *Personnel Psychology, 44,* 487-521.

Salthouse, T. A., Mitchell, D. R., Skovronek, E., & Babcock, R. L. (1989). Effects of adult age and working memory on reasoning and spatial abilities. *Journal of Experimental Psychology: Learning, Memory, and Cognition, 15,* 507-516.

Schneider, B. (1987). The people make the place. *Personnel Psychology, 40,* 437-453.

Schwartz, S. H. (1992). Universals in the content and structure of values: Theoretical advances and empirical tests in 20 countries. In M. Zanna (Ed.), *Advances in experimental social psychology* (pp. 1-65). New York: Academic Press.

Shore, L. M., Cleveland, J. N., & Goldberg, C. B. (2003). Work attitudes and decisions as a function of manager age and employee age. *Journal of Applied Psychology, 88,* 529-537.

Shore, L. M., & Goldberg, C. B. (2005). Age discrimination in the workplace. In R. L. Dipboye & A. Colella (Eds.), *Discrimination at work: The psychological and organizational bases* (pp. 203-226). Mahwah, NJ: Erlbaum.

Spencer, W. D., & Raz, N. (1995). Differential effects of aging on memory for content and context: A meta-analysis. *Psychology and Aging, 10,* 527-539.

Spokane, A. R. (1985). A review of research on person-environment congruence in Holland's theory of careers. *Journal of Vocational Behavior, 26,* 306-343.

Sterns, H. L., Barrett, G. V., & Alexander, R. A. (1985). Accidents and the aging individual. In J. E. Birren & K. W. Schaie (Eds.), *Handbook of the psychology of aging* (Vol. 2, pp. 703-724). New York: Van Nostrand Rinehold.

Sterns, H. L., & Miklos, S. M. (1995). The aging worker in a changing environment: Organizational and individual issues. *Journal of Vocational Behavior, 47*, 248-268.

Thomson, L., Griffiths, A., & Davison, S. (2000). Employee absence, age and tenure: A study of nonlinear effects and trivariate models. *Work & Stress, 14*, 16-34.

Tinsley, H. E. A. (2000). The congruence myth: An analysis of the efficacy of the person-environment fit model. *Journal of Vocational Behavior, 56*, 147-179.

Tranberg, M., Slane, S., & Ekeberg, S. E. (1993). The relation between interest congruence and satisfaction: A meta-analysis. *Journal of Vocational Behavior, 42*, 253-264.

Tsabari, O., Tziner, A., & Meir, E. I. (2005). Updated meta-analysis on the relationship between congruence and satisfaction. *Journal of Career Assessment, 13*, 216-232.

U.S. Census Bureau. (2005). *65+ in the United States*. Current Population Reports, P23-209. Washington, DC: U.S. Government Printing Office.

van der Velde, M. E. G., Feij, J. A., & van Emmerik, H. (1998). Change in work values and norms among Dutch young adults: Ageing or societal trends? *International Journal of Behavioral Development, 22*, 55-76.

Vancouver, J. B., & Schmitt, N. W. (1991). An exploratory examination of person-organization fit: Organizational goal congruence. *Personnel Psychology, 44*, 333-352.

Verhaeghen, P., Steitz, D. W., Sliwinski, M. J., & Cerella, J. (2003). Aging and dual-task performance: A meta-analysis. *Psychology and Aging, 18*, 443-460.

Verquer, M. L., Beehr, T. A., & Wagner, S. H. (2003). A meta-analysis of relations between person–organization fit and work attitudes. *Journal of Vocational Behavior, 63*, 473-489.

Vrugt, A. (1996). Stereotypes with respect to elderly employees: The contribution of attribute information and representativeness. *Journal of Community & Applied Social Psychology, 6*, 287-292.

Wang, M., Adams, G. A., Beehr, T. A., & Shultz, K. S. (2009). Bridge employment and retirement: Issues and opportunities during the latter part of one's career. In S. G. Baugh & S. E. Sullivan (Eds.), *Research in careers: Vol. 1. Maintaining focus, energy, and options over the career* (pp. 135-162). Charlotte, NC: Information Age.

Warr, P. (1994). Age and employment. In H. Triandis, M. Dunnette & L. Hough (Eds.), *Handbook of industrial and organizational psychology* (Vol. 4, pp. 485-550). Palo Alto, CA: Consulting Psychologists Press.

Warr, P. (2001). Age and work behaviour: Physical attributes, cognitive abilities, knowledge, personality traits, and motives. *International Review of Industrial and Organizational Psychology, 16*, 1-36.

Willis, S. L., & Schaie, K. W. (1999). Intellectual functioning in midlife. In S. L. Willis & J. D. Reid (Eds.), *Life in the middle: Psychological and social development in middle age* (pp. 233–247). San Diego, CA: Academic Press.

Wright, J. D., & Hamilton, R. F. (1978). Work satisfaction and age: Some evidence for the job change hypothesis. *Social Forces, 56*, 1140-1158.

CHAPTER 2

DEVELOPMENTAL RELATIONSHIPS AND THE NEW WORKPLACE REALITIES

A Life Span Perspective on Career Development Through Mentoring

S. Gayle Baugh and Sherry E. Sullivan

Professionals have long been encouraged to seek out mentoring in order to improve their career advancement. From the *Harvard Business Review* article explaining "Why Mentoring Matters in a Hypercompetitive World" (DeLong, Gabarro, & Lees, 2008) to *Business Week* magazine calling peer mentoring one of "The 10 Best Corporate Practices [of] 2008" (Ryan, 2008), practitioners continue to advocate the use of mentoring as a crucial strategy for attaining career success.

The importance of mentoring is generally recognized by practitioners and academics alike (for a review, see Molloy, 2006). As the workplace has changed, the study of mentoring has also changed, evolving from an examination of a single dyadic relationship to multiple sequential and simultaneous relationships (Allen & Finkelstein, 2003; Baugh, 2008;

Maintaining Focus, Energy, and Options Over the Career
pp. 27–50
Copyright © 2009 by Information Age Publishing
All rights of reproduction in any form reserved.

Baugh & Scandura, 1999; Higgins & Kram, 2001; Higgins & Thomas, 2001). Yet, despite these advances, little consideration has been given to the changing nature of the developmental needs presented by the protégé in today's turbulent and boundaryless career environment.

The purpose of this chapter is threefold. First, we briefly review the evolution of mentoring research from dyadic to multiple mentoring relationships. Second, we offer a change in perspective by suggesting that developmental relationships must respond to protégés' shifting needs with respect to three primary career parameters (authenticity, balance, and challenge) in order for the protégé to maintain focus, energy, and options over the life span. Third, based on this delineation, we suggest a dynamic agenda for future research on mentoring and developmental relationships.

FROM DYADIC TO MULTIPLE MENTORING RELATIONSHIPS

In the past, mentoring was defined as a one-on-one, hierarchical relationship between a more experienced organizational member with a newer, usually younger, employee, with the more experienced individual investing in the protégé's career through the provision of career and psychosocial support (Kram, 1985; Levinson, Darrow, Klein, Levinson, & McKee, 1978). Mentoring was often viewed as part of an organization's socialization and development process, whereby the mentor tried to meet the protégé's instrumental and relational needs in an effort to enhance the protégé's work adjustment, career outcomes, and contributions to the firm (Chao, 1997, 2007; Chao, Walz, & Gardner, 1992; Heimann & Pittenger, 1996; Payne & Huffman, 2005; Schrodt, Cawyer, & Sanders, 2003). Research has found that in addition to improved organization socialization, protégés relative to non-protégés enjoyed many benefits from the mentoring relationship, including career advancement, an increased ability to achieve goals, greater organizational knowledge, and increased visibility (Forret, Turban, & Dougherty, 1996; Lankau & Scandura, 2002; Scandura, 1992; Scandura, Tejeda, Werther, & Lankau, 1996; Veale & Wachtel, 1997) as well as higher job satisfaction and salary, lower turnover intentions, less work/nonwork conflict, and reduced work stress (Allen, Eby, Poteet, Lentz, & Lima, 2004; Allen, Russell, & Maetzke, 1997; Baugh, Lankau, & Scandura, 1996; Dreher & Ash, 1990; Forret & de Janasz, 2005; Higgins, 2000; Nielson, Carlson, & Lankau, 2001; Scandura & Viator, 1994; Sosik & Godshalk, 2000; Wallace, 2001).

Most research on mentoring has been predicated on the assumption that both mentors and protégés are pursuing traditional, linear careers—that is, individuals will work for only a few firms, will actively pursue hierarchical promotions, and will remain in the workforce relatively continuously over the course of their career (Super, 1957). More recent nontraditional career concepts, such as the boundaryless (Arthur, 1994; Arthur & Rousseau, 1996) and protean (Hall, 1996) career suggest that mentoring may occur across organizational boundaries (Baugh & Fagenson-Eland, 2005) or that there may be additional, relevant outcomes that should be explored, such as learning, growth, and development (Allen & Eby, 2003; Dymock, 1999; Hirschfield, Thomas, & Lankau, 2006; Lankau & Scandura, 2002, 2007).

These more recent career concepts (Arthur & Rousseau, 1996; Hall, 2002), which emphasize greater individual rather than organizational control over career mobility and career development, coupled with changes in the workplace, including globalization, rapid advances in technology and increasing job mobility (see Sullivan, 1999, for a review), have caused scholars to re-evaluate beliefs about mentoring. Today's turbulent work environment has caused scholars to question whether the traditional dyadic mentor-protégé relationship could still adequately meet the changing needs of a protégé (de Janasz, Sullivan, & Whiting, 2003; Higgins & Kram, 2001). The traditional, dyadic mentoring relationship may have fulfilled many protégé needs when both mentor and protégé worked within the same organization and workers focused on climbing the organizational career ladder (e.g., Super, 1957); however, given that workers are increasingly crossing the boundaries between organizations, industries, occupations, and even countries (Sullivan & Arthur, 2006), it seems unlikely that one person can continually meet the changing needs of a protégé in the contemporary work landscape (Berlew, 1991).

In order to account for an increasingly complex work environment, Baugh and Scandura (1999) suggested the concept of "multiple mentors," advocating that research should examine the impact on protégé outcomes of maintaining relationships with more than one mentor. Similarly, Higgins and Kram (2001) recommended that research be expanded beyond the traditional, dyadic mentoring relationship to the study of a protégé's constellation of developmental relationships, with different developers meeting different protégé needs (see Molloy, 2006, for a review). While each individual participant within this network of developers is not expected to offer the high levels of both instrumental and psychosocial support provided by the intense dyadic relationship described by Levinson et al. (1978), as a collective, this group should be better able to meet the protégé's changing array of needs over the life span than one mentor.

Further, the relationships within this developmental network may differ from the traditional model of mentoring in other ways. For example, developmental relationships may not incorporate the long time horizon of traditional mentoring relationships, which typically require 4 to 5 years to reach full development and can extend over decades (Chao, 1997; Dougherty, Turban, & Haggard, 2007; Kram, 1985). In contrast to the traditional dyadic mentoring relationship, which was originally studied as strictly a workplace phenomenon that unfolded within the boundaries of one organization (Levinson et al., 1978), developers may instead originate from many sources, including family, community, peer groups, or social systems. Some of these developers may be familiar with one another or even have strong network connections, such as coworkers assisting the same protégé. Other developers may have no connection beyond their individual relationship with the protégé (Allen & Finkelstein, 2003; Higgins & Kram, 2001).

Research has supported the notion that individuals have many developers in today's boundaryless career context (Chandler & Kram, 2007). It is unclear, however, if having more than one mentor actually enhances protégé outcomes or whether "too many cooks spoil the broth." For example, in one of the few published studies of multiple mentors, Baugh (2008) found positive effects of multiple mentoring in terms of protégé reports of enhanced career support, greater mentor helpfulness, and a higher number of reported promotions compared with protégés indentifying only one mentor. Although this study clearly demonstrated the benefits of multiple mentors, it did not investigate any negative outcomes. Baugh (2008) recommended that future research examine a broader range of outcomes and consider the potential negative outcomes that may result from multiple mentors.

Following this recommendation, Carraher, Sullivan, and Crocitto (2008) conducted a study of multiple, simultaneous mentoring across national boundaries. They found that having a host country mentor had a significant positive effect on the protégé's organizational knowledge, organizational identification, job performance, and teamwork, while having a home country mentor had a significant positive effect on promotability and organizational knowledge. Surprisingly, having a home country mentor had a significant, but negative, effect on organization identification. Also, contrary to findings of mentoring in a domestic setting, neither the home nor the host country mentor had a significant effect on either the protégé's job satisfaction or job tension. The findings of this study not only support the idea that no one mentor can adequately address the needs of a protégé, but also suggest that different developers may meet different needs for the protégé.

These empirical studies of multiple mentors also highlight the importance of examining the potential negative, as well as positive, outcomes of developmental relationships. Recent theoretical and empirical work on dyadic mentoring (Eby, 2007; Eby, Butts, Lockwood, & Simon, 2004; Eby

& McManus, 2004; Feldman, 1999; Scandura, 1998) has suggested that the mentoring experience may not be uniformly positive for either the protégé or the mentor. Given that most research has focused primarily on individual mentoring relationships, Baugh and Scandura (1999) have suggested that future research examine whether protégés with multiple mentors experience greater role conflict than protégés with only one mentor.

In sum, in the literature it is suggested that in today's changing, boundaryless workplace, it is likely that protégés will need a network of mentors or developers across their life span in order to obtain the necessary assistance for career advancement and satisfaction. However, one missing element in the discussion of a network of developers is the identification of the specific career issues these developers will focus on in order to help protégés to succeed. In the next section we present the Kaleidoscope Career Model (KCM) and suggest its integration with the literature on multiple mentoring in order to gain a fresh perspective on mentoring in the boundaryless work environment.

THE KALEIDOSCOPE CAREER MODEL

While some more recent research on mentoring and developmental relationships has incorporated newer perspectives on career development, the attempts at integrating mentoring and developmental relationships with career processes have been incomplete (e.g., de Janasz et al., 2003; Fagenson-Eland & Baugh, 2005). We propose that research on mentoring be reconsidered by integrating ideas on multiple mentoring with a non-traditional model of careers. Specifically, we suggest that the KCM (Mainiero & Sullivan, 2006) be used to examine how multiple mentors assist protégés in achieving work and nonwork outcomes across the boundaries of firms, industries, occupations, and countries over the course of the life span.

The KCM incorporates an understanding of how career motivations influence enactment of the career over an individual's life span (Mainiero & Sullivan, 2005, 2006). Just as a kaleidoscope uses three mirrors to create infinite patterns, the KCM has three "mirrors" or parameters (authenticity, balance, and challenge) that serve as career motivators over the life span. The three basic motivations of authenticity, balance, and challenge combine in different ways throughout an individual's life, reflecting the unique patterns of his or her kaleidoscope career.

The first parameter of the KCM is authenticity. Authenticity is defined by the quest for creating an alignment between an individual's inner values and his or her attitudes and behaviors (Cabrera, 2007; Cohen, 2003;

Svejenova, 2005). Individuals seeking authenticity desire a meaningful life as well as the time to pursue fulfilling nonwork activities, such as volunteerism, sports, and hobbies. They try to match themselves to organizations or work projects that reflect their personal values and beliefs. For example, many employees of the ice cream company Ben & Jerry's said that they chose to work for the firm over other companies, even those firms that offered greater compensation, because they believed that the corporate culture of Ben & Jerry's better matched their own personal values and goals (Wilson, 2000).

The second parameter of the KCM, balance, is defined as the seeking of a healthy equilibrium between work and nonwork demands. The extensive research on work/family conflict has examined how individuals struggle to achieve both satisfying work and nonwork lives (Byron, 2005; Greenhaus & Foley, 2007; Muse, Harris, Giles, & Feild, 2008). Individuals desiring balance recognize the importance of work as well as the importance of devoting time and energy to their family, friends, and community, with some individuals achieving a synergy between the work and nonwork aspects of their lives (Mainiero & Sullivan, 2006). Maternity and paternity leave, flexible schedules, telecommuting, and wellness programs are just a few of the initiatives firms have offered in an effort to help employees cope with work/nonwork conflict (Pitt-Catsouphes, Matz-Costa, & MacDermid, 2007).

The third parameter of the KCM, challenge, is defined as striving for stimulating work. Individuals with challenging jobs often discuss the intrinsic satisfaction they derive from solving the problems and puzzles presented to them on a daily basis (Brook & Brook, 1989). These individuals may look for employment that tests them mentally or physically on a regular basis and requires them to continue to learn and grow (e.g., Hudson & Inkson, 2006). For example, some firms have offered "intrapreneurship" programs in an effort to enhance employee challenge while encouraging the development of new, entrepreneurial products and processes (Chakravarthy & Lorange, 2008). The desire for challenge also includes striving for advancement in terms of salary and promotions.

According to the KCM, a person shifts the pattern of his or her career over the life span by rotating different aspects of work and life to arrange roles and relationships in new ways. At different points throughout life, one of the three parameters of the KCM takes on greater intensity, while the other two receive less emphasis. One of the parameters takes priority over the other two and has a greater impact on decisions and choices. The other two parameters lessen in intensity and recede to the background, but are still present and active, as all three parameters are necessary to create the current pattern of an individual's career (Mainiero & Sullivan, 2005, 2006). For instance, early in an individual's career, challenge may take center stage and be the motivational focus, while authenticity and balance, although still active, move into the background. Around mid-career, the individual's emphasis may shift such that more attention is given to balance, which becomes the individual's priority, while challenge joins authenticity as the parameters receiving less emphasis. In late career, authenticity may become the priority for the individual with balance joining challenge in the background and receiving less emphasis (Sullivan & Mainiero, 2007).

Research has supported the tenets of the KCM (Cabrera, 2007 and in press; Godshalk, Noble, & Line, 2007; Segers, Inceoglu, Vloeberghs, Bartram, & Henderickx, 2008; Smith-Ruig, this volume). For example, using a sample of 497 women, Cabrera (2007) reported that, as predicted by the KCM, women's career motives shift over the life span. Women in mid-career were most interested in balance, with the desire for authenticity increasing over the life span.

In the next section, we examine how the research on the evolution of mentoring from a dyadic relationship to a network of developers can be integrated with the KCM to provide a new perspective on mentoring. Using the lens of the KCM suggests that attention should be directed toward the content of mentoring, rather than to generic mentoring functions. Likewise, the integration of the mentoring and career literatures suggests that an individual enacting a nontraditional career path may receive greater career benefits from a network of developers, rather than from a traditional, dyadic mentoring relationship.

DEVELOPMENTAL RELATIONSHIPS AND THE KCM

Building from the KCM and integrating research on mentoring, we propose that no one mentor can adequately address an individual's need for authenticity, balance, and challenge over the life span. Instead, protégés will require the help of sequential and simultaneous mentors as they develop and mature in their career. Moreover, as the three parameters interact and shift in importance throughout individual development and maturation processes, mentoring needs will vary in type and intensity, depending upon which parameter is taking center stage in the protégé's life (see Feldman & Vogel, this volume, for a discussion of age-related adjustments). Therefore, using the KCM to examine mentoring relationships suggests that protégés will need a network of developers who will guide and support their development. The protégé's emphasis with respect to the three key career needs of authenticity, balance, and challenge will vary over time, and thus requisite mentor support will vary, as well. Protégés may assert different needs to their developers as their career changes, or alternatively, protégés may seek out different mentors or developers to support changes in interplay between the three career parameters.

Unlike most of the previous scholarship on mentoring, the KCM requires that the content of the developmental relationship, in addition to the functions that the mentor performs, must be examined. Much research to date has been directed toward identifying the functions of mentoring and the effect of those functions on career and personal outcomes (Dougherty et al., 2007; Kram, 1983, 1985; Levesque, O'Neill, Nelson, & Dumas, 2005; Mullen, 1998; Noe, 1988; Pellegrini & Scandura, 2005; Ragins & Cotton, 1999; Scandura, 1992; Schockett & Haring-Hidore, 1985; Tepper, Shaffer, & Tepper, 1996). There is fairly general agreement that mentoring includes vocational or career functions, which involve the protégé's skill development and career advancement, and psychosocial functions, which focus on the protégé's development of a sense of professional competence and identity. Role modeling is sometimes included as a psychosocial function (e.g., Kram, 1983) and sometimes identified as a separate function (e.g., Scandura, 1992). These generic descriptions, however, provide very little information about the content of the relationship between the protégé and the developer.

The KCM can help address this lack of research with respect to the issues or concerns that form the basis for any developmental relationship because the KCM indicates that the content of the developmental relationship should be dictated, for the most part, by the motivator that is the protégé's main focus. Thus, while the functions of developmental relationships may remain stable over time, the content of the protégé-developer interactions will change as a result of the shifts in the protégé's pattern of career motivators.

A protégé who is in the early part of his or her career and is primarily motivated by a desire for challenge will seek out a developer who can assist in obtaining stimulating work assignments that permit the protégé the chance to hone his or her skills on new and exciting opportunities. In addition to assuring that the protégé has challenging work assignments, appropriate career functions for a protégé focused on challenge would include (a) suggesting the protégé for special training or assignments, (b) making the protégé visible to higher level managers or others more advanced in the profession, and (c) coaching the protégé to develop new skills. Desired psychosocial functions might include support and encouragement for taking on novel tasks as well as nurturing the protégé's work-related self-esteem.

The emphasis on challenge that often characterizes early stages of the career may in time, for example, give way to concerns about balance. Thus, the content of the individual's developmental relationships must change to reflect this change in focus. Rather than concentrating on a developmental relationship that supports the pursuit of challenge, the protégé may instead find mentors or developers who can assist in finding a balance between work and nonwork interests. Appropriate career functions for a protégé whose priority is balance would include coaching the protégé to select the appropriate opportunities in the workplace that will facilitate balance between work and nonwork activities without sacrificing challenge in the work role, as challenge is still an active motivator, although of lesser intensity than balance. Psychosocial functions would include acceptance and confirmation of the protégé's desire to find a balance between work and outside activities and counseling to help to manage inter-role stress.

At some point, the individual's emphasis will shift to authenticity, with the developmental relationship focused on establishing congruence between personal values and workplace culture in order to permit the protégé to express core values through work activities. Career-related mentoring for a protégé focused on authenticity might be directed toward helping the protégé to identify appropriate settings and positions in which to find a fit with personal values as well as recommending the protégé for such positions. It may be that the developer even assists the protégé in changing firms or becoming self-employed in an effort to achieve a better fit between the protégé's values and his or her attitudes and behaviors. Psychosocial functions might include counseling to clarify needs and values, as well as acceptance and confirmation with respect to the importance of seeking fit with an organization's goals and values.

While mentors or developers can support a protégé with respect to the career parameter that is his or her current focus, a developmental relationship may, instead, be the catalyst for a shift in the protégé's motivational focus. A mentor or developer may serve as a change agent through active involvement in the protégé's career evolution, for example, by questioning the protégé's choices or helping to identify the values underlying them. A mentor or developer may facilitate change in the protégé's career by making the protégé cognizant of other important career parameters through role modeling.

Although we have focused on professionals following nontraditional career paths, the question arises as to whether a protégé following a more traditional career path would need such an array of developers, especially if the context of his or her career is relatively stable? For instance, despite the popularity of the boundaryless career concept, Smith-Ruig (this volume) found that half of the accountants in her sample still had traditional career patterns. While not specifically examined in her study, it may be that the accountants enacting more traditional career patterns within a more stable, traditional work context had fewer developers than the accountants with somewhat nontraditional, boundaryless careers. Acknowledging that not all individuals will experience the same level of boundarylessness (see Sullivan & Arthur, 2006, for a discussion) and that some individuals will continue to enact more traditional career paths, we still suggest that most protégés will need more than one developer over the life span. For instance, a protégé may find that a developmental relationship that was successful and satisfying in the past becomes less so as his or her motivational emphasis shifts. Likewise, as either party to the relationship experiences changes, one or both individuals may conclude that the costs of the relationship now exceed the benefits (Ragins & Cotton, 1993; Ragins & Scandura, 1994, 1999). Incompatibility, or "outgrowing the relationship," is cited as one of the primary reasons for the termination of mentoring relationships (Dougherty et al., 2007; Ragins & Scandura, 1997). While recognizing the need for multiple developers, however, we further propose that the number of developers may be smaller for those with traditional careers compared to those with less traditional, boundaryless careers. Those with boundaryless careers, operating in a relatively unstable and complex work and life context, will be more likely to need the assistance of a greater number of developers to help navigate his or her career path.

DEVELOPMENTAL RELATIONSHIPS IN ACTION

The dynamic nature of the network of developmental relationships and the changing foci of such relationships can become quite complex. However, it is possible to consider a "snapshot" of an individual's set of relationships at a particular point in time. Some examples might serve to illustrate how sequential and simultaneous developmental relationships may evolve and change over time.

For instance, in Figure 2.1 a protégé's network of developers over his or her life span is depicted. As can be seen in Figure 2.1, the protégé has developed relationships with individuals from diverse settings (e.g., work, social, community) and from different employment situations (e.g., across firms, across company levels, across company departments, across countries). Some developers are bosses, some are peers, and one is even the protégé's spouse. However, not all of these developers help the protégé at the same time or throughout his or her entire career. Some of the developers are active only to serve a particular career need, whereas other developmental relationships may evolve to serve two or even all three primary career needs over time. In Figure 2.1 the diverse and complex nature of possible developmental relationships over the course of an individual's life is illustrated.

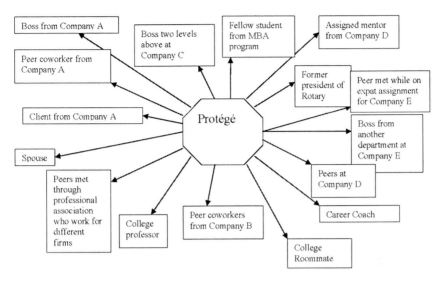

Figure 2.1.   Example of a protégé's developmental relationships over his/her life span.

In Figure 2.2, the protégé's developers at Time 1 are presented. Upon completing his or her undergraduate degree and obtaining his or her first job, the protégé engaged in four relationships simultaneously. For the most part, these relationships involved the career parameter of challenge, which was the protégé's motivational focus. Two of these developers were of higher rank (e.g., boss, professor), while two were peers. The professor helped the protégé obtain a challenging job, while the boss guided the protégé in the completion of demanding work assignments. The coworker/peer, to a lesser extent than the boss, helped the protégé learn how to obtain more challenging assignments, while also providing some guidance with respect to coping with work/nonwork demands (at that time, balance was an active motivator, but was a less intense career need than challenge for the protégé). The college roommate/peer assisted with work/nonwork balance issues as well as serving as a sounding board as to whether the protégé was staying authentic to himself or herself in the workplace (authenticity, like challenge, was also of less intensity than challenge but still active at that time). As the protégé's job situation changed over time (i.e., the protégé changed employers or work functions, or there was a shift among the career parameters), some of these developmental relationships might fade or disappear, some might continue or transform, and new relationships would arise.

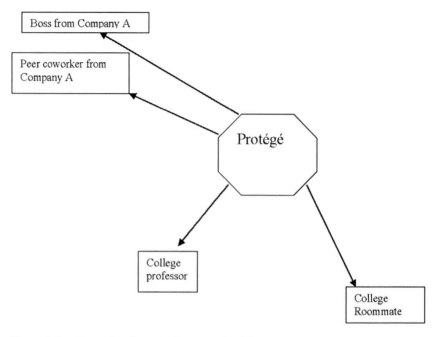

Figure 2.2.   Example of protégé's network of developers at Time 1.

In Figure 2.3, the protégé's developmental relationships are illustrated at Time 2, when the protégé's need for balance is shifting to the foreground, while challenge is receding in intensity. In the period since Time 1, the protégé, now employed with Company E, has worked for several different firms, developed new relationships, and changed the nature of some relationships. The boss from Company A and the college professor are still serving as developers but the frequency of interaction with the protégé is reduced, since those relationships served the need for challenge, which is currently receding in importance to the protégé. The peers from Company A who were developers at Time 1 are no longer in the picture, in part because of physical separation and in part due to changing needs. A client relationship created while working at Company A has transformed into a developmental relationship, as the former client now provides the protégé with important work connections, including introducing the protégé to a professional career coach. Similarly, the formal mentor assigned to the protégé from Company D continues to mentor the protégé. New developers, outside of the boundaries of the current employer, have entered into the protégé's life. These developers include the protégé's spouse, a fellow student in the protégé's MBA program, and

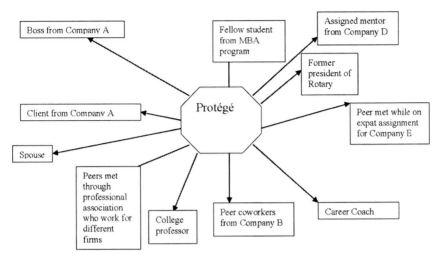

Figure 2.3.   Example of a protégé's developmental relationships at Time 2.

a career coach, all of whom guide the protégé's efforts in satisfying the emerging need for work/nonwork balance. The former president of the local Rotary Club also assists the protégé. The relationship with the Rotary Club president began during a period in which the protégé was questioning the match between his or her beliefs and the company's culture due to some ethical problems with corporate policies. The protégé invested less in his relationship, however, as balance was still his or her motivational emphasis.

The developmental relationships illustrated in Figures 2.1, 2.2, and 2.3 provide a picture of sequential as well as simultaneous multiple mentoring relationships at different points in the protégé's career. These figures help illustrate how different mentors or developers focus on the parameters of authenticity, balance, and challenge as the emphasis on these parameters evolves over the protégé's career. Empirical support can be found for the evolution of developmental relationships over time. For instance, Terjesen and Sullivan (2007) found examples of both sequential and simultaneous mentoring in their study of individuals making the transition from a member of an organization to a self-employed entrepreneur. Some of those making the transition continued developmental relationships from their previous organizational careers, although the nature of the relationships changed. These individuals also identified new developers to include in their network. Some mentoring relationships from previous organizational careers, however, did not continue once the individual became self-employed. While this study did not explore the effect of changes in the protégé's career parameters on the network of relationships, it is certainly suggestive and entirely consistent with the notion that developmental relationships may be time-bounded.

So far in this section we have discussed how developmental relationships can change in response to shifting career motivators over time. The KCM suggests that all three parameters are active simultaneously, but that one parameter will move to the foreground and be the individual's priority, while the other two parameters will be less intense and recede to the background. Over the life span, these three parameters shift in priority. It is important to note that while the KCM highlights individual differences in the enactment of careers, there are predictable career patterns. Based on 52 individual interviews as well as responses from 27 individuals who participated in online focus groups, Sullivan and Mainiero (2007) identified two major career prototypes, which they labeled the *alpha kaleidoscope career pattern* and the *beta kaleidoscope career pattern*. About 40% of the sample displayed the alpha pattern and 60% displayed the beta pattern.

Individuals with an alpha career pattern focused on challenge first, with concerns about authenticity taking center stage at midlife, and a later shift to an emphasis on balance. In contrast, individuals with a beta career pattern began by focusing on challenge, with balance emerging to prominence around midlife, and authenticity rising in importance in later life. In both patterns, all three parameters were active and interacted with each other over the course of the life span; thus, we suggested that protégés required different developers throughout life to meet their shifting needs for authenticity, balance, and challenge. At different points in life, depending upon career pattern, the protégé would need more assistance in order to meet the need of the parameter that was currently the highest priority. It is important for both individuals and organizations to be aware of changing individual needs with respect to developmental relationships so that both formal and informal relationships can be focused in a manner that will maximize their effectiveness and fulfill the protégé's needs.

Based upon the preceding discussion, we suggest the following five propositions:

Proposition 1:   Individuals will differ in their self-assessed need for developmental relationships and those assessments will change over the life span, depending on which of the career parameters (authenticity, balance, challenge) is the individual's priority at that time.

Proposition 2:   Individuals who desire developmental relationships will seek out multiple developmental relationships over their life span, including both sequential and simultaneous relationships, with different developers focusing on different career parameters at different points in time.

Proposition 3:   As the pattern of protégé career needs changes, the constellation of developmental relationships will change accordingly. Protégés will invest more in those developmental relationships that address the career parameter which is of greatest priority at that point in his or her career, investing less in developmental relationships related to the other two career parameters.

Proposition 4:   Individuals enacting traditional career patterns will have fewer developmental relationships than individuals enacting boundaryless career patterns.

Proposition 5:   The history of developmental relationships will mirror the career pattern that an individual exhibits (alpha or beta). Thus, an individual with an alpha career pattern will seek developers that will focus on challenge in early career, authenticity as the individual matures and moves toward midcareer, and balance in the latter part of the career. An individual with a beta career pattern will seek developers that will focus on challenge in early career, balance around midcareer, and authenticity in the latter part of the career.

RESEARCH AGENDA

Despite a great deal of speculation and theorizing about multiple developmental relationships, relatively little empirical research has been completed to explore networks or patterns of relationships. In addition to the five propositions, we offer three major suggestions for enhancing our general understanding about mentoring and developmental relationships.

First, scholars need to clearly delineate how they are defining mentoring and how different types of mentors (or developers) are being identified (e.g., Baugh & Sullivan, 2005). Using the lens of the KCM and considering the shifting needs of protégés that mentors may address highlights the fact that developmental relationships will differ in breadth and intensity both across developers and over time. Instead of using the generic term *mentoring* to describe all these various types of relationships, scholars must clearly identify a developer's investment in the relationship (e.g., 6 months versus 1 year versus 5 years), in addition to identifying which career needs a developer is addressing (e.g., authenticity, balance, challenge). Also, both the protégé's and developer's perceptions regarding the relationship should be examined to determine if the parties agree that they are engaged in some form of developmental relationship. By clarifying the nature of the relationship, the differences and similarities among the multiple developmental relationships the protégé is engaged in can be fully explored.

The lack of consensus with respect to the characterization of mentoring relationships that has plagued academic research is amplified in the proliferation of definitions utilized by the participants in research studies. This ambiguity in identification has no doubt resulted in inaccurate interpretation of research findings among mentoring scholars and limits the extent to which findings can be cumulated or compared (Baugh & Sullivan, 2005). Future research should measure various aspects of developmental relationships to determine the type and strength of mentoring provided. For example, an individual may consider legendary baseball player Joe DiMaggio a "mentor" in the sense of being a role model, but this type of "mentoring" relationship is much different from the intensive, usually longer term, face-to-face mentoring described by Levinson et al. (1978) and should not be identified in research in the same way. When evaluating findings across studies, scholars must be sure that similar mentoring experiences are being compared, as the antecedents and consequences of a role model "mentoring relationship," a Levinsonian mentoring relationship, and a more generalized developmental relationship (e.g., peer to peer) may be much different.

Mentoring relationships are developed for different reasons by protégés with different career needs. We join others (e.g., Baugh & Scandura, 1999; Crocitto, Sullivan, & Carraher, 2005; Mezias & Scandura, 2005) in suggesting that researchers must assess the different purposes that mentors serve, specifically in helping protégés to navigate the important career parameters of authenticity, balance, and challenge, rather than categorizing all developmental relationships with the same "mentoring" label. Future research needs to capture the frequency, intensity, effectiveness, and method (e.g., face-to-face versus electronic) of communication between the protégé and his or her mentors as well as which parameters of the KCM are the focus of the communication at different points over the course of the protégé's career.

Second, given the increased mobility of individuals across functions, organizations, occupations, industries, and even countries, it is important to investigate how mentor relationships are developed, transformed, and maintained over time. In the past, research focused on studying traditional dyadic relationships that were typically developed and maintained within the context of one firm, sometimes under the guidance of formalized organizational programs (e.g., Baugh & Fagenson-Eland, 2007). As both developers and protégés are more likely in today's global workplace to cross many boundaries over their careers, scholars should examine if and how developmental relationships that span many boundary crossings are different from relationships that occur within the context of one firm. Not only must further research be conducted on boundaryless developmental relationships as opposed to traditional mentoring relationships, but investigations of how a protégé develops and maintains a developmental network across time and boundaries are also needed.

Third, a focus on multiple developmental relationships and developmental networks leads to some complex but also very intriguing questions. For example, what effect does agreement or disagreement among developers with respect to their advice and suggestions have on the protégé? The impact of the extent of agreement among the different developers with respect to their advice and counsel as well as the effect of the intensity of each developmental relationship on the protégé's receptiveness to each developer's influence should also be examined. Could it really be that too many cooks (developers) really do spoil the broth? Research has yet to examine whether multiple simultaneous developers can have negative as well as positive effects on protégés, especially if these individuals provide divergent advice or collectively place overly stringent demands on the protégé's time.

Along this same line of thinking, we should also investigate the effect of multiple developmental relationships on the developer. An awareness of the protégés' multiple relationships may affect the willingness of individuals to assume the role of a developer, especially engaging in a more intense relationship such as the traditional, master-apprentice mentoring dyad described by Levinson et al. (1978). Given previous research findings that those with no mentoring experience overestimate the cost-to-benefit ratio of being a mentor (Ragins & Scandura, 1999), one might speculate that inexperienced individuals could perceive that their contributions are superfluous or less important if a protégé has a network of developers. Thus, the willingness of individuals to provide developmental support may decrease just as the protégé's needs for individuals to serve in these developmental roles are increasing as a result of today's dynamic career landscape.

Similarly, the increasingly turbulent career scene and the greater mobility of some workers may lead potential mentors to shy away from investing in such relationships. Potential mentors may have greater difficulty in judging the quality of a potential protégé because the increased mobility of workers may make it more difficult to gain information by which to evaluate the potential protégé's abilities and competence. Long-tenured employees considering initiating a developmental relationship with newer employees may assess the risk of devoting the time and effort to developmental relationships as too high, especially (a) if the protégé is unlikely to have a long tenure with the firm (and thus be less likely to "pay back" the assistance) and (b) if the organization provides no rewards for being mentor. Further, those individuals who are willing to serve as developers or mentors are likely to find that they are engaged in multiple relationships with protégés who may present different patterns of career needs (e.g., alpha or beta), thus presenting additional challenges, and perhaps requiring more time and creating more stress for the mentor.

And while we have focused on the kaleidoscope career pattern and shifting career parameters of the protégé, it is important to consider the career pattern and motivators of the developer. Are the outcomes of protégé-developer relationships affected by the match or mismatch between protégé and developer career needs? For instance, it may be more likely that relationships between two peer developers, both having challenge as their priority, will result in fewer positive outcomes than a relationship between a protégé focused on challenge and a developer focused on authenticity. While the two peers may provide assistance to each other, the potential competition for similar positions may cause mistrust or unease between the parties. In contrast, the developer searching for authenticity may view helping the protégé obtain challenging work as a means to create a legacy that reflects his or her personal values in terms of being a good organizational or professional citizen by helping to develop others. Future research should examine whether different combinations of protégé-developer career foci (e.g., protégé and developer both focused on balance versus protégé focused on challenge, developer focused on balance) produce different positive (or negative) outcomes for both the protégé and the developer.

In a similar fashion, the career parameter that is the developer's priority at a particular time may influence the type and number of developmental relationships he or she is willing to develop. For instance, a developer who is focused on achieving balance may have less time to devote to protégés and may engage in fewer developmental relationships than when he or she is focused authenticity. Analogous questions can be explored regarding the congruence between the career patterns (e.g., alpha, beta) of the protégé and developer. For example, do developmental relationships between parties with the same basic pattern (e.g., alpha-alpha; beta-beta) produce better outcomes than between parties with different patterns (e.g., alpha-beta; beta-alpha)? Does the inclusion of these relationships within the boundaries of a firm (or occupation or country) versus outside of such boundaries moderate these relationships?

Overall, integrating the literature on developmental relationships and mentoring with the KCM should enhance our capability to ask original and meaningful questions in both spheres of interest. In this chapter, we have integrated these two streams of research, offered some research propositions, and suggested some general avenues for future investigation. We hope that this new perspective will inspire others to consider the dynamic nature of mentoring over an individual's life span and to apply similar integrative approaches to the empirical study of mentoring and career development in our increasingly complex work environment.

REFERENCES

Allen, T. D., & Eby, L. T. (2003). Relationship effectiveness for mentors: Factors associated with learning and quality. *Journal of Management, 29,* 469-486.

Allen, T. D., Eby, L. T., Poteet, M. L., Lentz, E., & Lima, L. (2004). Career benefits associated with mentoring for protégés: A meta-analysis. *Journal of Applied Psychology, 89,* 127-136.

Allen, T. D., & Finkelstein, L. M. (2003). Beyond mentoring: Alternative sources and functions of developmental support. *Career Development Quarterly, 51,* 346-355.

Allen, T. D, Russell, J. E. A., & Maetzke, S. B. (1997). Formal peer mentoring: Factors related to protégés satisfaction and willingness to mentor others. *Group & Organization Management, 22,* 488-507.

Arthur, M. B. (1994). The boundaryless career: A new perspective for organizational inquiry. *Journal of Vocational Behavior, 15,* 295-306.

Arthur, M. B., & Rousseau, D. M. (Eds.). (1996). The boundaryless career as a new employment principle. In *The boundaryless career* (pp. 3-20). New York: Oxford University Press.

Baugh, S. G. (2008). Sequential and multiple simultaneous relationships: Is more really better? In N. Twigg (Ed.), *Proceedings of the Southwest Academy of Management, 27-34.* Conway, SC: Coastal Carolina University.

Baugh, S. G., & Fagenson-Eland, E. A. (2007). Formal mentoring programs: A "poor cousin" to informal relationships? In B. R. Ragins & K. E. Kram (Eds.), *Handbook of mentoring at work: Theory, research, and practice* (pp. 249-272). Los Angeles: SAGE.

Baugh, S. G., & Fagenson-Eland, E. A. (2005) Boundaryless mentoring: An exploratory study of the functions provided by internal versus external organizational mentors. *Journal of Applied Social Psychology, 35,* 939-955.

Baugh, S. G., Lankau, M. J., & Scandura, T. A. (1996). An investigation of the effects of protégé gender on responses to mentoring. *Journal of Vocational Behavior, 49,* 309-323.

Baugh, S. G., & Scandura, T. A. (1999). The effect of multiple mentors on protégé attitudes toward the work setting. *Journal of Social Behavior and Personality, 14,* 503-522.

Baugh, S. G., & Sullivan, S. E. (2005). Mentoring and career development. *Career Development International, 10,* 425-428.

Berlew, L. D. (1991). Multiple mentor model: A conceptual framework. *Journal of Career Development, 17,* 213-221.

Brook, J. A., & Brook, R. J. (1989). Exploring the meaning of work and nonwork. *Journal of Organizational Behavior, 10*, 169-178.

Byron, K. (2005). A meta-analytic review of work-family conflict and its antecedents. *Journal of Vocational Behavior, 67*, 169-198.

Cabrera, E. F. (in press). Protean organizations: Reshaping work and careers to retain female talent. *Career Development International*.

Cabrera, E. F. (2007). Opting out and opting in: Understanding the complexities of women's career transitions. *Career Development International, 12*, 218-237.

Carraher, S. M., Sullivan, S. E., & Crocitto, M. M. (2008). Mentoring across global boundaries: An empirical examination of home and host country mentors on expatriate effectiveness. *Journal of International Business Studies, 39*, 1310-1326.

Chakravarthy, B., & Lorange, P. (2008). Driving renewal: The entrepreneur-manager. *Journal of Business Strategy, 29*(2), 14-28.

Chandler, D. E., & Kram, K. E. (2007). Mentoring and developmental networks in the new career context. In H. Gunz & M. Peiperl (Eds), *Handbook of career studies* (pp. 241-267). Los Angeles: SAGE.

Chao, G. T. (1997). Mentoring phases and outcomes. *Journal of Vocational Behavior, 51*, 15-28.

Chao, G. T. (2007). Mentoring and organizational socialization: Networks for work adjustment. In B. R. Ragins & K. E. Kram (Eds.), *Handbook of mentoring at work: Research, theory, and practice* (pp. 179-196). Los Angeles: SAGE.

Chao, G. T., Walz, P. M., & Gardner, P. D. (1992). Formal and informal mentorships: A comparison on mentoring functions and contrast with nonmentored counterparts. *Personnel Psychology, 45*, 619-636.

Cohen, B. N. (2003). Applying existential theory and intervention to career decision making. *Journal of Career Development, 29*, 195-210.

Crocitto, M. M, Sullivan, S. E., & Carraher, S. M. (2005). Global mentoring as a means of career development and knowledge creation: A learning based framework and agenda for future research. *Career Development International, 10*, 522-535.

de Janasz, S., Sullivan, S. E., & Whiting, V. (2003). Mentor networks and career success: Lessons for turbulent times. *Academy of Management Executive, 17*(4), 78-82.

DeLong, T. J., Gabarro, J. J., & Lees, R. J. (2008). Why mentoring matters in a hypercompetitive world. *Harvard Business Review, 86*(1), 115-121.

Dougherty, T. W., Turban, D. B., & Haggard, D. L. (2007). Naturally occurring mentoring relationships involving workplace employees. In T. D. Allen & L. T. Eby (Eds.), *Blackwell handbook of mentoring: A multiple perspectives approach* (pp. 139-158). Malden, MA: Blackwell.

Dreher, G. F., & Ash, R. A. (1990). A comparative study of mentoring among men and women in managerial, professional, and technological positions. *Journal of Applied Psychology, 75*, 539-546.

Dymock, D. (1999). Blind dates: A case study of mentoring as workplace learning. *Journal of Workplace Learning: Employee Counseling Today, 11*, 312-317.

Eby, L. T. (2007). Understanding relational problems in mentoring: A review and proposed investment model. In B. R. Ragins & K. E. Kram (Eds.), *Handbook of mentoring at work: Theory, research, and practice* (pp. 323-344). Los Angeles: SAGE.

Eby, L. T., Butts, M., Lockwood, A., & Simon, S. A. (2004). Protégés' negative mentoring experiences: Construct development and nomological validation. *Personnel Psychology, 57,* 411-447.

Eby, L. T., & McManus, S. E. (2004). The protégé's role in negative mentoring experiences. *Journal of Vocational Behavior, 65,* 255-275.

Feldman, D. C. (1999). Toxic mentors or toxic protégés? A critical re-examination of dysfunctional mentoring. *Human Resource Management Review, 9,* 247-278.

Feldman, D. C., & Vogel, R. M. (2009). The aging process and person-environment fit. In S. G. Baugh & S. E. Sullivan (Eds.), *Research in careers: Vol. 1. Maintaining focus, energy, and options over the career* (pp. 1-26). Charlotte, NC: Information Age.

Forret, M. & de Janasz, S. (2005). Protégé work-family conflict: Does type of mentor and organizational culture make a difference? *Career Development International, 10,* 478-492.

Forret, M., Turban, D., & Dougherty, T. (1996). Making the most of mentoring. *Human Resource Management International Digest, 4,* 9-12.

Greenhaus, J. H., & Foley, S. (2007). The intersection of work and family. In H. Gunz & M. Peiperl (Eds.), *Handbook of career studies* (pp. 131-152). Los Angeles: SAGE.

Godshalk, V. M., Noble, A. M., & Line, C. (2007, August). *High achieving women: An exploratory study of the differences between kaleidoscope career types.* Paper presented at the annual meeting of the Academy of Management, Philadelphia, PA.

Hall, D. T. (1996). *The career is dead—Long live the career: A relational approach to careers.* San Francisco: Jossey-Bass.

Hall, D. T. (2002). *Careers inside and outside of organizations.* Los Angeles: SAGE.

Heimann, B., & Pittenger, K. K. S. (1996). The impact of formal mentorship on socialization and commitment of newcomers. *Journal of Managerial Issues, 8,* 108-117.

Higgins, M. C. (2000). The more, the merrier? Multiple developmental relationships and work satisfaction. *Journal of Management Development, 19,* 277-296.

Higgins, M. C., & Kram, K. E. (2001). Reconceptualizing mentoring at work: A developmental network perspective. *Academy of Management Review, 26,* 264-288.

Higgins, M. C., & Thomas, D. A. (2001). Constellations and careers: Toward understanding the effects of multiple developmental relationships. *Journal of Organizational Behavior, 22,* 223-247.

Hirshfield, R. R., Thomas, C. H., & Lankau, M. J. (2006). Achievement and avoidance motivational orientations in the domain of formal mentoring: Looking both ways in predicting the personal learning of mentors and protégés. *Journal of Vocational Behavior, 68,* 524-537.

Hudson, S., & Inkson, K. (2006). Volunteer overseas development workers: The hero's adventure and personal transformation. *Career Development International, 11,* 304-320.

Kram, K. E. (1983). Phases of the mentor relationship. *Academy of Management Journal, 26*, 608-625.

Kram, K. E. (1985). *Mentoring at work: Developmental relationships in organizational life*. Glenview, IL: Scott, Foresman.

Lankau, M. J., & Scandura, T. A. (2002). An investigation of personal learning in mentoring relationships: Content, antecedents, and consequences. *Academy of Management Journal, 45*, 779.

Lankau, M. J., & Scandura, T. A. (2007). Mentoring as a forum for personal learning in organizations. In B. R. Ragins & K. E. Kram (Eds.), *Handbook of mentoring at work: Theory, research, and practice* (pp. 95-122). Los Angeles: SAGE.

Levesque, L. L., O'Neill, R. M., Nelson, T., & Dumas, C. (2005). Sex differences in the perceived importance of mentoring functions. *Career Development International, 10*, 429-443.

Levinson, D. J., Darrow, C. N., Klein, E. B., Levinson, M. H., & McKee, B. (1978). *The seasons of a man's life*. New York: Knopf.

Mainiero, L. A., & Sullivan, S. E. (2005). Kaleidoscope careers: An alternative explanation for the opt-out revolution. *Academy of Management Executive, 19*(1), 106-123.

Mainiero, L. A., & Sullivan, S. E. (2006). *The opt-out revolt: Why people are leaving companies to create kaleidoscope careers*. Palo Alto, CA: Davies-Black.

Mezias, J., & Scandura, T. A. (2005). A needs-driven approach to expatriate adjustment and career development: A multiple mentoring perspective. *Journal of International Business Studies, 36*, 519-538.

Molloy, J. C. (2006). Developmental networks: Literature review and future research. *Career Development International, 10*, 536-547.

Mullen, E. J. (1998). Vocational and psychosocial mentoring functions: Identifying mentors who serve both. *Human Resource Development Quarterly, 9*, 319-331.

Muse, L., Harris, S.G., Giles, W., & Feild, H. (2008). Work-life benefits and positive organizational behavior: Is there a connection? *Journal of Organizational Behavior, 29*, 171-192.

Nielson, T. R., Carlson, D. S., & Lankau, M. J. (2001). The supportive mentor as a means of reducing work-family conflict. *Journal of Vocational Behavior, 59*, 364-381.

Noe, R. A. (1988). An investigation of the determinants of successful assigned mentoring relationships. *Personnel Psychology, 41*, 457-479.

Payne, S. C., & Huffman, A. H. (2005). A longitudinal examination of the influence of mentoring on organizational commitment and turnover. *Academy of Management Journal, 48*, 158-169.

Pellegrini, E. K., & Scandura, T. A. (2005). Construct equivalence across groups: An unexplored issue in mentoring research. *Educational and Psychological Measurement, 65*, 323-335.

Pitt-Catsouphes, M., Matz-Costa, C., & MacDermid, S. M. (2007). HRD responses to work-family stressors. *Advances in Developing Human Resources, 9*, 527-543.

Ragins, B. R., & Cotton, J. L. (1993). Gender and willingness to mentor in organizations. *Journal of Management, 19*, 97-111.

Ragins, B. R., & Cotton, J. L. (1999). Mentor functions and outcomes: A comparison of men and women in formal and informal mentoring relationships. *Journal of Applied Psychology, 84*, 529-550.

Ragins, B. R., & Scandura, T. A. (1994). Gender differences in expected outcomes of mentoring relationships. *Academy of Management Journal, 37*, 957-971.

Ragins, B. R., & Scandura, T. A. (1997). The way we were: Gender and the termination of mentoring relationships. *Journal of Applied Psychology, 82*, 945-953.

Ragins, B. R., & Scandura, T. A. (1999). Burden or blessing? Expected costs and benefits of being a mentor. *Journal of Organizational Behavior, 20*, 493-510.

Ryan, L. (2008, January 7). Best corporate practices 2008. *BusinessWeek online.* Retrieved March 30, 2008, from www.businessweek.com

Scandura, T. A. (1992). Mentorship and career mobility: An empirical investigation. *Journal of Organizational Behavior, 13*, 169-174.

Scandura, T. A. (1998). Dysfunctional mentoring relationships and outcomes. *Journal of Management, 24*, 449-467.

Scandura, T. A., Tejeda, M., Werther, W., & Lankau, M. J. (1996). Perspectives on mentoring. *Leadership and Organization Development Journal, 17*, 50-58.

Scandura, T. A., & Viator, R. (1994). Mentoring in public accounting firms: An analysis of mentoring-protégé relationships, mentorship functions, and protégé turnover intentions. *Accounting, Organizations, and Society, 19*, 717-734.

Schockett, M. R., & Haring-Hidore, M. (1985). Factor analytic support for psychosocial and vocational mentoring functions. *Psychological Reports, 57*, 627-630.

Schrodt, P., Cawyer, C. S., & Sanders, R. (2003). An examination of academic mentoring behaviors and new faculty members' satisfaction with socialization and tenure and promotion processes. *Communication Education, 52*, 17-29.

Segers, J., Inceoglu, I., Vloeberghs, D., Bartram, D., & Henderickx, E. (2008). Protean and boundaryless careers: A study on potential motivators. *Journal of Vocational Behavior, 73*, 212-230.

Smith-Ruig, T. (2009). Mapping the career journey of accountants in Australia. In S. G. Baugh & S. E. Sullivan (Eds.), *Research in careers: Vol. 1. Maintaining focus, energy, and options over the career* (pp. 163-196). Charlotte, NC: Information Age.

Sosik, J. J., & Godschalk, V. M. (2000). Leadership styles, mentoring functions received, and job-related stress: A conceptual model and preliminary study. *Journal of Organizational Behavior, 21*, 365-383.

Sullivan, S. E. (1999). The changing nature of careers: A review and research agenda. *Journal of Management, 25*, 457-484.

Sullivan, S. E., & Arthur, M. B. (2006). The evolution of the boundaryless career concept: Examining physical and psychological mobility. *Journal of Vocational Behavior, 69*, 19-29.

Sullivan, S. E., & Mainiero, L. A. (2007). The changing nature of gender roles, alpha/beta careers, and work-life issues: Theory-driven implications for human resource management. *Career Development International, 12*, 238-263.

Super, D. (1957). *Psychology of careers.* New York: Harper & Brothers.

Svejenova, S. (2005). "The path with the heart": Creating the authentic career. *Journal of Management Studies, 42*, 947-974.

Tepper, K., Shaffer, B. C., & Tepper, B. J. (1996). Latent structure of mentoring function scales. *Educational and Psychological Measurement, 56*, 848-857.

Terjesen, S. A., & Sullivan, S. E. (2007, August). *Leaving corporate boundaries: Leveraging mentors in career transitions to entrepreneurship.* Paper presented at the meeting of the Academy of Management, Philadelphia.

Veale, D., & Wachtel, J. (1997). Coaching and mentoring at Coca-Cola Foods. *Human Resource Management International Digest, 5*, 12-15.

Wallace, J. E. (2001). The benefits of mentoring for female lawyers. *Journal of Vocational Behavior, 58*, 366-391.

Wilson, M. (2000). More than just causes. *Chain Store Age, 76*(8), 37-42.

CHAPTER 3

GENERATIONAL DIFFERENCES IN ATTITUDES, BELIEFS, AND PREFERENCES ABOUT DEVELOPMENT AND LEARNING AT WORK

**William A. Gentry, Tracy L. Griggs,
Jennifer J. Deal, and Scott P. Mondore**

It is becoming common in most large organizations for the workforce to include employees who range in age from those in their 70s (born in the 1930s) to those in their 20s (born in the 1980s) (Harris, 2005). Indeed, the average age of the U.S. workforce has risen over the last 2 decades and it continues to increase with improvements in the overall health of older workers, the possibility of cuts to Social Security retirement benefits, and the enforcement of age discrimination legislation that outlaws mandatory retirement for older workers (Noe, Hollenbeck, Gerhart, & Wright, 2006). As the age of the workforce increases, so does appreciation for generational differences within the workforce, including differences in work styles, well-being, and development (Smola & Sutton, 2002). Managers and researchers face the challenge of understanding generational differ-

Maintaining Focus, Energy, and Options Over the Career
pp. 51–73
Copyright © 2009 by Information Age Publishing
51

ences in order to effectively work with, manage, motivate, and develop workers from different generations (Allerton, 2001; Chester, 2002; Lancaster & Stillman, 2002). The purpose of our study is to examine generational differences in preferences for learning and development at work.

Research from Maurer (2001) suggests that workers from older generations (e.g., Baby Boomers and earlier generations) do not participate in as many developmental processes as workers in younger generations (e.g., "Generation X"). Reasons for the suggested decline in interest include (a) the tendency for older generations to believe that impending retirement precludes them from participating, (b) older workers' decreased confidence that they can still learn new things and continue to develop at an older age, and (c) management's view of older workers being not as worthy an investment as younger workers (Maurer, 2001). Consequently, it is unclear whether decreased participation of older generations in developmental processes is an indication of older workers not wanting to be developed or a result of the perception that older workers should not pursue development.

Our research builds on previous research concerning generational differences, particularly as it applies to beliefs about developmental opportunities. We intend to examine whether differences exist among generations in their attitudes and beliefs about development and learning at work. Moreover, we detail how workers of different generations say they would like to receive development in soft skills (people skills) and hard skills (technical skills), and what developmental opportunities workers intend to take advantage of in the future. Findings of our study will have implications for the best ways to manage and develop workers of all generations.

Our study is important for several reasons. First, it is common for organizations to offer training and development that is designed to meet a specific organizational need, rather than that which meets the broader developmental needs and desires of the employee. Our research draws attention to the differences in employee needs and preferences with regard to training and development by addressing the kinds of training and development that employees prefer.

Second, findings of our research are important because a critical part of training and development is needs assessment. Training needs assessment includes knowing the workers who are to be trained, their needs, preferences, current skill levels, and barriers to learning (Noe et al., 2006). Many organizations may already be considering the age or generation of their trainees when they organize the content of training. For needs assessment to be helpful, it will be important for organizations to understand the reality of generational similarities and differences so they do not waste either employees' time or the company's money on training that is inappropriate or unnecessary.

Next, our research is important because organizations spend billions of dollars every year on training and development for employees (Rivera & Paradise, 2006). Organizations risk wasting money on training for employees that is not utilized in the actual job. Tailoring the delivery to different generations based on their preferences or offering options in terms of delivery will likely improve the chances that the *transfer of training* will occur. Research has shown that both pretraining motivation and the reputation of the training/development have a direct impact on transfer of training (Facteau, Dobbins, Russell, Ladd, & Kudisch, 1995). For example, if an older employee goes through a laundry list of developmental opportunities that are delivered via a computer or through outdoor experiences, with limited pretraining motivation, transfer of training may be limited and the cost justification for the training will not materialize. Therefore, an additional reason to offer different options is that employees can self-select into training for which they have greater pretraining motivation, thereby increasing the chance for behavioral change to occur.

Finally, training in Fortune 500 companies tends to be highly diverse in its content and normally offers multiple delivery methods in the same modules so that all audiences receive the portion of training that is most closely associated with their preferences. Thus, consideration of multiple learning styles and preferences for training content might be considered a best practice for training in all organizations.

GENERATIONAL CATEGORIES

A generation is a group of people or societal subculture that is distinguishable from other groups by their shared birth years, similar life events, values, and their historical and social life experiences (Jurkiewicz & Brown, 1998; Kupperschmidt, 2000; Mannheim, 1972; Smola & Sutton, 2002; Strauss & Howe, 1991; Thau & Heflin, 1997). Consistent with Deal (2007), our study examines the following groups: "Silents: (born between 1925 and 1945), "Early Boomers" (born between 1946 and 1954), "Late Boomers" (born between 1955 and 1963), and "Gen Xers" (born between 1964 and 1986). However, given that most research on generational groups has not differentiated between Early Boomers and Late Boomers, our literature review will cover only three generational groups: Silents, Baby Boomers, and Gen Xers.

The Silent generation was born before the end of World War II. Silents are stereotypically described as dependable, loyal, trustworthy, risk-avoidant, and conservative (Egri & Ralston, 2004; Strauss & Howe, 1991;

Thau & Heflin, 1997). Though many people in this generation are retired, those still working may be powerful and influential in organizations.

Baby Boomers were born after the end of World War II until 1963, coinciding with the increase in birth rate as many troops came home from the war. Baby Boomers are stereotypically described as change agents and consensus-builders, overly occupied with their jobs (sometimes at the expense of their families), and as valuing personal development and self-fulfillment (Egri & Ralston, 2004; Kupperschmidt, 2000; Parker & Chusmir, 1990; Smola & Sutton, 2002; Strauss & Howe, 1991; Thau & Heflin 1997).

Members of Generation X (Gen Xers) were born after the end of the Baby Boom through 1986. The name Generation X comes from a book by Hamblett and Deverson (1964) and from Coupland (1991), who applied it to this group. Stereotypically, Gen Xers are materialistic, apathetic, highly individualistic, risk-takers, self-reliant, and entrepreneurial. In addition, they are comfortable with change and diversity. They are also described as placing low importance on job security (because many of them saw their parents, who had been loyal to their company, downsized or laid-off), and valuing personal freedom, challenging work, and a balance between their work and their life away from work (Craig & Bennett 1997; De Meuse, Bergmann, & Lester, 2001; Deal, 2007; Egri & Ralston, 2004; Jurkiewicz & Brown, 1998; Kupperschmidt, 2000; Tulgan, 1995).

RESEARCH COMPARING GENERATIONS

Much of the research on generational differences at work suggests that each generation is very different from one another. For instance, Gen Xers have different work values than other generations, want to be promoted faster than other generations, and are less loyal and more self- or "me"-focused (Smola & Sutton, 2002), reinforcing the stereotype that Gen Xers continually ask "what's in it for me?" (Karp, Sirias, & Arnold, 1999). In contrast, Baby Boomers are more likely than other generations to feel that work is one of the most important parts of a person's life (Smola & Sutton, 2002). Furthermore, Gen Xers place more importance on autonomy, independence, variety, excitement, and challenge than Baby Boomers, and both of these generations place more importance on the aforementioned values than the Silent generation (Egri & Ralston, 2004). While Gen Xers and Baby Boomers value achieving personal success through competence more than those in the Silent generation, the Silent generation values self-control, safety, stability, and respect more than Baby Boomers and Gen Xers (Egri & Ralston, 2004).

Older and younger workers also differ in their beliefs about the nature of careers, career development, and the "psychological contract" between employees and employers (Brousseau, Driver, Eneroth, & Larsson, 1996; De Meuse et al., 2001; Hirsch & Shanley, 1996; Putnam, 2000; Robinson & Jackson, 2001; Valcour & Tolbert, 2003). Older workers, such as Baby Boomers, are more likely to identify with the concept of a traditional career model, with relatively few and typically hierarchical job changes throughout their career (Hirsch & Shanley, 1996). Within a traditional career model, workers subscribe to a psychological contract in which their employer provides job security, status, and pay in return for their loyalty and hard work (Solomon, 1992). The nature of this reciprocal relationship also places the responsibility for career development on the employer because many older workers expect that in exchange for their loyalty, the employer will provide them with opportunities for upward development and mobility within the same organization (Greenhaus, Callanan, & Godshalk, 2000).

Younger generations, such as Gen Xers, are less likely to embrace a traditional career model. Instead, they are more likely to subscribe to the idea that careers are protean or boundaryless (Brousseau et al., 1996; Hirsch & Shanley, 1996). Protean careers are characterized by frequent change, self-invention, autonomy, and self-direction (Hall, 2002). The term boundaryless is often used to describe the organizational boundary-spanning nature of these careers (Arthur & Rousseau, 1996). That is, workers using this model may change jobs more frequently, both within and outside of the organization. In addition, under the boundaryless career model, younger workers appear to emphasize psychological success that results from achieving life goals, which are not limited to their work achievements but also include their achievements within other life spheres, such as family and other nonwork roles (Greenhaus et al., 2000). Younger generations appear to place far less importance on symbols of occupational status and instead desire flexibility and a sense of meaning from their work (Greenhaus et al., 2000). Another key aspect of the protean career is self-direction. The protean career follows the personal career choices of the individual, not the needs or goals of an organization (Hall, 2002). Thus, in this model, the responsibility for career development is not placed on the employer but, rather, on the employee. Because workers in this model may expect to make several major job or career changes over their life span, they tend to be more prepared for career transitions and place value on career development opportunities that make them more marketable both within and outside their current firm (Solomon, 1992).

Differences among generational groups have become one way to understand how to manage, motivate, work with, and develop different generations of employees. New managerial and human resource management practices and development strategies may need to be implemented to account for generational differences at work (Egri & Ralston, 2004; Jurkiewicz & Brown, 1998; Kupperschmidt, 2000). On one hand, older workers may be motivated by rewards and incentives in the form of status and pay. On the other hand, younger workers may be more motivated by challenging and personally meaningful work opportunities, and value their personal life away from work. As a result, different types of benefits and work environments (such as flexible work arrangements or telecommuting) may need to be considered (Rodriguez, Green, & Ree, 2003; Smola & Sutton, 2002).

Differences among generations also suggest that while both older and younger workers may seek developmental opportunities, generational groups may seek different kinds of development. For instance, if older workers are more motivated than younger workers by external rewards and status, they may focus on more targeted areas of development, including technical skills and issues pertinent to their life, such as mid-life stress and health (Noe et al., 2006; Wright, 2005, 2006). If younger workers are more focused on a need to find personally meaningful work, rather than upward mobility within the same organization, they may focus on acquiring broad transferable skills and seek opportunities to develop within the context of an ever-changing career (Greenhaus et al., 2000).

Though previous research has found that generational differences exist, others have noted similarities among generations. For instance, in a study of public sector employees, Jurkiewicz (2000), with few exceptions, found that many more similarities than differences existed among workers of different generations in what employees want in their jobs (i.e., work-related motivational factors). Similarly, Gen X and Baby Boomer IT professionals were more homogeneous than different in their thoughts on work involvement, work attachment, commitment to the organization, and commitment to the profession (Davis, Pawlowski, & Houston, 2006).

OBJECTIVES OF OUR STUDY

Different generational groups work within organizations. To become more informed about how to manage and work with these generations, our research examines whether different generations have different perceptions regarding their needs for development and learning at work. Although previous research has noted that the rate of participation in developmental opportunities is lower for older generations than younger ones (Maurer, 2001), there is a lack of research that examines whether differences exist regarding each generation's own attitudes, beliefs, and preferences for development and learning at work.

Development is a key process in an employee's success and involves all types of learning, including developing skills on the job, growing in self-awareness, developing relationships, and developing as a leader (Noe et al., 2006). Development is so important that the absence of development is cited as a key factor leading to career derailment (Leslie & Van Velsor, 1996). Moreover, executives who are successful in their job and career are often those who can learn from their past and who desire developmental opportunities in order to adapt and change across a variety of situations (Van Velsor, Moxley, & Bunker, 2004).

Previous research has examined the career outcomes associated with development for individual employees. But research also suggests that developing employees can positively affect organizational outcomes, as well. According to Eisenberger and colleagues' research on organizational support theory (Aselage & Eisenberger, 2003; Eisenberger, Armeli, Rex-winkel, Lynch, & Rhoades, 2001; Eisenberger, Cummings, Armeli, & Lynch 1997; Eisenberger, Huntington, Hutchison, & Sowa, 1986; Rhoades & Eisenberger, 2002; Rhoades, Eisenberger, & Armeli, 2001), employees want to know whether or not their organization values their contributions and cares for their well-being and development. Employees develop perceptions of organizational support that help them to fulfill their own needs for emotional support, affiliation, esteem, and approval. Based on social exchange theory and the norm of reciprocity (Blau, 1964; Eisenberger et al., 1986), in return for their perceived support from the organization, employees endeavor to help their organization reach highly-valued organizational goals and objectives. When employees feel that their organization values them and cares for their development and well-being, they return the favor by increasing their own performance and decreasing withdrawal behaviors such as lateness, absenteeism, or apathy. Hence, the more organizations provide opportunities for development to their employees, the more their employees will reciprocate by performing at a high standard.

Developing employees at work is important both for individuals and for the organizations. Generational theories suggest that differences exist among the generations with regard to their attitudes, beliefs, and preferences for development and learning at work. However, other research observes more similarities than differences among generations (e.g., Davis et al., 2006; Deal, 2007; Jurkiewicz, 2000). We seek to answer the following research questions in order to discover whether similarities or differences exist among generations:

Research Question 1: Are there differences among generations in their attitudes and beliefs about development and learning at work?

Research Question 2: Are there differences among generations in their preferences for learning soft skills (e.g., influencing; people skills) and hard skills (e.g., accounting; technical skills) for developmental needs?

Research Question 3: Are there differences among generations in the type of development they intend to engage in over the next year?

METHOD

Participants and Procedures

There were several ways through which we identified participants for our study. Participants filled out the survey from which the data came for a variety of reasons, including (a) their organization agreed to take part, (b) the survey was part of the pre-work for a leadership development program they were attending, or (c) they were taking a university course that gave them access to free developmental tools that were available to those who filled out the survey.

Results reported here are from a subsample of a larger dataset and focus on those in the librarian profession. Individuals received an initial e-mail asking for participation followed by a second e-mail. Actual response rates are not available because the link to the online survey was circulated so widely that we were unable to determine how many people received the link. Participants were 771 library workers who have only lived in the United States. Of the 771 workers, 93 were Silents, 320 were Early Baby Boomers, 155 were Late Baby Boomers, and 203 were Gen Xers. Because of the size of the Baby Boomer sample, we split them into two separate groups. (Deal (2007) also examined Baby Boomers in this manner.) In addition, 83.9% were women and 82.5% identified themselves as white. With regard to educational background, 88.5% of participants had at least a bachelor's degree (69.3% had a master's degree, 1.5% had more than a master's degree), and fewer than 9% had less than a bachelor's degree (e.g., associate's degree or high school diploma). Participants were found at various organizational levels. Just under 50% were from management levels (7.50% were from the top or executive levels, 40.92% were from upper middle management or middle management levels), about one third identified themselves as professionals (33.82%), and the rest self-identified as first level employees (6.97%), hourly employees (8.42%), or said organizational level was not relevant to their situation (2.37%). With regard to organizational tenure, 7.35% had been with the organization less than a year, 15.88% for 1-3 years, 12.34% for 3-5 years, 15.75% for 6-10 years, 15.75% for 11-15 years, 10.63% for 16-20 years, and 22.31% had been with their organization more than 21 years. Participants varied on tenure in their current position, with the majority (50.35%) between 0 and 3 years. The vast majority of respondents (87.75%) reported working at least 36 hours a week.

Respondents were asked to participate in a 20-minute online (Web-based) survey and were informed that results would be used for research purposes only. Data were analyzed with identifying information removed.

Measures

Each participant voluntarily completed a survey that included a series of questions about general lifestyle issues, work patterns, employee work attitudes, areas for development, interest in training options, values, learning tactics, and leadership attributes. Questions used for the purposes of our study focused on attitudes and beliefs about development and learning at work, preferred methods for soft and hard skill development, and what developmental opportunities workers intended to participate in over the following year. The survey was developed over the course of 2 years after substantial review of the literature, discussions with people in industry, and conversations with experts in the field. The subject areas for development came from a review of the literature, current lists of the typical training areas available at the time, and from conversations with industry experts to attempt to validate the list. Nine experts were asked to review the survey before it was administered.

To answer Research Question 1, participants responded to the following questions on a 5-point Likert scale with 1 = *strongly agree* to 5 = *strongly disagree*: (a) It is important to me to learn on the job; (b) On the job, I am developing the skills I need for the future; and (c) I believe that my organization will develop me as an employee. To answer Research Question 2, participants were asked how they wanted to receive both soft skills (e.g., influencing; people skills) and hard skills (e.g., accounting; technical skills) training and development, and were allowed to choose five of 15 options for each (soft skills and hard skills): *Web-based training; workbooks/manuals; satellite/broadcast TV/distance learning programs; computer-based training; case studies; outdoor experiential programs; computer-based games or simulations; books/reading; classroom instruction–live; games or simulations (non-computer-based); discussion groups; peer interaction/feedback; on-the-job; assessment and feedback*; and *one-on-one coaching*. Finally, to answer Research Question 3, participants were asked on a 5-point Likert scale with 1 = *very likely* to 5 = *very unlikely* how likely they were to engage in the following developmental initiatives within the next year: *leadership; international business knowledge; international customs/cultural adaptability; entrepreneurialism; diplomacy/politics at work; vision; performance appraisal; team building; problem solving/decision making; public speaking/presentation skills; hiring/interviewing; time management; quality/process improvement; managing change; strategic planning; diversity; self-awareness; conflict management; career coaching skills; management/business skills; communication skills; career planning; sales; life balance; creativity; ethics; foreign language; computer training;* and *skills training in field of expertise*.

RESULTS

Research Question 1

We conducted a series of one-way ANOVAs (alpha set at .05, missing values excluded analysis by analysis) to determine whether differences existed among employees of different generations with regard to their attitudes and beliefs about development and learning at work. Group means for each question can be found in Table 3.1. For the question "It is important to me to learn on the job" ANOVA results revealed no significant differences among the generations, $F (3, 762) = .854, p = $ ns. Each generation strongly believed in the importance of learning on the job. For the question "On the job, I am developing the skills I need for the future" ANOVA results revealed no significant differences among the generations, $F (3, 761) = .485, p = $ ns. Though not as strongly endorsed as the previous question, each generation believed they were developing skills needed for the future. Last, for the question "I believe that my organization will develop me as an employee" ANOVA results revealed no significant differences among the generations, $F (3, 759) = .944, p = $ ns. Again, though not as strongly endorsed as the previous questions, the generations tended to agree that their organizations were developing them as employees. In summary, employees across generations believed in the importance of learning on the job, believed they were developing skills for the future, and believed that their organizations were developing them as employees. This finding supported the notion that generations are more similar than they are different.

**Table 3.1.   Means and Standard Deviations
of Each Generational Group for Research Question 1**

Generational Group	n	M	SD
It is important to me to learn on the job			
Silents	92	1.33	0.70
Early Baby Boomers	318	1.35	0.66
Late Baby Boomers	155	1.27	0.47
Gen Xers	201	1.38	0.78
Overall	766	1.34	0.67
On the job, I am developing the skills I need for the future			
Silents	93	2.05	0.95
Early Baby Boomers	316	1.94	0.90
Late Baby Boomers	155	2.01	0.91
Gen Xers	201	2.01	1.02
Overall	765	1.99	0.94
I believe that my organization will develop me as an employee			
Silents	92	2.41	1.03
Early Baby Boomers	317	2.37	0.93
Late Baby Boomers	154	2.52	1.02
Gen Xers	200	2.47	0.98
Overall	763	2.43	0.97

Note: Differences in subsample sizes are due to missing data. Missing values were
excluded analysis by analysis.

Research Question 2

The second research question dealt with how employees preferred to
receive soft skills and hard skills training. We ran a series of chi-square
analyses to determine whether there were generational differences, with
the row variables being the different preferences for soft skills training
and the column variables being generational groups (Table 3.2). We
repeated the same analysis with hard skills training for the row variables
(Table 3.3).

Soft skills training and development. In Table 3.2, chi-square results are
displayed for preferences for soft skills training. The least popular
method overall was *satellite/broadcast TV/distance learning programs*, and the
most popular was *on-the-job* learning (see the first column, "Overall %
Yes"). For a majority of the initiatives, there were no statistically significant

**Table 3.2.   Percentages and Chi-Square Analyses
for Research Question 2: Soft Skills Training/Development**

Initiative	Overall % Yes	Silents % Yes	EBs % Yes	LBs % Yes	Gen Xers % Yes	χ^2	Φ
On-the-job training	80.0	80.6	80.6	74.2	83.3	4.71	
Discussion groups	66.5	78.5	66.9	67.7	59.6	10.47*	0.12
Peer interaction/ feedback	58.8	62.4	59.4	63.2	52.7	4.89	
Classroom instruction – live	57.7	52.7	63.4	59.4	49.8	10.70*	0.12
One-on-one coaching	53.6	49.5	53.8	58.7	51.2	2.73	
Books/reading	49.5	55.9	50.0	46.5	48.3	2.26	
Assessment and feedback	38.4	34.4	36.9	38.7	42.4	2.30	
Case studies	20.2	26.9	17.8	22.6	19.2	4.37	
Workbooks/manuals	16.3	11.8	15.3	14.8	21.2	5.37	
Web-based training	13.6	2.2	15.6	11.6	17.2	14.29**	0.14
Computer-based training	13.4	19.4	12.8	13.5	11.3	3.70	
Games or simulations (non-computer-based)	7.3	2.2	6.6	9.0	9.4	5.89	
Computer-based games or simulations	6.9	7.5	4.7	5.8	10.8	7.71	
Outdoor experiential programs	6.7	3.2	5.6	8.4	8.9	4.59	
Satellite/broadcast TV/ distance learning programs	5.1	7.5	5.0	6.5	3.0	3.68	

Note: EBs = Early Baby Boomers. LBs = Late Baby Boomers. *p < .05. **p < .01.

differences among the generations in their preferences for how to receive soft skills development. Statistically significant differences among the generations were found with respect to three types of training. First, there were group differences in the preference for *Web-based training* [χ^2 (3) = 14.29, p = .003, Φ = .14]. Among the four groups, Silents endorsed *Web-based training* the least (2.2% said "Yes") while Gen Xers endorsed *Web-based training* the most (17.2% said "Yes"). Second, there were group differences in the preference for *classroom instruction – live* [χ^2 (3) = 10.70, p = .013, Φ = .12]. For this particular preference, Gen Xers endorsed *class-*

**Table 3.3. Percentages and Chi-Square Analyses
for Research Question 2: Hard Skills Training/Development**

Initiative	Overall % Yes	Silents % Yes	EBs % Yes	LBs % Yes	Gen Xers % Yes	χ^2	Φ
Classroom instruction – live	77.7	80.6	83.4	74.8	69.5	15.23**	0.14
On-the-job training	73.4	75.3	73.1	70.3	75.4	1.33	
Workbooks/manuals	53.3	50.5	53.4	59.4	49.8	3.60	
Books/reading	51.1	45.2	51.6	49.7	54.2	2.24	
One-on-one coaching	50.1	45.2	50.0	54.8	48.8	2.44	
Computer-based training	46.3	51.6	45.0	47.1	45.3	1.39	
Web-based training	28.9	17.2	27.8	31.0	34.5	9.77*	0.11
Peer interaction/feedback	26.5	33.3	25.3	27.1	24.6	2.86	
Discussion groups	26.3	34.4	28.8	25.2	19.7	8.80*	0.11
Assessment and feedback	22.4	23.7	20.9	23.9	23.2	0.74	
Case studies	11.2	9.7	10.3	9.0	14.8	3.83	
Computer-based games or simulations	10.6	10.8	7.8	12.3	13.8	5.24	
Satellite/broadcast TV/ distance learning programs	9.2	8.6	10.3	11.0	6.4	2.99	
Games or simulations (non-computer-based)	4.0	2.2	2.8	6.5	4.9	4.86	
Outdoor experiential programs	1.3	0.0	1.6	0.6	2.0	2.63	

Note: EBs = Early Baby Boomers. LBs = Late Baby Boomers. *$p < .05$. **$p < .01$.

room instruction – live the least (49.8% said "Yes") and "Early Baby Boomers" endorsed *classroom instruction – live* the most (63.4% said "Yes"). Finally, there were group differences in the preference for *discussion groups* [χ^2 (3) = 10.47, $p = .015$, Φ = .12]. Gen Xers endorsed *discussion groups* the least (59.6% said "Yes") while Silents endorsed it the most (78.5% said "Yes").

Hard skills training and development. In Table 3.3, the chi-square results are displayed for preferences for hard skills training. The least popular method for hard skills training for all generations was *outdoor experiential programs*, and the most popular was *classroom instruction – live* (see "Overall % Yes" column). For a majority of the initiatives, there were no statistically significant differences among the generations in their preferences for how to receive hard skills development. The statistically significant differences among the generations were the same as those found in the soft skills training questions: (a) *Web-based training* [χ^2 (3) = 9.77, p = .021, Φ = .11], which was least endorsed by Silents (17.2% said "Yes") and most endorsed by Gen Xers (34.5% said "Yes") among the four groups; (b) *classroom instruction – live* [χ^2 (3) = 15.23, p = .002, Φ = .14], which was least endorsed by Gen Xers (69.5% said "Yes") and most endorsed by "Early Baby Boomers" (83.4% said "Yes") among the four groups; and (c) *discussion groups* [χ^2 (3) = 8.80, p = .032, Φ = .11], which was least endorsed by Gen Xers (19.7% said "Yes") and most endorsed by Silents (34.4% said "Yes") among the four groups.

Research Question 3

The third research question focused on what kinds of development employees intended to engage in during the following year. The results are displayed in Table 3.4. The most likely types of development were *skills training in my field of expertise* and *computer training*, while the least likely were *international business knowledge* and *sales*. Using one-way ANOVAs (alpha set at .05, missing values excluded analysis by analysis) to determine whether differences existed among employees of different generations, for a majority of the initiatives, there were no differences among generations in their preferences for the types of development they intended to engage in over the next year. There were three development initiatives that were statistically significantly different among the generations. The first was *leadership* [F (3, 754) = 3.52, p = .015, η^2 = .01]. The Least Significant Difference (LSD) post hoc test revealed that the significant difference was between Silents and Gen Xers, with the latter being more likely to intend to engage in leadership development. The second was *career planning* [F (3, 756) = 13.76, p < .001, η^2 = .05]. The LSD post hoc test revealed that all groups were significantly different from each other, except between Silents and Early Baby Boomers. Younger generations were more likely to believe that they would engage in career planning development than older generations. Finally, there was a statistically significant difference among the generations in *foreign language* [F (3, 753) = 5.06, p = .002, η^2 = .02]. The LSD post hoc test revealed that Gen Xers were different from all other generations, and that they were more likely to believe that they would engage in development concerning foreign languages than the other, older generations.

Table 3.4. Descriptives and ANOVA Results for Different Development Initiatives for Research Question 3

Development Initiative	Overall M (sd)	Silents M (sd)	EBs M (sd)	LBs M (sd)	Gen Xers M (sd)	F	η^2
Skills training in field of expertise	1.90 (1.00)	2.02 (1.06)	1.86 (0.94)	2.00 (1.04)	1.84 (1.04)	1.35	
Computer training	2.01 (1.01)	1.97 (0.93)	1.92 (0.92)	2.15 (1.16)	2.05 (1.03)	1.92	
Problem solving/decision making	2.32 (1.00)	2.27 (1.00)	2.26 (1.03)	2.48 (1.00)	2.32 (0.95)	1.70	
Team building	2.40 (1.04)	2.27 (1.04)	2.36 (1.06)	2.45 (1.02)	2.49 (1.03)	1.26	
Leadership	2.47 (1.20)	2.76 (1.23)	2.49 (1.21)	2.50 (1.18)	2.28 (1.17)	3.52*	.01
Managing change	2.55 (1.12)	2.56 (1.22)	2.43 (1.12)	2.59 (1.05)	2.71 (1.13)	2.61	
Communication skills	2.61 (1.06)	2.64 (1.06)	2.57 (1.04)	2.69 (1.03)	2.58 (1.10)	0.47	
Conflict management	2.62 (1.05)	2.77 (1.21)	2.54 (1.02)	2.69 (1.00)	2.61 (1.06)	1.40	
Diversity	2.67 (1.10)	2.51 (1.02)	2.63 (1.08)	2.79 (1.20)	2.72 (1.09)	1.59	
Performance appraisal	2.71 (1.17)	2.69 (1.20)	2.63 (1.18)	2.78 (1.15)	2.80 (1.14)	1.15	
Quality/process improvement	2.73 (1.13)	2.72 (1.18)	2.64 (1.12)	2.88 (1.05)	2.77 (1.16)	1.61	
Vision	2.73 (1.14)	2.72 (1.23)	2.70 (1.14)	2.76 (1.11)	2.77 (1.12)	0.19	
Strategic planning	2.75 (1.20)	2.72 (1.27)	2.65 (1.18)	2.85 (1.19)	2.86 (1.20)	1.64	
Time management	2.77 (1.13)	2.85 (1.22)	2.69 (1.13)	2.89 (1.08)	2.76 (1.14)	1.19	
Public speaking/presentation skills	2.78 (1.17)	2.71 (1.28)	2.77 (1.18)	2.85 (1.14)	2.77 (1.12)	0.30	
Self-awareness	2.84 (1.12)	2.82 (1.13)	2.78 (1.15)	2.93 (1.05)	2.88 (1.11)	0.73	
Management/business skills	2.91 (1.14)	2.97 (1.22)	2.88 (1.15)	2.98 (1.08)	2.87 (1.12)	0.44	
Creativity	2.91 (1.23)	2.64 (1.19)	2.98 (1.21)	2.99 (1.25)	2.87 (1.24)	2.03	
Career coaching skills	2.95 (1.08)	2.93 (1.11)	2.94 (1.08)	2.91 (1.05)	3.01 (1.10)	0.30	
Diplomacy/politics at work	3.05 (1.16)	3.24 (1.21)	3.11 (1.16)	3.00 (1.06)	2.89 (1.18)	2.41	
Ethics	3.07 (1.18)	2.93 (1.23)	3.13 (1.18)	3.09 (1.16)	3.04 (1.17)	0.71	
Hiring/interviewing	3.10 (1.22)	3.07 (1.30)	3.02 (1.25)	3.22 (1.12)	3.15 (1.21)	1.11	
Life balance	3.14 (1.22)	3.11 (1.33)	3.20 (1.21)	3.18 (1.22)	3.03 (1.20)	0.95	
Career planning	3.28 (1.16)	3.70 (1.18)	3.44 (1.12)	3.19 (1.15)	2.90 (1.12)	13.76***	.05
Foreign language	3.39 (1.30)	3.52 (1.33)	3.45 (1.27)	3.58 (1.28)	3.09 (1.33)	5.06**	.02
International customs/cultural adaptability	3.61 (1.25)	3.36 (1.35)	3.64 (1.22)	3.71 (1.27)	3.60 (1.22)	1.64	
Entrepreneurialism	3.96 (1.15)	3.99 (1.15)	4.00 (1.13)	4.04 (1.13)	3.84 (1.19)	1.05	
International business knowledge	4.19 (1.01)	4.20 (1.09)	4.23 (0.94)	4.22 (0.97)	4.11 (1.09)	0.70	
Sales	4.30 (0.93)	4.26 (1.06)	4.35 (0.87)	4.36 (0.88)	4.18 (1.01)	1.77	

Note: EBs = Early Baby Boomers. LBs = Late Baby Boomers. *p < .05. **p < .01. ***p < .001.

DISCUSSION

Organizations are made up of workers from different generations, from Silents to Baby Boomers to Gen Xers. While some research suggests that differences exist among these generations (e.g., Brousseau et al., 1996; Egri & Ralston, 2004; Hirsch & Shanley, 1996; Smola & Sutton, 2002), others suggest the differences are minimal (e.g., Davis et al., 2006; Jurkiewicz, 2000). Our study investigated whether differences existed among library workers of different generations with regard to their attitudes, beliefs, and preferences about development. Our results tend to support previous research that found greater similarities than differences among generations in preferences for learning and development.

With regard to the first research question, there were no statistically significant differences among the generations regarding the importance of learning and developing on the job. All generations thought it was important to learn on the job. They all also believed that they were developing skills needed for the future and that the organization was developing them as employees, though this point was endorsed to a slightly lesser extent. Our findings seem to run counter to research that suggests substantial differences exist among generations when it comes to the issue of learning (e.g., Brousseau et al., 1996; Egri & Ralston, 2004; Hirsch & Shanley, 1996; Smola & Sutton, 2002). Our research suggests that when it comes to workplace learning and development, there are more similarities than differences among the generations.

With regard to the second research question, preferences for how to receive both soft and hard skills training and development were also similar among the generations. For instance, for soft skills training and development, a majority of people wanted *on-the-job training, discussion groups, peer interaction/feedback, live classroom instruction,* and *one-on-one coaching*. Few employees desired *satellite/broadcast TV/distance learning programs, outdoor experiential programs, computer* or *non-computer based games or simulations*. For hard skills training and development, a majority of respondents indicated that they wanted *live classroom instruction, on-the-job training, workbooks/manuals, books/reading,* and *one-on-one coaching*. Few employees indicated that they desired *outdoor experiential programs, satellite/broadcast TV/distance learning programs,* and *computer* or *non-computer based games or simulations*. These results indicate that there are definite, preferred methods by which employees want to receive both soft and hard skills training and development, and that there are more similarities than differences among the generations with regard to those preferences. Where differences existed among the generations, the effect sizes (Φ) were rather small, so the practical significance of these differences may be small. The trend suggests that younger generations (i.e., Gen

Xers) may be more likely to prefer *Web-based training* and are less likely to prefer *live classroom instruction* and *discussion groups* than the older generations. These findings fit with common beliefs that younger workers are more technology oriented than older generations, because they have grown up with technology and have become comfortable using it. With younger generations growing up with technology and perhaps living in a more virtual world, learning preferences may focus more on visual, electronic, and virtual learning, and less on face-to-face learning (Proserpio & Gioia, 2007).

Regarding the third research question, participants had stronger preferences for some developmental opportunities than others. Employees in our study wanted development in *skills training in their field of expertise* and in *computer training*, and did not prefer developmental opportunities in *international business knowledge* or in *sales*. Again, there were more similarities among the generations than there were differences. The effect sizes (η^2) were small (except for *career planning*), so the practicality of these differences must be considered.

It is interesting to note that younger generations such as Gen Xers were more likely to say they intended to participate in *leadership development, career planning*, and *foreign language* than older generations. Career theory and the changing global context within which we work may help explain these findings. For instance, the boundaryless career model suggests that Gen Xers highly regard career development and professional development opportunities, because these options make them more marketable not only within their organization but also externally (Solomon, 1992). Boundaryless career models also suggest that Gen Xers are less job-focused and more career-focused (Greenhaus et al., 2000; Hirsch & Shanley, 1996). These factors could explain why *leadership development* and *career planning* are more highly regarded by Gen Xers than other generations. However, it should also be acknowledged that this effect might simply be the result of life stage differences for older and younger workers. Older workers may be less interested in career development opportunities because they have already made their career plans or because they are nearing the end of their career and do not desire further development.

Finally, with the world of work becoming increasingly global (Gupta & Govindarajan, 2000; Javidan & House, 2002), workers show a greater appreciation for understanding and working with others who speak different languages. This shift may explain why Gen Xers see development in a *foreign language* as making them more marketable in their careers.

Limitations and Future Research

There are several limitations to our study. First, we could not control for certain demographics such as organizational level and gender, which could have influenced results. Our sample (librarian workers) may limit the generalizability of findings to other sectors, such as private, for-profit organizations. However, published research has used librarian samples to generalize findings to a broader population (e.g., Cogliser & Schriesheim, 2000; Day, Cross, Ringseis, & Williams, 1999; Green, Anderson, & Shivers, 1996; Williams, Gavin, & Williams, 1996). Data from librarians may not be generalizable to all employment and organization types, however, the research must start from a position of strength. The demographics of librarians point towards a group that is highly educated (compared to the average U.S. worker) and has a certain thirst for knowledge, as they have decided to work in an environment surrounded by books. Among other U.S. workers, librarians are presumed to cast a very critical eye toward training and development opportunities—having participated in the learning process for years. Our sample also consisted of individuals born in and currently living in the United States. Our results may not generalize to individuals outside of the United States and, therefore, future research might focus on more globally diverse groups.

Future research should also include younger generations, such as "Generation Y" or "Millenials." Recent research suggests that these younger generations, similar to Gen Xers, may follow a kaleidoscope career model (Sullivan & Mainiero, 2007), wherein careers are defined by the workers' own values, not prescribed by the organization's values. Careers are dynamic, and employees, particularly those in younger generations, want the best fit based on their own priorities at work and away from work (Sullivan & Mainiero, 2007). Future research should examine whether these attitudes and beliefs differ among other generations at work.

In addition, our research only asked about attitudes, beliefs, and preferences with regard to learning and development. Future research should attempt to determine *why* people want the development they want and should examine *how* these differences (or similarities) affect their actual participation in these developmental activities in the workplace.

Finally, future research should consider a longitudinal approach. Our research examined a cross section of workers. Future research should attempt to gather data on the same employees across years of employment. From this proposed longitudinal study, one could determine how attitudes and beliefs might change over time within the individual, rather than what the differences are among groups of people of different generations at one point in time. The findings of a cross-sectional survey cannot rule out that observed group differences may be due to age, rather than generational differences. The most that our research can say about age differences is that they might exist. Indeed, it is important to disentangle differences due to age and differences due to generational groups. Future research should attempt to test this notion by examining longitudinal data from the same cohort across the life span.

Implications

There are three primary conclusions that can be drawn from our research. First, the results of our study suggest that all generations believe development is important. In contrast to current stereotypes, even older generations want to be developed, and have specific preferences for how they want to be developed and what they want to learn. Second, our research suggests that most employees—regardless of generation—want to be developed. Finally, the preferences for and types of development may vary in their popularity for employees, but they do not vary among generations. In other words, younger and older employees alike favor certain developmental initiatives and opportunities.

The results from our study imply that a vast majority of workers—regardless of age—believe (a) that development is important on the job, (b) that they are developing the skills needed on the job, and (c) that their organization is developing them. Because of the importance that development has on individuals' careers (Leslie & Van Velsor, 1996; Van Velsor et al., 2004), employees, no matter their age, deserve the opportunity to learn and be developed at work. However, just as development is important from the perspective of the individual, it is also important for the continued viability of organizations. Organizations should also promote continuous learning and espouse the belief that development is important for their own employees. According to organizational support theory, such an organizational strategy is likely to improve an organization's performance, as well as the organization's retention of employees (Aselage & Eisenberger, 2003; Eisenberger et al., 2001; Eisenberger et al., 1997; Eisenberger et al., 1986; Rhoades & Eisenberger, 2002; Rhoades et al., 2001). The more employees feel their organization supports and cares for their well-being and development, the more those same employees will return the favor by performing effectively. Organizations should pay attention to findings such as these, for such findings give a snapshot of what employees want for development and how employees feel they can best be developed.

According to our research, there are methods that all generations prefer for receiving soft and hard skills training and development, and there are certain developmental opportunities in which all generations of employees intend to participate in the near future. Organizations, in particular training and development departments, need to be mindful that some practices and methods for learning and development are preferred by all generations for soft skills and hard skills (e.g., *on-the-job training* or *live classroom instruction*) and some are not desired by any generation (e.g., *outdoor programs, distance learning, games,* or *simulations*). In addition, employees of all generations intended to participate in certain developmental opportunities (e.g., *skills training in field of expertise* and *computer training*) and not in others (e.g., *international business knowledge* and *sales*). In the interest of effective learning and development, the thoughts and opinions of workers, and the preferences for how they best learn, should be taken into account by organizations and their training and development departments when designing developmental opportunities.

Though research states that participation rates for development are lower for older workers than younger workers (Maurer, 2001), the results of our study suggest that older workers do not have any less desire to be developed than do younger workers, and that certain developmental opportunities are desired for employees regardless of their generation. With this in mind, perhaps companies should consider a change in the way that they target and promote developmental opportunities for their workers. Developmental opportunities should not just be targeted at younger or "fast-track" employees; rather, they should be available and encouraged among workers of all ages, including those seeking midcareer renewal (Power, this volume) or employment that bridges work and retirement (Wang, Adams, Beehr, & Schultz, this volume).

REFERENCES

Allerton, H. E. (2001). Generation why. *T+D, 55*(11), 56-60.

Arthur, M. B., & Rousseau, D. M. (1996). *Boundaryless careers: A new employment principle for a new organizational era.* New York: Oxford University Press.

Aselage, J., & Eisenberger, R. (2003). Perceived organizational support and psychological contracts: A theoretical integration. *Journal of Organizational Behavior, 24,* 491-509.

Blau, P. (1964). *Exchange and power in social life.* New York: Wiley.

Brousseau, K. R., Driver, M. J., Eneroth, K., & Larsson, R. (1996). Career pandemonium: Realigning organizations and individuals. *Academy of Management Executive, 10*(4), 52-66.

Chester, E. (2002). *Employing generation why?: Understanding, managing, and motivating your new workforce.* Lakewood, CO: Tucker House.

Cogliser, C. C., & Schriesheim, C. A. (2000). Exploring work unit context and leader-member exchange: A multi-level perspective. *Journal of Organizational Behavior, 21,* 487-511.

Coupland, D. (1991). *Generation X: Tales for an accelerated culture*. New York: St. Martin's.

Craig, S. C., & Bennett, S. E. (1997). *After the boom: The politics of Generation X*. New York: Rowman and Littlefield.

Davis, J. B., Pawlowski, S. D., & Houston, A. (2006). Work commitments of Baby Boomers and GenXers in the IT profession: Generational differences or myth? *Journal of Computer Information Systems, 46*, 43-49.

Day, D. V., Cross, W. E., Jr., Ringseis, E. L., & Williams, T. L. (1999). Self-categorization and identity construction associated with managing diversity. *Journal of Vocational Behavior, 54*, 188-195.

De Meuse, K. P., Bergmann, T. J., & Lester, S. W. (2001). An investigation of the relational component of the psychological contract across time, generation, and employment status. *Journal of Managerial Issues, 13*, 102–118.

Deal, J. J. (2007). *Retiring the generation gap: How employees young and old can find common ground*. San Francisco: Jossey-Bass.

Egri, C. P., & Ralston, D. A. (2004). Generation cohorts and personal values: A comparison of China and the U.S. *Organization Science, 15*, 210-220.

Eisenberger, R., Armeli, S., Rexwinkel, B., Lynch, P. D., & Rhoades, L. (2001). Reciprocation of perceived organizational support. *Journal of Applied Psychology, 86*, 42-51.

Eisenberger, R., Cummings, J., Armeli, S., & Lynch, P. (1997). Perceived organizational support, discretionary treatment, and job satisfaction. *Journal of Applied Psychology, 82*, 812-820.

Eisenberger, R., Huntington, R., Hutchison, S., & Sowa, D. (1986). Perceived organizational support. *Journal of Applied Psychology, 71*, 500-507.

Facteau, J. D., Dobbins, G. H., Russell, J. E. A., Ladd, R. T., & Kudisch, J. D. (1995). The influence of general perceptions of the training environment on pretraining motivation and perceived training transfer. *Journal of Management, 21*, 1-25.

Green, S. G., Anderson, S. E., & Shivers, S. L. (1996). Demographic and organizational influences on leader-member exchange and related work attitudes. *Organizational Behavior and Human Decision Processes, 66*, 203-214.

Greenhaus, J. H., Callanan, G. A., & Godshalk, V. M. (2000). *Career management* (3rd ed.). New York: Dryden.

Gupta, A. K., & Govindarajan, V. (2000). Managing global expansion: A conceptual framework. *Business Horizons, 43*(2), 45-54.

Hall, D. T. (2002). *Careers inside and outside of organizations*. Thousand Oaks, CA: SAGE.

Hamblett, C., & Deverson, J. (1964). *Generation X*. Oxford: Gold Medal Books.

Harris, P. (2005). Boomer vs. echo boomer: The work war? *T+D, 59*(5), 44-50.

Hirsch, P. M., & Shanley, M. (1996). The rhetoric of boundaryless—Or, how the newly empowered managerial class bought into its own marginalization. In M. B. Arthur & D. M. Rousseau (Eds.), *The boundaryless career: A new employment principle for a new organizational era* (pp. 218-233). New York: Oxford University Press.

Javidan, M., & House, R. J. (2002). Leadership and cultures around the world: Findings from GLOBE: An introduction to the special issue. *Journal of World Business, 37*, 1-2.

Jurkiewicz, C. L. (2000). Generation X and the public employee. *Public Personnel Management, 29*(1), 55-74.

Jurkiewicz, C. L., & Brown R. G. (1998). GenXers vs. boomers vs matures: Generational comparisons of public employee motivation. *Review of Public Personnel Administration 18*, 18-37.

Karp, H., Sirias, D., & Arnold, K. (1999). Teams: Why generation X marks the spot. *The Journal for Quality and Participation, 22*, 30-33.

Kupperschmidt, B. R. (2000). Multigeneration employees: Strategies for effective management. *The Health Care Manager, 19*, 65-76.

Lancaster, L. C., & Stillman, D. (2002). *When generations collide*. New York: Harper-Business.

Leslie, J. B., & Van Velsor, E. (1996). *A look at derailment today: North America and Europe*. Greensboro, NC: Center for Creative Leadership.

Mannheim, K. (1972). The problem of generations. In P. G. Altbach & R. S. Laufer (Eds.), *The new pilgrims: Youth protest in transition* (pp. 101-138). New York: David McKay.

Maurer, T. J. (2001). Career-relevant learning and development, worker age, and beliefs about self-efficacy for development. *Journal of Management, 27*, 123-142.

Noe, R. A., Hollenbeck, J. R., Gerhart, B., & Wright, P. M. (2006). *Human resource management: Gaining a competitive advantage* (5th ed.). New York: McGraw-Hill.

Parker, B., & Chusmir, L. (1990). A generational and sex-based view of managerial work values. *Psychological Reports, 66*, 947–950.

Power, S. J. (2009). Midcareer renewal: A research agenda for the twenty-first century. In S. G. Baugh & S. E. Sullivan (Eds.), *Research in careers: Vol. 1. Maintaining focus, energy, and options over the career* (pp. 107-133). Charlotte, NC: Information Age.

Proserpio, L., & Gioia, D. A. (2007). Teaching the virtual generation. *Academy of Management Learning & Education, 6*(1), 69-80.

Putnam, R. D. (2000). *Bowling alone: The collapse and revival of American community*. New York: Simon and Schuster.

Rhoades, L., & Eisenberger, R. (2002). Perceived organizational support: A review of the literature. *Journal of Applied Psychology, 87*, 698-714.

Rhoades, L., Eisenberger, R., & Armeli, S. (2001). Affective commitment to the organization: The contribution of perceived organizational support. *Journal of Applied Psychology, 86*, 825-836.

Rivera, R. J., & Paradise, A. (2006). *State of the industry in leading enterprises: ASTD's annual review of trends in workplace learning and performance*. Alexandria, VA: American Society for Training & Development.

Robinson, R. V., & Jackson, E. F. (2001). Is trust in others declining in America? An age-period-cohort analysis. *Social Science Research, 30*, 117-145

Rodriguez, R. O., Green, M. T., & Ree, M. J. (2003). Leading generation X: Do the old rules apply? *Journal of Leadership and Organizational Studies, 9*, 67-75.

Smola, K. W., & Sutton, C. D. (2002). Generational differences: Revisiting generational work values for the new millennium. *Journal of Organizational Behavior, 23*, 363-382.

Solomon, C. M. (1992). Managing the baby busters. *Personnel Journal, 71*(3), 52-59.

Strauss, W., & Howe, N. (1991). *Generations: The history of America's future, 1584–2089.* New York: Quill William Morrow.

Sullivan, S. E., & Mainiero, L. A. (2007). Kaleidoscope careers: Benchmarking ideas for fostering family-friendly workplaces. *Organizational Dynamics, 36*(1), 45-62.

Thau, R. D., & Heflin, J. S. (1997). *Generations apart: Xers vs. boomers vs. the elderly.* Amherst, NY: Prometheus Books.

Tulgan, B. (1995). *Managing generation X: How to bring out the best in young talent.* New York: Nolo.

Valcour, P. M., & Tolbert, P. S. (2003). Gender, family, and career in the era of boundarylessness: Determinants and effects of intra- and interorganizational mobility. *International Journal of Human Resource Management, 14*, 768-787.

Van Velsor, E., Moxley, R. S., & Bunker, K. A. (2004). The leader development process. In C. McCauley & E. Van Velsor (Eds.), *The Center for Creative Leadership handbook of leadership development* (2nd ed., pp. 204-233). San Francisco: Jossey-Bass and Center for Creative Leadership.

Wang, M., Adams, G. A., Beehr, T. A., & Shultz, K. S. (2009). Employment and retirement: Issues and opportunities during the latter part of one's career. In S. G. Baugh & S. E. Sullivan (Eds.), *Research in careers: Vol. 1. Maintaining focus, energy, and options over the career* (pp. 135-162). Charlotte, NC: Information Age.

Williams, L. J., Gavin, M. B., & Williams, M. L. (1996). Measurement and non-measurement processes with negative affectivity and employee attitudes. *Journal of Applied Psychology, 81*, 88-101.

Wright, J. (2005). Coaching mid-life, baby boomer women in the workplace. *Work: Journal of Prevention, Assessment & Rehabilitation, 25*, 179-183.

Wright, J. (2006). Crisis and opportunity: Coaching older workers in the workplace. *Work: Journal of Prevention, Assessment & Rehabilitation, 26*, 93-96.

CHAPTER 4

CAREER PLATEAUING
IN OLDER WORKERS

Contextual and Psychological Drivers

Dianne Bown-Wilson and Emma Parry

Against a background of demographic, social, and economic change, issues relating to the careers of older employees are escalating in importance. People are living and working longer (Loretto, Vickerstaff, & White, 2005; McNair, Flynn, Owen, Humphreys, & Woodfield, 2004). At the same time, technology, globalization, and resource limitations are fundamentally altering the shape of career structures and the nature of "career" throughout the duration of working life.

As the purpose of this volume is to examine ways of maintaining energy, focus, and options over the career life span, it would hardly seem complete without an examination of some of the key issues relating to the latter years of work. As this is a broad field, we have chosen to concentrate specifically on what we believe is one of the most significant and under-researched areas relevant to older workers: the relationship between (older) age and the highly familiar phenomenon of career plateauing.

Maintaining Focus, Energy, and Options Over the Career
pp. 75–105

Our focus in this chapter is to address what we believe are three fundamental questions that lie at the heart of career plateauing in older employees:

1. *Who decides* the nature of older individuals' careers? Do employers continue to play the greatest role in decisions about the nature of their older employees' careers, or do individuals deliberately take steps to resist further hierarchical progress, engineering themselves into positions where they are psychologically comfortable?

2. *What matters* most to older employees? Are they motivated by continuing *extrinsic* rewards characterized by promotion and status, or do they increasingly seek *intrinsic* psychological satisfaction, potentially resulting in external perceptions of plateauing?

3. *How desirable* are later life career plateaus and how dependent is this desirability on whether the career plateau is the result of employer actions (circumstance) or individual employee decisions (choice)?

A career plateau in its simplest form is that point in a career at which the individual recognizes that further hierarchical mobility seems unlikely (Ference, Stoner, & Warren, 1977). This is an objective view based on the absence of further vertical promotion and associated increases in pay and status. Bardwick (1986) and Allen, Russell, Poteet, and Dobbins (1999) extended this definition to cover the notion of job content plateauing, which occurs when there is no longer scope for growth within an individual's job and it has ceased to be personally challenging. Applebaum and Finestone (1994) chose to represent this difference as the distinction between organizational plateauing and personal plateauing. Therefore, we can suggest that a career plateau represents a situation in which employee mobility, whether upward, horizontal, geographical, or even psychological, is unlikely.

Although plateauing is more likely to occur in older workers (Armstrong-Stassen, 2008), younger workers may also reach a point at which mobility is difficult. The key difference between the two groups is that younger employees who find themselves in this position usually have the option to change jobs and seek advancement elsewhere. This option is more difficult for older employees because, to a large extent, employers are often reluctant to recruit older people (Daniel & Heywood, 2007; Greller & Stroh, 2004).

The opportunity to focus on career plateauing among older workers is timely. Much has changed in the careers arena since a body of work on career plateauing was undertaken in the 1970s and 80s, but little new material has emerged to elucidate how such changes are currently impacting both older individuals' careers and employer policies and practices. In particular, there is a lack of clarity concerning the relative influence exerted on later life careers by age-related changes, employee motivation, length of tenure, and employer attitudes. There is even a question as to whether, in today's employment context, career plateauing as a concept remains the same for older individuals as that which may be experienced in midcareer.

In the past, linear theories of career, such as those of Super (1957) and Levinson, Darrow, Klein, Levinson, and McKee (1978), have tended to view career plateauing as an almost inevitable process whereby the individual naturally gravitated towards doing less and marking time on the way to retirement in the final few years of working life (Veiga, 1981). We suggest that this scenario is no longer the case. Today, a combination of economic pressures on both businesses and individuals, flattening career structures in which employees peak earlier, and longer working lives mean that the "latter" stage of an individual's career could be as long as 30 years. As a result, career plateauing is increasing in frequency and duration as employees retire later (Ettington, 1997).

This situation presents employers with a number of challenges.

1. How can they manage the performance of an increasing number of older people who, for a wide variety of reasons, want or need to work beyond what has been regarded as normal retirement age?

2. How can they prevent key older individuals from leaving the workplace prematurely, taking with them irreplaceable skills and experience?

3. How can they maintain and increase the motivation and engagement of older employees who previously would have been left to coast along quietly until retirement?

4. How can they identify employees who will represent a good return on investment if additional training and development programs are provided?

5. How can they recognize and develop policies and programs to meet the specific needs of older workers, such as flexible working, while avoiding the dangers of prioritizing the needs of older employees above those of other employee groups?

6. And perhaps most challenging of all, how can employers address the long-standing problem of creating promotion opportunities for younger workers without the practical and psychological difficulties of dismissing long-serving employees (Brennan et al., 2007)?

Improved knowledge about the interrelationship of age and career plateauing could assist employers in addressing these issues.

There are also numerous challenges for older employees themselves.
There is inadequate evidence at this time concerning individual perspectives on the relationship between age, career progression, and career plateauing that employees can use to shape their current or future career.
Existing research has been largely quantitative in nature (e.g. Ettington,
1997; Evans & Gilbert, 1984; Lussier & Wister, 1995) and either undertaken from an employer perspective or focused on the needs and aspirations of older employees *as a group* rather than as individuals. It has also
largely considered employees' reactions to becoming plateaued, rather
than the causes of plateauing and individual motivational implications
(Armstrong-Stassen, 2008).

Developing good practice concerning successful adaptation to new initiatives in later life could encourage change among older employees. Further guidance as to how older employees should *feel* and what might be
appropriate actions and responses in a changed and changing workplace
environment may be helpful and reinvigorating, although no research to
date appears to have been undertaken to provide this guidance.

In this chapter we will examine what is known about how individual
differences and contemporary contextual workplace variables affect
career plateauing in later life and what this means for older workers and
their employers. This process will involve a review of the literature from
both organizational and employee perspectives, recommending areas for
further investigation. By considering the differing pressures on both
employers and older employees, we will highlight where future research is
needed to allow employers to gain insight into which approach to managing plateaued employees will work best for particular individuals in particular contexts.

OLDER WORKERS' CAREERS

The concept of age is a complex one. Potentially it may encompass
notions of relative and functional age as well as pure chronological age.
There is no clearly recognized and accepted definition of *older* employees
to use as a starting point. Despite its frequent inclusion as a diversity
issue, *older age* is not an attribute that is either present or not, as with gender or ethnicity; its meaning relies heavily on both context and individual
self-image. As a result, the term is often used simply to refer to those who
are no longer young or in the upward phases of career development. In
relation to career plateauing, the age at which workers' careers tend to
plateau may vary by industry or job role. It may also depend on an indi-

vidual's age relative to colleagues and to organizational norms of what constitutes *old* or *senior*. We choose to follow the definition provided by Greller and Simpson (1999), who refer to late career as covering workers 50 to 70 years of age. The emphasis on career stage rather than the exact nature of individuals at that stage in terms of physical, mental, and social acuity is, we believe, a helpful one.

Research into workplace aging has commonly focused on "older workers' careers" as the unit of analysis. Frequently, the composition of the older worker cohort, particularly in terms of education, gender, and social situation is disregarded or unclear (Greller & Simpson 1999). Also, when considering careers, much hinges on the type of career, nature of work, and the context in terms of sector and size of business within which it is located, elements which at times receive insufficient attention. This is particularly true of the distinction between older workers, some of whom may consider their working lives as representing a series of jobs rather than a formalized career, and "older managers," who generally will experience careers in terms of some kind of structure.

Regardless of the lack of a consistent definition of "older workers," in today's workplace numerous decisions are made, formally or informally, consciously or unconsciously, concerning the treatment of "older employees" (Taylor & Walker, 1994). Despite legislation designed to abolish discriminatory practices based on age (introduced in the U.K. as recently as 2006 but much earlier in the U.S.), negative attitudes toward older individuals in the workplace persist (Loretto & White, 2006). *Ageism*—a process of systematic stereotyping of and discrimination against people because they are old (Butler & Lewis, 1973)—and *age discrimination*—where age is the deciding factor when an employer takes decisions to recruit, promote, retrain, or retire/dismiss an employee (Brennan et al., 2007)—are continuing problems (Parry, 2006).

It is ageism, perhaps more than any other factor, that has a continuing influence on the career options of older plateaued workers, exerting unique pressures on individuals in terms of the decisions they make. This situation is highlighted here in the first of a number of real life scenarios based on the career experiences of individuals we have encountered through our work. These individuals' careers embody many of the issues common to employees in the latter years of working life.

Alan, 55, is a mid-level manager for a national utilities company. University educated, he started his career as an engineer but has since spent most of his 22 years with the organization in supervisory roles. The company was acquired by a larger multi-national firm some 6 years ago, leading to a radical change of culture. Alan feels his "face no longer fits," although he has survived two waves of layoffs and resisted heavy hints about early retirement, both of which have resulted in the disappearance of most of his age cohort. He is now one of the oldest manag-

ers and, although open to change, finds he is frequently bypassed for training and overlooked for redeployment and project work. In the past 5 years he has applied unsuccessfully for over 40 external positions but has received only three interviews. Family and financial pressures mean that he needs to continue working for at least another 10 years before retirement. He puts his lack of success down to his age and summarizes his position in two words: "totally stuck."

As we shall see later, Alan's experiences reveal the existence for many older workers of a career spectrum between "stuck" and "safe." Both positions are located within the current employment context, with *safe* representing a relatively secure position where there is inherent job satisfaction and ongoing challenge. The opposite situation is particularly problematic for older workers; if an employee feels *stuck* earlier in his or her career history, then he or she can leave the organization and go elsewhere.

A NEW MODEL OF CAREER PLATEAUING IN OLDER WORKERS

Several factors contribute to our belief that a new model is needed to help explain the interrelationship of factors contributing to career plateauing in older individuals. As suggested previously, much research to date has been quantitative, undertaken from an organizational perspective and using age as one of a number of variables that may or may not correlate with some dependent outcome (e.g., Ettington, 1997; Evans & Gilbert, 1984; Lussier & Wister, 1995). In addition, career plateauing continues to be defined as an absence of progression rather than the presence of certain other positive factors and, as a result, tends to be viewed as a negative occurrence. For example, an organizationally plateaued older worker who has chosen not to pursue further opportunities for advancement may find intrinsic satisfaction from feelings of mastery with respect to his or her position. Rather than face the challenge of new organizational goals, the individual may prefer the inherent reward and stimulation provided by such challenges as mentoring relationships. Similarly, this employee may choose not to invest more time in further organizational career development at the expense of personal and family interests.

For the employer, employees who are content to operate at a hierarchically plateaued level, while remaining engaged and committed, should not present a problem. These employees can provide the workforce with an element of stability and knowledge retention to counter the mobility of younger workers.

We propose a model of the factors determining career plateauing in older workers in Figure 4.1. This model suggests a structure to examine the role of career attributes, career motivators, and career decisions in determining whether older workers' careers are plateaued or progressing.

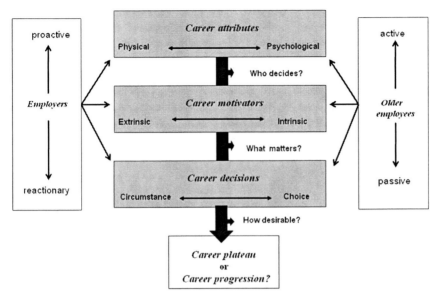

Figure 4.1. Factors contributing to career plateauing or progression in older employees.

This model also stresses the role played by employers and older employees themselves in the process.

Our model is designed to address the three questions central to this chapter: First, who decides the nature of older individuals' careers? Second, what matters most to older employees? Finally, how desirable are later life plateaus? Overarching these questions is the issue of whether employers and older employees share a common view of the nature of career plateauing, its desirability, and the impact it may have on ongoing performance, engagement, and job satisfaction. A lack of research concerning these issues (Armstrong-Stassen, 2008; Greller & Stroh, 1995; Kooij, de Lange, Jansen, & Dikkers, 2008) means that so far there are no comprehensive answers. Throughout the remainder of this chapter we will examine each of these issues in turn from the perspective of both the employer and the older worker, highlighting recommendations for future research.

An examination of cases such as Amanda's, which follows, highlights the gaps that exist for many older employees between appearances and the underlying reality.

Amanda, 52, is one of a team of HR managers in the U.K. subsidiary of a multinational branded food company. The company is performance driven and prides itself on its lean production methods, teamwork, charismatic leadership, and high levels of employee engagement. A rigorous performance management regime, which Amanda helped to introduce shortly after she joined the organization 11 years ago, provides all workers with ambitious objectives backed by stringent monitoring. Although she loves her job and would like to continue with the organization, Amanda finds the relentless pressure for improved performance increasingly difficult to cope with, but she feels unable to admit that she no longer harbors any ambition for further responsibilities and rewards. Ideally, she would like to take a step down to a less stressful role but knows that in a company where plateauing is an unthinkable option, such a request would be tantamount to career suicide.

CAREER ATTRIBUTES: WHO DECIDES ON THE STRUCTURE OF AN EMPLOYEE'S CAREER?

We will now focus on a dichotomy present in our model—that of the role of employers and employees in deciding on the structure and progression of an employee's career. Employers can decide to promote older workers or to withhold promotion. Older workers can proactively seek promotion and accept opportunities for further advancement or they can decline further progression. The focus of this section is an examination of who is responsible for making decisions regarding the mobility of older workers' careers.

The Employer Perspective

Career plateauing can occur at any stage in an employee's career. Within traditional hierarchical career structures, plateauing has generally been regarded as a negative phenomenon created and controlled by the employer (Near, 1984). In situations where the employer withdraws incremental opportunities for advancement or mobility, a plateaued employee is categorized as being in an undesirable or disadvantaged position (Ference et al., 1977).

Career plateauing in linear career models (Levinson et al., 1978; Super, 1957) is thought of as being employer created and controlled, meaning that it can be explained in terms of physical factors largely external to the employee. In a traditional organizational setting, we can also assume that competition for promotion is generally among those from the same age cohort. More recent career literature has suggested that the traditional linear career structure is in decline, generating much academic discussion around what we are to understand by the concept of *career* in today's working environment. "Boundaryless" and "protean" theories have emerged embodying the notion of self-managed careers and horizontal movement—often across employers—with allegiance to oneself rather than an employing body (DeFillippi & Arthur, 1996; Hall, 1976). The emergence of these new theories has caused the focus for career control and progression to shift from the employer to individuals. It also created the possibility that older workers may be competing for further advancement with workers who may be younger.

In the contemporary workplace where older and younger employees are more likely to be working alongside each other, older employees may find themselves unable to compete, due to a comparative lack of training and development, and unable to move elsewhere to develop their career due to ageism. This assumes that in such situations older workers actively want to move. Our review of the literature produced little information concerning older workers' motivation for further career progression in boundaryless workplace settings.

The change in the theorized nature of careers leads us to an important question: What is the role of career plateauing within boundaryless and protean careers? In linear career models, such as those of Super (1957) and Levinson et al. (1978), plateauing represents the failure of an individual to continue upward mobility. We suggest that in boundaryless and protean career models, plateauing may also refer to a lack of horizontal movement both within and across organizations as well as across industries, occupations, and geographical regions. It may also cover a failure of individuals to continue to develop skills or experience that will allow them to initiate future career development moves. In this case, plateauing may represent a general stagnation, rather than simply a lack of upward mobility. Feelings of progression or plateauing are likely to be closely linked to each individual's psychological state (Sullivan & Arthur, 2006). For example, we suggest that individuals may start to identify themselves as "older" and start to look toward retirement as a final goal. They may simply feel they have done enough and not want further progression. They may want to improve their work-life balance and devote more time to interests and commitments outside the workplace. None of these states mean that the individuals reduce commitment to their work role; it is simply that their priorities change.

A common thread running through recent approaches to careers is the shift in responsibility for career development from the policies and programs of the employer to the psychological drivers of the individual. This shift is in line with the view that "people create meanings out of life experiences to build a sense of psychological success" (Arthur & Rousseau, 1996, p. 372) and is represented by the first question in our model: *Who decides the nature of later life careers?* As psychological mobility—whether across external borders or internal boundaries—is key to the notion of psychological success, and as control for this mobility rests with the individual, questions are raised as to whether career plateauing may be, to a degree, an irrelevant concept under these new models (Ettington, 1998). If employees themselves feel psychologically successful, regardless of their external situation, we are led to challenge what it means to classify them as plateaued.

We would endorse a cautious approach when considering the significance of career theories. Theoretical changes mean that we are in danger of viewing the world of work as a dichotomous situation. On one side we have "the past," representing careers that were predictable, secure, and linear in organizations with rigid hierarchical structures operating in a stable environment. On the other side we have "today's" organizations, creating careers that are unpredictable, vulnerable, and multidirectional in organizations and environments that are insecure and constantly changing. This dichotomy represents an extreme scenario; we tend to follow the view of Baruch (2006), who maintains

> while much has shifted from the traditional and conventional mode, many organizations still perform within a relatively stable environment and apply well established strategies, keeping a significant share of the traditional [career] system intact. (p. 125)

The new theories have engendered fresh ideas concerning the very nature of careers and have provided novel avenues for research. For example, examining the evolution of the boundaryless career concept, Sullivan and Arthur (2006) investigated the concept of mobility across both *physical* and *psychological* boundaries. They found that, although much research has been undertaken into the concept of physical mobility, comparatively few studies address the notion of psychological mobility and the perceived capacity for change which underlies it.

We now need to take a more wide-ranging approach to our understanding of careers by considering individuals' own psychological states. Arnold (1997) highlighted this new emphasis in more general terms by noting that "careers are subjective as well as objective—they include people's interpretation of what happens to them as well as what happens objectively" (p. 1). This approach highlights what we believe is a much neglected area—how older employees themselves define "older," their perceptions of what it means to be older, and how they view their position and their own rationale for how it has occurred, particularly with reference to the stereotypical attitudes of others.

Age stereotypes. Undoubtedly, it is still the case that decision making about older individuals' capabilities and careers can often be heavily influenced by employers' innate attitudes manifested in both negative (ageist) and positive stereotypes (Loretto & White, 2006). Rosen and Jerdee (1977) demonstrated how these stereotypes could unconsciously play a part in a number of different management decisions, concluding that employers create self-fulfilling prophesies by making decisions on the basis of an expected decline in older workers' motivation for advancement. Older workers then sense that their efforts fail to lead to further career progress, leading to a decline in motivation.

More recently, Duncan and Loretto (2004) and Taylor and Walker (1994) found the continued existence of negative and inaccurate age attitudes by employers, particularly in relation to employers' notions of appropriate ages for certain jobs. Specifically, they confirmed that individuals may be neglected and marginalized by their employer and bypassed in decisions relating to development and promotion as they age (Loretto & White, 2006). The extent to which this marginalizing creates career plateaus or is symptomatic of attitudes towards existing plateaued employees is uncertain. Also unclear is the degree to which such practices result from employers' innate negative attitudes (ageism) or simply an inability to recognize the age implications of many of their policies and practices.

HR policies and practices. HR policies and practices have traditionally played a significant role in the creation and continuation of career plateaus and a large number of studies have examined the relationship between HR policies and practices and employee age (Armstrong-Stassen, 2008; Greller & Simpson, 1999; van der Heijden, Schalk, & van Veldhoven, 2008). We will examine these policies and practices in relation to a number of individual factors.

Pay and promotion represent two areas of concern. Decisions relating to pay and promotion often result from appraisal and performance management systems that provide employers and line managers with a rational means of justifying their decisions. However, as Ferris and King (1992) maintain, these rationales may mask prejudice and erroneous assumptions. Although research supports the notion that older individuals have the capacity to continue contributing fully at work (Appelbaum, Serena, & Shapiro, 2005; Sterns & Miklos, 1995), employers may assume that older employees no longer wish to "play the game" by seeking material reward and promotion in the same way as younger colleagues. Decisions are made that relegate them, on this basis, to a plateaued situation (Greller & Stroh, 1995). Decisions about retirement continue to be largely financially based (Arnold, 1997; Vickerstaff, 2006) and financial status is a key factor that often causes older individuals keep working and to accept a plateaued situation, rather than endanger their pension rights.

Another area of concern is training and development. The availability of training and development has also been shown to differ according to the age of an employee. Sullivan, Carden, and Martin (1998) maintained that under boundaryless and protean careers, employees no longer trade loyalty for job security but, rather, exchange performance for training so that they may remain marketable. However, research demonstrates that older employees generally receive fewer training and development opportunities, placing them in a poor competitive position relative to younger colleagues (Gentry, Griggs, Deal, & Mondore, this volume; Loretto & White, 2006; McNair et al., 2004).

Performance management is another area of concern. We have found that the performance management of older individuals is a topic that is more and more in the spotlight due to the growing trend toward people extending their working life (Hedge, Borman, & Lammlein, 2006). Employers often find performance management complex. Both employers and older employees can misunderstand its purpose and may resist its application. For example, Rupp, Vodanovich, and Crede (2006) found that older employees may receive more severe penalties as a consequence of poor performance (transfer, demotion) than younger colleagues, who instead receive recommendations for training. Lawrence (1987) addressed the issue of "typical ages" for organizational roles and showed that the probability of receiving high performance ratings increased for managers who were seen as younger than typical ages and decreased for managers who were seen as older. There is also the reluctance of younger managers to effectively address performance issues in older individuals (Finkelstein & Burke, 1998), with the oft-quoted comment, "How can I evaluate the performance of someone who is older than my dad?"

The Older Worker Perspective

What meaning and impact do new career theories have for the lives of older employees? For most older workers, the concept of career, based on their lived experience, is likely to be one of a traditional linear structure (including a beginning, middle, and end). There is an increasing focus on their own career's relatively imminent end-point as represented by cessation of work or retirement.

Although the career framework of many older employees may have been quite traditional, the majority will have had to adapt in recent years to the changes that have taken place around them. Many may have been laid off, redeployed or, like Alan, who we discussed previously, survived massive restructuring, while colleagues and peers were forced toward rapid exit. As Hansson, DeKoekkoek, Neece, and Patterson (1997) suggest, downsizing and restructuring have resulted in increased demands on workers of all ages to find ways to adapt to an environment of increased uncertainty and decreased job or career security. Hansson et al.'s proposal is of particular relevance, given the recent downturn in global economies, which has led to reduced job security.

Few older employees will have failed to recognize the need for a certain degree of psychological mobility and flexibility if they are to remain employed. But the degree to which this requirement is accepted or resisted may depend on each individual's orientation toward change. Inkson (2006) viewed protean and boundaryless careers as involving "action" rather than "structure" and likened them to the common metaphor of a journey. With respect to boundaryless careers, he concluded that "boundaries are crossed because people have the will and the personal resources (the protean orientation of adaptability) to cross them" (p. 55).

For those who do not have the personal resources to adapt a protean stance, *promotion stress*, defined as the experienced feelings of anxiety, concern, or tension with one's career reality (in terms of the level one has reached in an organization), can be a problem for plateaued individuals, leading to lower satisfaction and commitment (Carlson & Rotondo, 2001). Carlson and Rotondo maintained that stress depends on factors external to the individual, such as what the organization values and how it rewards its employees. However, this study showed that stress levels were lower for later career stages, which suggests that other factors may come into play among older workers that counteract these external pressures. They acknowledged that "research examining the unique form of stress accompanying limited promotion is sparse" (p. 100) and suggested that this was an area ripe for further investigation.

Resistance to change is not always a negative reaction, however, as Mark's story shows:

Mark, 53, is an accountant. Once qualified, he spent 8 years in the finance division of a large company before deciding that his interests lay in a more hands-on role in a smaller organization. Within that company he held the only internal financial role. Since then, he has changed employers four times in order to advance his career and move into higher paid positions with greater responsibility. As he has a close personal relationship with his current boss (the company owner), who tells him he would be difficult to replace, Mark has no plans for further advancement and envisions working for at least another 10 to 15 years, although he has made provision for a good pension and could retire at any time.

Mark's story highlights, as we mentioned earlier, how decisions regarding further career mobility can lie equally with employees and employers. Applebaum and Finestone (1994) make the distinction between *organizational* and *personal* plateaus with *organizationally plateaued* individuals being those with the capability to progress and perform well, but who are held back by the lack of job opportunities or management attitudes, while *personally plateaued* individuals are seen as not desiring a higher level job, due to a lack of either ability or motivation. Personally plateaued individuals may choose not to progress if, for example, advancement or mobility conflicts with family or personal interests (Near, 1980).

As we suggested earlier, in light of more recent career theories, plateauing may include the absence of mobility in general, with lack of psychological mobility being a key factor. Further investigation of these concepts could help explain older individuals' attitudes toward career development in later life. In terms of new theories that, by definition, propose that contemporary careers have no physical boundaries and may also have no psychological boundaries (Arthur & Rousseau, 1996), progress results from an individual's own psychological drivers. Clarification about what it means to be plateaued in later life in today's workplace may be achieved through focusing on older workers' motivations and feelings—an area that is ripe for investigation (Sullivan & Arthur, 2006).

Older employees' career plateaus may be influenced by a range of individual variables, although little evidence-based theory exists in these areas (Briscoe, Hall, & DeMuth, 2006). For some, such as Sarah, the implications of being an aging female were clear relatively early in her career. Referring back to our model, the factors affecting Sarah's career were contextual. Her realization of them enabled her to make decisions in order to avoid plateauing and other problems in later life.

Sarah is 57. After graduating from the university she started her career as a receptionist in an advertising agency. Within a year, she was promoted to junior copywriter and from there enjoyed a 25-year career within several agencies, rising to the heights of senior management. However, by her early 40s she realized what she had always known—advertising was a young, macho industry and she was getting old. She now runs her own consulting business providing creative services and copywriting to small businesses and sees no reason to either expand or retire, enjoying the control she retains over the amount of work she chooses to undertake.

As would be expected, gender and ethnicity are closely linked to how people see themselves and may affect (a) the propensity of the individual to become plateaued, (b) the personal meaning of a career plateau, and (c) the individual's reaction to plateauing. Gender has been identified as a significant issue in career development and so may also be relevant to career plateauing. Studies have shown that in addition to differing from men in terms of status and reward, women's needs and drivers with respect to career success are also quite dissimilar to men's (Gallos, 1989; O'Neil, Hopkins, & Bilimoria, 2008; Roberts & Friend, 1998).

For example, research by Sturges (1999) into personal conceptions of career success held by male and female managers identified four orientational categories—climbers, experts, influencers, and self-realizers—with participant responses analyzed according to age and gender. Results showed that women were more likely than men to describe what success meant to them in terms of internal criteria, whereas for men position and pay were seen as indispensable markers of career success, closely related to status. Although in this study the "older" group only extended to individuals in their 40s, for both sexes the findings suggest that as individuals age, factors such as influence and autonomy become more important than material criteria for career success (Sturges, 1999). This finding, however, may be the result of the fact that *influence* and *autonomy* are generally less available to younger employees, who may lack the skills and experience necessary to exert influence or to work autonomously. Sturges' findings, therefore, require further investigation.

Research Implications

Further research is needed into the importance of various career attributes to older individuals in order to clarify a number of issues. For instance, we need to examine the degree to which older individuals recognize changes in career contexts; that is, from linear to boundaryless situations, and the impact that they feel these changes have on their career.

The importance of physical and psychological aspects of careers to older workers also needs further investigation. It may be that the existing typology of different career plateaus (e.g., between voluntary and involuntary or individually and organizationally defined plateaus) could be extended to include the importance to groups of individuals of particular physical and psychological aspects of their career in later life. This typology might, for example, identify those who are motivated to improve their work-life balance, as opposed to those who want to develop their career in different realms of influence (e.g., through temporary project management assignments). It may reveal that there are those who are motivated to learn new skills but lack the support to pursue their interest. There may be another group of individuals who want to work beyond the common retirement age of their peers without blocking the career aspirations of more junior colleagues. This typology may provide a useful tool for practice through helping employers and older employees recognize and address possible later life career options on an individual basis.

Little is known about how much individuals feel that their career position is due to age-related changes that have occurred within themselves or due to other factors, such as employer attitudes that may be invidiously limiting their options. It is important to distinguish between older workers who are willing to advance but are unable to do so, due to lack of opportunities, for instance, and those who are able to advance but do not want to. Little is known on an individual basis about how amenable older workers might be to further promotion if such opportunities were available. How much would they want to participate in programs such as mentoring, project work, or bridge employment in order to alleviate some of the negative aspects of plateauing, such as lack of stimulation? Research is needed in order to identify the key individual, contextual, or moderating factors that make employees able but not willing to seek advancement. Equally important, more needs to be known about what might prevent older workers from seeking progression or advancing when they are willing to do so. We also need to examine whether there is agreement between employers and individuals as to what constitutes a career plateau in later life and how this phenomenon is recognized and acknowledged.

CAREER MOTIVATORS: WHAT MATTERS TO OLDER EMPLOYEES?

In this section we will focus on the question in the second section of our model: What matters to older employees in their career? Much existing research on later life careers has been from an employer perspective (e.g., Claes & Heymans, 2008; Ettington, 1997). Few studies address the issue of what drives older employees. The issue of the relative importance for older workers of continuing incremental extrinsic rewards compared to the intrinsic satisfaction of the work itself is important in understanding older employees' motivation and commitment to working. It is also important for understanding how it affects their attitude toward continuing progression.

There is a need to pinpoint what matters most under certain circumstances, such as changing family commitments or organizational restructuring. As mentioned above, there is a need to determine whether, based on motivational categories, it is possible to identify different groups of older workers. If so, this categorization may assist employers to better engage, manage, and support older workers when continuing promotion and pay increases are no longer available.

The Employer Perspective

Traditional theories of motivation (e.g., Maslow, 1954) have tended to focus on intrinsic and extrinsic motivators as independent variables in driving behavior. Intrinsic motivators are those that derive from the inherent value of the work itself; e.g., achievement, meaning, responsibility, and autonomy. Extrinsic motivators arise from the desire to obtain outcomes that are apart from the work itself; e.g., pay and benefits, status, and working conditions (Amabile, 1993). In practice, of course, such a stark separation rarely exists. In today's workplace many employers attempt to underpin extrinsic rewards with factors that create job satisfaction as well as employee engagement and commitment.

Several studies have shown that work-life balance and the ability to work flexibly are both key aspirations for older employees (Lissenburgh & Smeaton, 2003; Loretto et al., 2005; McNair et al., 2004). In response, enlightened employers are increasingly introducing flexible and part-time working arrangements to enable older individuals to keep working. However, these changes raise the question of whether these new types of working arrangements should be seen as continuing a plateaued situation, or—as may be felt by employees themselves—as new roles as part of a boundaryless or protean career. In such circumstances, a significant variable in terms of older individuals' motivation and communication appears to be how employers react to employees' needs, although as yet little evidence exists for the role this reaction plays.

For employers, understanding motivation in later life careers is undoubtedly a challenging topic. In her study of successful career plateauing, Ettington (1998) showed that the effects of plateauing can be examined through the lens of several established theories of motivation. She related plateauing to expectancy-value theory (Vroom, 1964) and to goal-setting theory (Locke & Latham, 1984), through the assertion that plateauing removed or reduced work-related goals and outcomes. Within the framework of equity theory, Adams (1965) maintained that plateauing can damage older employees' motivation by failing to award them the same promotions received by others.

Additionally, Ettington's (1998) study recognized that promotional opportunities do not have the same importance for all. For example, she suggested that those with a managerial orientation as opposed to a technical orientation may suffer more if they fail to advance. Ettington explained this finding within the framework of Schein's (1985) *career anchors* (aspects of an individual's occupation of fundamental significance to them). According to this explanation, those with a managerial orientation place a high value on advancement.

In the area of career motivators perhaps more than any other there is a clear divide between proactive employers and laissez-faire or reactive employers. Proactive employers recognize the likely motivational implications of the cessation of opportunities for ongoing promotion and pay increases and actively seek to motivate plateaued individuals. Laissez-faire employers take no action. Reactive employers may use the situation as an invidious strategy to drive older employees toward early retirement through neglecting their needs for advancement, development, or recognition.

The Employee Perspective

An employee's motivation may significantly affect his or her career progression. However, little is known about how motivation changes with age and which variables are important in relation to changing workplace environments. The drivers that motivate older employees may be complex. Sterns and Miklos (1995) identify three sets of factors that they see as affecting behavioral change in older individuals. The first two are normative: biological and/or environmental determinants bearing a strong relationship to chronological age and historical influences which affect most members of a cohort in similar ways. The third set comprises nonnormative unique career and life changes, including individual health and stress-inducing events.

Sterns and Miklos (1995) surmise that older adults may have a different perspective on work than younger adults. In later life, survival needs are likely to be less urgent and older workers may have a greater knowledge about the likelihood of effort paying off. Whether or not goals change, a greater reality is adopted about the likelihood of achieving those goals, particularly external goals such as further promotion. Overall, as a result, the intrinsic rewards of work founded in job satisfaction grow in importance. They also suggest that with age, factors such as health, outside interests, and family and other responsibilities may have a greater and more diverse effect on individual motivation than in earlier years. In later life increasing numbers of individuals find themselves caring for children, grandchildren, and parents. It is becoming more common for grandparents to rear their grandchildren, due to their own children's work responsibilities, causing many individuals to face caring for young families until quite late in life. The over 50s also often have to provide care for elderly parents and other individuals. The case of Anne clearly illustrates this point.

Anne, 61, was divorced 7 years ago. She has worked as a senior secretary for a firm of lawyers in her hometown for 10 years, having rejoined the workforce when her youngest child left school. She enjoys the work but acknowledges she is capable of more. Her employers have encouraged her to train as a paralegal; however, because Anne's mother is in failing health and Anne also provides back-up support in caring for her grandchildren, she is reluctant to take on additional commitment. Anne would like to continue working for as long as she is able as she enjoys the social interaction and needs the income to supplement what will be a "virtually nonexistent" pension.

Anne's case is a good example of how external circumstances and responsibilities may lead to a shift in older workers' career goals. Realizing that they need to compromise in order to balance work and family or life demands, older workers may end up trading off one against the other.

As individuals age, they may recognize that there are other components to general life satisfaction than just work and, therefore, may have changing priorities that will affect their career motivation and the decisions that result. This change in priorities, in essence, leads to the "what matters" question in our model.

Within the diverse range of people that comprises the "over 50s," older individuals' views about their position, attitudes, and aspirations are likely to vary significantly according to job role and status, nature of work, and previous experience. Degrees of acceptance of aging and an individual's relationship toward his or her own aging identity may also be key factors in later life self-image, ongoing aspirations, and success. In the absence of a clear indication of the influence of age norms—a common shared view of the "right age" at which one should do certain things (Greller & Simpson, 1999)—researchers such as Freund (1997) postulate that age norms provide benchmarks against which older individuals set their own objectives and judge their success.

Motivation, of course, can be either toward rewards and accomplishment or away from negative experiences; therefore, the overall situation of older individuals must be viewed through this lens. For example, it is generally thought that retirement for those with good pensions or other sources of income is motivated by the desire to stop working and lead the good life, traveling and pursuing hobbies and interests. However, that may not be the case; in the light of constrained choices, ageist attitudes and possible loss of confidence and self-esteem, retirement may not be motivated by such positive goals (Duncan, 2003). Older individuals who may have preferred to continue working in some capacity are driven toward retirement. Although they are reluctant to give up the social network, self-esteem, and feelings of value that working provides, they may find these benefits are no longer available if their needs and position are overlooked and they are no longer considered worthy of development.

Undoubtedly, extrinsic factors play a significant role in motivating the majority of individuals in the early stages of their career (Amabile, 1993; Sturges, 1999), but evidence suggests that older employees may not be affected by these factors in the same way as younger people (Loretto et al., 2005). Although extrinsic and intrinsic rewards are separate constructs that operate in different ways, rather than as opposite ends of a single spectrum, it nevertheless appears that the importance of these rewards may change in later working life. Aspects of employment such as innate meaning, quality of relationships, inclusion, stimulation, and continuing opportunity to contribute may assume a greater motivational significance than earlier in the career (Sturges, 1999). A further finding suggests that those managers who are successful in terms of advances in pay and promotion may value these external criteria for success less once they have achieved them (Sturges, 1999).

The motivation of some older individuals may thus change over time, causing them to be less driven by extrinsic factors for success. But there is a need to investigate the extent to which motivational changes are context specific. For example, for many older individuals, financial concerns predominate the nearer they are to retirement, leading them to value financial rewards in terms of how much they contribute to future financial security (Irving, Steels, & Hall, 2005; Vickerstaff, 2006). Others may be facing increasing financial demands at a time of life when these burdens were traditionally easing. As members of the *sandwich generation*, caring for children as well as parents, their concerns are for immediate returns to fund their day-to-day commitments (Phillipson & Smith, 2005).

Many older employees who lose motivation with respect to their current position may nevertheless be highly motivated to continue working through, for example, changing careers, operating as consultants, or setting up in business. However, despite the emergence of boundaryless career theory, evidence continues to show that changing jobs over the age of 50 is difficult for many (Daniel & Heywood, 2007). In consequence, perhaps some older individuals' motivation may adjust relative to what they come to realize is and isn't possible or likely in terms of future career options.

Research Implications

Research is needed into the sets of circumstances influencing when different groups of older employees accept that they are irrevocably plateaued. Investigation is also required into how this situation affects their motivation. If, as evidence suggests, many older workers have realized and accepted their situation much earlier in their career—the oft-quoted mid-life crisis (Golembiewski, 1978)—it is possible that they may be quite sanguine and accepting of their situation by the time they are 50 and older. They may even view themselves as being in an entirely different post-plateaued situation. If so, how do they describe this condition? Is it possible to identify a typology of different career types at this stage based on career motivators?

Further research is also needed into the success of employer programs that aim to anchor the value of work, work goals, and reward structures in aspects of an individual's work unrelated to future hierarchical progress, such as participation in mentoring schemes. What is the motivation for older employees in participating in these developmental activities? What are employers' expectations with respect to desired outcomes? How do younger employees view such programs and activities in terms of their own future? Research is also needed to identify which categories of rewards—intrinsic and extrinsic—are particularly appealing to older employees and the amount of influence these rewards exert on their attitudes and behavior.

CAREER DECISIONS: ARE CAREER PLATEAUS CAUSED BY CHOICE OR CIRCUMSTANCE?

In this section, we will focus on the dichotomy at level three within our model—the question of whether career plateaus result from choice or circumstance and who ultimately makes the decision concerning the form and nature of an individual's later life career. We will first consider whether career plateaus remain a negative phenomenon or if they have become a relatively acceptable inevitability which, in some circumstances, are actually chosen by employees. Second, we will examine the extent to which employers and older employees share a common view of this phenomenon. The answer to this question is likely to depend on the degree to which the career plateau is the result of employer actions (circumstance) or individual employee decisions (choice). Of course, individual circumstance—such as responsibility for caring for young, elderly, or ill family members—may also play a role in the career decisions made by older employees, but for the purposes of this discussion we shall regard these as causal factors influencing personal choices.

There is an assumption in much of the literature that career plateauing is always a negative phenomenon for both employers and employees. This attitude is a barrier that needs to be overcome. Career plateaus can have many positive attributes. For example, allowing an employee who wants to stay in his or her current role until retirement to remain plateaued may be beneficial to both the employer and the employee. It may help maintain a stable core of staff to balance the mobility of younger workers and, if well-managed, provide a context of security and manageable stress for older individuals themselves (Ettington, 1997).

For instance, in Jeremy's case, the fact that he is happy to remain plateaued in his role as a chief planning officer allows the organization to retain an experienced individual in this role:

Jeremy, 55, is a regional government chief planning officer. He has been with the governmental organization for 24 years and attained his current role 6 years ago, having risen progressively through the internal ranks. He is now at the top of his area of specialization and has no higher role to aspire to, unless he wishes to become chief executive (he doesn't). Otherwise, he can only gain further pay and status by moving geographically to another county council. As he is already well paid, his family is settled, and his career success is heavily reliant on his network of local contacts, geographic relocation is unlikely. He is planning to retire at 63.

The Employer Perspective

The fundamental characteristics of hierarchical career plateauing, such as lack of promotion and the cessation of increases in salary and job-related status for older employees, are not necessarily part of a calculated process by employers. Indeed, it has been suggested that there is little that employers can do to prevent later life managerial career plateauing. Bardwick (1986) graphically demonstrated that "in every large and complex organization the number of positions at the highest decision making level is always less than 1% of the number of employees ... if only 1% will not plateau, 99% will" (p. 36). Additionally, many older individuals, especially managers like Jeremy, will simply have reached the top of the hierarchy or scale within their organization for their specialization and will have become plateaued as a result.

Nevertheless, it is important that employers ensure that career plateaus are not caused purely by unilateral employer decisions that leave older employees feeling sidelined, powerless, and belittled. Traditionally, employers' attitudes towards plateaued older workers have been underpinned by two factors. First, there is a common attitude that plateauing and age are inevitable bedfellows, with increased age leading naturally to declining performance, resistance to change, and inflexibility. Second, there may be an expectation that older employees' responses to being plateaued will mirror those of younger plateaued employees. Elsass and Ralston (1989) point out, however, that the motivational differences between plateaued and non-plateaued managers grow less distinct with age, with the result that older workers' motivation is generally more focused on the intrinsic rewards of their job

Of course, any individual at any age who has been in a job for too long with no change of focus, no developmental training, and no new objectives may experience boredom and stagnation. Reduced productivity, disengagement, frustration, cynicism, and disaffection are only some of the symptoms of plateaued individuals. These may impact their own position and also have detrimental influences on their colleagues and the wider organizational culture (Allen et al., 1999).

A common response of younger employees in this situation is to leave the organization. Reactionary employers, should this suit their purposes, may adopt a strategy of neglecting or sidelining older workers in order to encourage them to leave. But unlike younger individuals, older employees will almost certainly find it difficult to secure new employment. Alternatively, employees may remain in the organization but be unmotivated and therefore not performing to the best of their abilities. The key point here is that older employees may be disaffected not so much as a result of their plateaued situation *per se* but because of the lack of training, development, and job enrichment opportunities that have led to this situation in the first place.

As long ago as 1977, Ference and colleagues suggested four states of managerial careers: learners, stars, solid citizens, and deadwood. The latter two states refer to those who are plateaued, with solid citizens being seen as effective, while the deadwood individuals are obsolete. Obviously, a different management approach may be required with respect to each group; the solution may not always be to move them up or out. In terms of their knowledge, experience, skills, and value to the organization, many older employees are likely to be solid citizens. In the absence of recognition of their value, they may feel more like unwanted deadwood.

The Employee Perspective

A key question is whether older individuals can be described as plateaued if they no longer seek or desire promotion and are content to derive job satisfaction from other intrinsic, job-related factors? For example, they may regard their current position as their *calling* and resist promotion which will take them away from that. Such would be the case if an engineer declined a promotion to an administrative managerial role because he or she wanted to continue working with machines. Alternatively, an employee may refuse a promotion if he or she sees it as beyond his or her level of expertise and does not want to undertake additional training.

As we saw earlier in the case study of Amanda, it may be that for many employees, work motivation changes with age so that plateauing may actually be desirable. What is not known is the extent to which career plateauing is a general, natural, and irreversible phenomenon or how much it depends on such factors as stress, career history, current role, and other contributory factors.

In fact many older plateaued individuals seem happy with their position, having become aware of it gradually and adjusted their expectations accordingly (Greller & Simpson, 1999; Howard & Bray, 1988). This adjustment may depend, however, on the extent to which they perceive themselves to be plateaued (Armstrong-Stassen, 2008). Job satisfaction among older employees is generally reported to be higher than at earlier stages of life (Warr, 1992) and it is felt that this increase may be due to older workers accepting what they see as inevitable and realizing what works for them. The case of Jim is a good example of a satisfied older employee:

Jim, 59, is a sales manager. He has worked in business-to-business sales for three different employers since leaving school at 16. He spent the majority of his early career "on the road" selling to customers. He has been with his current employer for 18 years and has spent the last 13 years in an office-based position, preparing sales forecasts and reports as well as training. Although he recognizes that this role doesn't play to his strengths, the job is less tiring than previously and it is a relief to have decreased pressure to meet targets. He enjoys the camaraderie of his colleagues and the network of contacts he has established over the years and acknowledges that he no longer wants to make the effort that would be required to rebuild these aspects if he went elsewhere. He has not, as yet, decided when to retire.

Like Jim, many older workers, rather than feeling stuck, may choose the relative safety and security of their existing position in preference to facing a new challenge where they may have to test their skills and confidence in direct competition with younger colleagues (Hansson et al., 1997). Constructs such as Baltes and Baltes' (1990) selective optimization with compensation model demonstrate how individuals may make choices and decisions about how to use limited resources in order to deal successfully with developmental opportunities and losses, particularly as they occur with respect to aging. This model accentuates the significance of using compensatory processes (i.e., new alternative means) to maintain a certain level of functioning in a specific domain when faced with losses (Baltes & Dickson, 2001). For example, some older individuals may decide to downscale their ambition in order to withstand stress better and avoid burnout as their energy levels start to lessen. In doing so they may be weighing the benefits and disadvantages of career progression and deciding that their best option—for themselves, their colleagues, and their employer—may lie in remaining *in situ*.

From the perspective of those individuals who have reached a stage of life when they are motivated more by internal psychological drivers such as accomplishment, enjoyment, integrity, balance, and influence than physical advancement, perhaps a new terminology for plateauing is required. In those situations where older individuals are content to stop striving for further extrinsic reward but are still keen to pursue the inherent interest and challenge within their role, the term *plateau* could be replaced by a more appropriate word. This might reflect a *post-plateau* situation. Perhaps a concept of *place* (i.e., reaching a place of accomplishment or security) would be a more meaningful construct.

Research Implications

Whether there is such a thing as *positive* career plateauing has been considered in recent literature. For instance, Ettington (1998) defined *successful* career plateauing as "effective job performance and high job satisfaction despite a low likelihood of promotion" (p.72). In a quantitative study of 373 middle managers, she acknowledged the importance of adopting both an *objective* and *subjective* approach to measuring plateauing, but was able to shed little light on causes of plateauing and its links to employee motivation. A key area for future research is, therefore, the extent to which employers and older individuals recognize and appreciate the existence of *positive plateauing* and can identify its benefits.

Little is known about the desirability of plateauing for older individuals—the third question in our model—and the frequency with which they actively and consciously choose plateauing over the opportunity for future advancement. Similarly, we have scant knowledge about the circumstances under which this choice occurs. For example, how much is plateauing related to changes that are associated purely with age, such as tiredness or a shift of focus towards retirement? How much is it related to changes in focus, such as a greater emphasis on caring responsibilities or outside interests, or factors that are related to length of time in the job, such as boredom and lack of impetus?

Undoubtedly a gap exists in empirical research in terms of asking older individuals about their feelings about these questions and many other matters (Giles & Reid, 2005). For example, to what extent do older workers feel they actually control their career direction, rather than being entirely at the behest of their employers? What factors prevent older employees from taking advantage of opportunities to find meaning and motivation? What do older workers feel their employers should be doing in order to facilitate their satisfaction and engagement? How do older individuals feel about communicating their needs and desires to their employer and what might inhibit them from doing so? How important is the role played by external influences, such as the media, in providing role models for how they should act and feel? Research into how older employees evaluate and choose their own career directions and the extent to which they acknowledge and take responsibility for their own futures would be helpful for both employers and older individuals alike.

CONCLUSIONS

Significant demographic and social changes that have already begun are predicted to intensify in the coming decades. These changes are leading to longer working lives. However, at present, comparatively little information is available to guide employers or workers as to which policies, practices, attitudes, and behaviors they should adopt to deal with the physical management of longer later-life careers. Similarly, little guidance exists to help employers ensure productivity, engagement, and commitment in those who, willingly or not, face many more years of work than they may have envisioned at the outset of their career.

Numerous gains can be achieved by organizations prepared to include plateaued workers in their review and development of in-company talent (Guest & Shacklock, 2005). Achieving these benefits may involve acknowledging that older individuals have needs other than increases in pay and promotion and may prefer to derive satisfaction in their employment from those things that they are individually enthusiastic about. In order to make this shift, a better understanding of both individuals and their employment context is required. Questions remain about the validity of existing career theories in the reality of today's workplace, particularly when so little evidence exists about the interrelationship of career plateauing and age.

In the future, a strategic, radical, and far-sighted approach will be required on the part of both employers and older individuals to better manage later working lives. This approach will need to focus on flexibility and planning over a longer period of time than the immediate pre-retirement years. Longer working lives and earlier plateauing will mean that younger workers also will need to look ahead to the later stages of their career from a much earlier stage.

In this chapter, through the introduction of a new model, we have attempted to clarify how individual differences and contemporary contextual workplace variables may affect career plateauing in older workers. We have addressed what the questions underpinning this model might mean for older individuals and their employers. We have examined the situation from both an organizational and employee perspective, recommending areas where future research is needed. Our ultimate aim is to assist employers to gain insight into which approach to managing older plateaued employees may work best for which individuals in what contexts.

We believe that a better understanding of the factors at work in late-stage career progression and plateauing and how these may be acknowledged by employers could help in better maintaining each individual's focus, energy, and options over the remainder of his or her working life. However, this understanding is unlikely to come from treating all older employees as a single group. We maintain it lies in identifying and addressing individual needs through, for example, tailored person-related training, role development, and even flexible working provisions. Such an approach would depend on identifying a typology of different later-life careers based on individual needs and drivers. It could help narrow the gap between employer and employee perspectives on the value of older workers (Duncan & Loretto, 2004; Phillipson & Smith, 2005). At an individual level improved focus may help transform what may have been considered an intransigent situation for an older employee into a period of career renewal and reinvigoration.

From an academic perspective this area is in its infancy and there is a need to draw together the more recent theories of career with what we know about the management of older workers so that we can comprehensively examine the factors that affect career plateauing in this group of employees.

REFERENCES

Adams, J. S. (1965). Inequity in social exchange. In L. Berkowitz (Ed.), *Advances in experimental psychology* (Vol. 2, pp. 267-299). New York: Academic Press.

Allen, T. D., Russell, J. E. A., Poteet, M. L., & Dobbins, G. H. (1999). Learning and development factors related to perceptions of job content and hierarchical plateauing. *Journal of Organizational Behavior, 20,* 1113-1137.

Amabile, T. M. (1993). Motivational synergy: Toward new conceptualizations of intrinsic and extrinsic motivation in the workplace. *Human Resource Management Review, 3,* 185-201.

Appelbaum, S. H., & Finestone, D. (1994). Revisiting career plateauing: Same old problems—Avant garde solutions. *Journal of Managerial Psychology, 9*(5), 12-21.

Appelbaum, S. H., Serena, M., & Shapiro, B.T. (2005). Generation X and the Boomers: An analysis of realities and myths. *Management Research News, 28*(1), 1-33.

Armstrong-Stassen, M. (2008). Factors associated with job content plateauing among older workers. *Career Development International, 13,* 594-613.

Arnold, J. (1997). *Managing careers into the 21st century.* London: Paul Chapman.

Arthur, M. B., & Rousseau, D. M. (1996). *The boundaryless career: A new employment principle for a new organizational era.* New York: Oxford University Press.

Baltes, P. B., & Baltes, M. M. (Eds.). (1990). Psychological perspectives on successful aging: The model of selective optimization with compensation. In *Successful aging: Perspectives from the behavioral sciences* (pp. 1-34). Cambridge, England: Cambridge University Press.

Baltes, B. B., & Dickson, M. W. (2001). Using life-span models in industrial-organizational psychology: The theory of selective optimization with compensation. *Applied Developmental Science, 5,* 51-62.

Bardwick, J. M. (1986). *The plateauing trap.* New York: AMACOM.

Baruch, Y. (2006). Career development in organizations and beyond: Balancing traditional and contemporary viewpoints. *Human Resource Management Review, 16,* 125-138.

Brennan, C., Carmichael, F., Ingham, B., Prashar, A., Dobson, J., Sharifi, S., & Porcellato, L. (2007). *Ageism and employment: A survey of the literature in the context of current research agendas.* Unpublished manuscript: Salford Business School, United Kingdom.

Briscoe J., Hall, D., & DeMuth, R. (2006). Protean and boundaryless careers: An empirical exploration. *Journal of Vocational Behavior, 69,* 30-47.

Butler, R. N., & Lewis, M. I. (1973). *Aging and mental health: Positive psychosocial approaches*. St. Louis, MO: Mosby.

Carlson, D. S., & Rotondo, D. M. (2001). Differences in promotion stress across career stage and orientation. *Human Resource Management, 40*, 99-110.

Claes, R., & Heymans, M. (2008). HR professionals' views on work motivation and retention of older workers: A focus group study. *Career Development International, 13*, 95-111.

Daniel, K., & Heywood, J. S. (2007). The determinants of hiring older workers: UK evidence. *Labour Economics, 14*, 35-51.

DeFillippi, R. J., & Arthur, M. B. (1996). Boundaryless contexts and careers: A competency based perspective. In M. B. Arthur & D. M. Rousseau (Eds)., *The boundaryless career*. New York: Oxford University Press.

Duncan, C. (2003). Assessing anti-ageism routes to older worker re-engagement. *Work, Employment and Society, 17*, 101-120.

Duncan, C., & Loretto, W. (2004). Never the right age? Gender and age-based discrimination in employment. *Gender, Work and Organization, 11*, 95-115.

Elsass, P. M. & Ralston, D. (1989). Individual responses to the stress of career plateauing. *Journal of Management, 15*, 35-47.

Ettington, D. R. (1997). How human resource practices can help plateaued managers succeed. *Human Resource Management, 36*, 221-234.

Ettington, D. R. (1998). Successful career plateauing. *Journal of Vocational Behavior, 52*, 72-88.

Evans, M. G., & Gilbert, E. (1984). Plateaued managers: Their need gratifications and their effort-performance expectations. *Journal of Management Studies, 21*, 99-108.

Ference, T. P., Stoner, J. A., & Warren, E. K. (1977). Managing the career. *Academy of Management Review, 2*, 602–612.

Ferris, G. R., & King, T. R. (1992). The politics of age discrimination in organizations. *Journal of Business Ethics, 11*, 341-350.

Finkelstein, L. M., & Burke, M. J. (1998). Age stereotyping at work: The role of rater and contextual factors on evaluations of job applicants. *The Journal of General Psychology, 125*, 317–345.

Freund, A.M. (1997). Individuating age salience: A psychological perspective on the salience of age in the life course. *Human Development, 40*, 287-292.

Gallos, J. V. (1989). Exploring women's development: Implications for career theory, practice, and research. In M. B. Arthur, D. T. Hall, & B. S. Lawrence (Eds.), *Handbook of career theory* (pp. 110-132). Cambridge, England: Cambridge University Press.

Gentry, W. A., Griggs, T. L., Deal, J. J., & Mondore, S. P. (2009). Generational differences in attitudes, beliefs, and preferences about development and learning at work. In S. G. Baugh & S. E. Sullivan (Eds.), *Research in careers: Vol. 1. Maintaining focus, energy, and options through the career* (pp. 51-74). Charlotte, NC: Information Age.

Giles, H., & Read, S. A. (2005). Ageism across the lifespan: Towards a self-categorization model of aging. *Journal of Social Issues, 61*, 389-404.

Golembiewski, R. T. (1978). Mid-life transition and mid-career crisis: A special case for individual development. *Public Administration Review, 38*, 215-222.

Greller, M. M., & Simpson, P. (1999). In search of late career: A review of contemporary social science research applicable to the understanding of late career. *Human Resource Management Review, 9,* 309-347.

Greller, M. M., & Stroh, L. K. (1995). Careers in midlife and beyond: A fallow field in need of sustenance. *Journal of Vocational Behavior, 47,* 232-247.

Greller, M. M., & Stroh, L. K. (2004). Making the most of "late career" for employers and workers themselves: Becoming elders not relics. *Organizational Dynamics, 33,* 202-214

Guest, R., & Shacklock, K. (2005). The impending shift to an older mix of workers: Perspectives from the management and economics literatures. *International Journal of Organizational Behavior, 10,* 713-738.

Hall, D. T. (1976). *Careers in organizations.* Glenview, IL: Scott, Foresman.

Hansson, R. O., DeKoekkoek, P. D., Neece, W. M., & Patterson, D. W. (1997). Successful aging at work: Annual Review, 1992-1996: The older worker and transitions to retirement. *Journal of Vocational Behavior, 51,* 202-233.

Hedge, J. W., Borman, W. C., & Lammlein, S. E. (2006). *The aging workforce: Realities, myths, and implications for organizations.* Washington, DC: American Psychological Association.

Howard, A., & Bray, D. W. (1988). *Managerial lives in transition: Advancing age and changing times.* New York: Guilford.

Inkson, K. (2006). Protean and boundaryless careers as metaphors. *Journal of Vocational Behavior, 69,* 48-63.

Irving, P., Steels, J., & Hall, N. (2005). *Factors affecting the labour market participation of older workers,* Research Report No. 281, Department for Work and Pensions, Leeds: HMSO.

Kooij, D., de Lange, A., Jansen, P., & Dikkers, J. (2008). Older workers' motivation to continue to work: Five meanings of age: A conceptual review. *Journal of Managerial Psychology, 23,* 364-394.

Lawrence, B. S. (1987). An organizational theory of age effects. In N. DiTomaso & S. B. Bacharach (Eds.), *Research in the sociology of organizations* (Vol. 5, pp. 37-71). Greenwich, CT: JAI Press.

Levinson, D. J., Darrow, C. N., Klein, E. B., Levinson, M. H., & McKee, B. (1978). *The seasons of a man's life.* New York: Knopf.

Lissenburgh, S., & Smeaton, D. (2003). *The role of flexible employment in maintaining labour market participation and promoting job quality.* York: Joseph Rowntree Foundation.

Locke, E. A., & Latham, G. P. (1984). *Goal setting: A motivational technique that works.* Englewood Cliffs, NJ: Prentice Hall.

Loretto, W., Vickerstaff, S., & White, P. (2005). *Older workers and options for flexible work.* Universities of Kent and Edinburgh, UK. Equal Opportunities Commission Working Paper Series.

Loretto, W., & White, P. (2006). Employers' attitudes, practices and policies towards older workers. *Human Resource Management Journal, 16,* 313–330.

Lussier, G., & Wister, A. V. (1995). A study of workforce aging of the British Columbia Public Service, 1983-1991. *Canadian Journal on Aging, 14,* 480-497.

Maslow, A. H. (1954). *Motivation and personality* (3rd ed.). New York: Harper and Row.

McNair, S., Flynn, M., Owen, L., Humphreys, C., & Woodfield, S. (2004). *Changing work in later life: A study of job transitions*. SEEDA Report. Centre for Research into the Older Workforce (CROW), University of Surrey, Guildford, UK.

Near, J. P. (1980). The career plateau: Causes and effects. *Business Horizons, 23*(5), 53-57.

Near, J. P. (1984). Reactions to the career plateau. *Business Horizons, 27*(4), 75-79.

O'Neil, D. A., Hopkins, M. M., & Bilimoria, D. (2008). Women's careers at the start of the 21st century: Patterns and paradoxes. *Journal of Business Ethics, 80*, 727-743.

Parry, E. (2006, June). *Factors affecting the elimination of age discrimination in the workplace*, ACREW/KCL Conference, Prato, Italy.

Phillipson, C., & Smith, A. (2005). *Extending working life: A review of the research literature*. Research Report No. 299, Department for Work and Pensions, Leeds: HMSO.

Roberts, B. W., & Friend, W. (1998). Career momentum in midlife women: Life context, identity, and personality correlates. *Journal of Occupational Health Psychology, 3*, 195-208.

Rosen, B., & Jerdee, T. H. (1977). Too old or not too old. *Harvard Business Review, 55*(6), 97-106.

Rupp, D. E., Vodanovich, S. J., & Crede, M. (2006). Age bias in the workplace: The impact of ageism and causal attributions. *Journal of Applied Social Psychology, 36*(6), 1337-1364.

Schein, E. H. (1985). *Career anchors: Discovering your real values* (1st ed.). London: Pfeiffer & Co.

Sterns, H. L., & Miklos, S. M. (1995). The aging worker in a changing environment: Organizational and individual issues. *Journal of Vocational Behavior, 47*, 248-268.

Sturges, J. (1999). What it means to succeed: Personal conceptions of career success held by male and female managers at different ages. *British Journal of Management, 10*, 239-252.

Sullivan, S. E., & Arthur, M. B. (2006). The evolution of the boundaryless career concept: Examining physical and psychological mobility. *Journal of Vocational Behavior, 69*, 19-29.

Sullivan, S. E., Carden, W. A., & Martin, D. F. (1998). Careers in the next millennium: Directions for future research. *Human Resource Management Review, 8*, 165-185.

Super, D. E. (1957). *The psychology of careers*. New York: Harper.

Taylor, P., & Walker, A. (1994). The ageing workforce: Employers' attitudes towards the employment of older people. *Work, Employment and Society, 8*, 569-591.

van der Heijden, B. I. J. M., Schalk, R., & van Veldhoven, M. J. P. M. (2008). Ageing and careers: European research on long-term career development and early retirement. *Career Development International, 13*, 85-94.

Veiga, J. F. (1981). Plateaued versus non-plateaued managers: Career patterns, attitudes and paths. *Academy of Management Journal, 24*, 566-578.

Vickerstaff, S. (2006). Entering the retirement zone: How much choice do individuals have? *Social Policy and Society, 5,* 507-517.

Vroom, V. (1964). *Work and motivation.* New York: Wiley.

Warr, P. (1992). Age and occupational well-being. *Psychology and Aging, 7,* 37-45.

CHAPTER 5

MIDCAREER RENEWAL

A Research Agenda
for the Twenty-first Century

Sally J. Power

The long-standing model of career progression, articulated by Super in 1957, involved four stages: exploring, establishing, maintaining, and disengaging. It was a linear model, as was common for that era of careers research, and assumed stable, long-term employment (Sullivan & Crocitto, 2007). The maintenance stage in particular was seen primarily as a stable period where the individual "does not attempt to break new ground, to open up new fields of work" (Super, 1957, p. 147).

Interest in changes occurring within the maintenance stage or midcareer[1] began to increase with the blossoming of the study of adult development in the 1970s and after (Gould, 1978; Levinson, Darrow, Klein, Levinson, & McKee, 1978; Vaillant, 1977). Scholarly research such as studies concerning midlife crisis became popular, as the perspective offered in *Seasons of a Man's Life* by Levinson et al. (1978) spread among academics and practitioners alike (Hill & Miller, 1981; Kets de Vries, 1978; Lawrence, 1980; McGill, 1977; Smith, 1975). By the 1990s even more changes in employment dynamics suggested that career theory, par-

Maintaining Focus, Energy, and Options Over the Career
pp. 107–133
Copyright © 2009 by Information Age Publishing
All rights of reproduction in any form reserved.

ticularly related to those older individuals already established in the work-place, needed to be reconsidered (Cascio, 2000; Herr, 1996; Jones, 1996; Sullivan, 1999; Watts, 1996).

Employees are becoming more mobile across employers. In his latest study of employment insecurity, Farber (2008) reports that the percentage of men in the private sector with 10 years of employment at one company declined from about 50% to 35% between 1973 and 2006. Twenty-year employment at one employer fell from 35% to 20% for this same group in the same period. Other research has suggested increased mobility rates among additional groups, as well. For example, there have been at least two studies suggesting increases among women moving in and out of the workforce throughout their career (e.g. Cabrera, in press; Mainiero & Sul-livan, 2006). Also, Wang, Adams, Beehr, and Schultz (this volume), using Health and Retirement Study data, found that approximately half of those who retired between 1992 and 1996 re-entered the workforce at least once in the 8 years following retirement. About 66% of those who re-entered the workforce transferred in and out of the workforce more than once. Such increased mobility as well as internal organizational changes, such as downsizing and the flattening of structures (Anand & Daft, 2007), and the increase in contract work (Barley & Kunda, 2003) have helped to redefine the maintenance stage. Although the maintenance stage or mid-career was once viewed as a time of relative stability (Super, 1957), it is now seen as a time marked by changes and career transitions (Hall & Mirvis, 1995; Power, 2006; Reitman & Schneer, 2003). In this chapter I will focus on what is arguably the ideal in midcareer or maintenance stage transition: *career renewal*, defined here as the achievement on the part of individuals in midcareer of greater positive involvement in their work and/or feelings of greater subjective career success (i.e., intrinsic out-comes) as the result of some career or personal transition.

Over the last 50 years, scholars from numerous disciplines, including government (Gardner, 1964, 1991), social work (Bargal, 1982), psycho-therapy (Jaffe, 1985; Tien, 1989), education (Mezirow, 1991), adult devel-opment (Hudson, 1991), career counseling (Bejian & Salomone, 1995) and management (Hall & Mirvis, 1995) have studied renewal. Despite the research that has been completed on renewal, the literature remains frag-mented. Scholars studying renewal have rarely built upon the works of one another and there is no consensus regarding how to define renewal.

In this chapter the lack of integration and consensus is addressed. Based on a critical analysis of the literature, I will suggest a definition of career renewal as well as an integrative model of the career renewal pro-cess. I also argue that more research on midcareer renewal is called for in the twenty-first century for three prime reasons. First, the actual number of career transitions occurring in midcareer has likely increased (Cabrera, in press; Mainiero & Sullivan, 2006; Wang et al., this volume) and even more older workers are planning to continue working past retirement age (Groeneman & Pope, 2008), thus elongating midcareer. Second, more individuals have faced a number of negative repercussions (e.g., downsizings) from career transitions in the last 20 years, including reduced income (Baumol, Blinder, & Wolff, 2003; Farber, 2005) and psychological difficulties (Uchitelle, 2006; Wanberg, 1995). But theorists have pointed out that greater mobility can allow individuals greater self-actualization and renewal as a result of their choices (Arthur, Inkson, & Pringle, 1999; Power & Rothausen, 2003). A focus on the mechanisms of career renewal might provide some insight into how we can increase the positive outcomes of some of these transitions. Third, current employees are telling employers that they have a "hunger for renewal" (Morison, Erickson, & Dychtwald, 2006, p. 81). Morison et al. (2006) reported that only 33% of employees between the ages of 35 and 54 felt energized by their work but more than 40% reported feelings of burnout.

Although there are more opportunities now for studying renewal because of changes in workforce demographics and economic turbulence, there are also serious research challenges, including the need to develop measures of renewal and to find methods for overcoming the difficulties of obtaining midcareer research participants. The purpose of this chapter is to critically analyze past studies of renewal and, based on that analysis, integrate past research into a model of midcareer renewal. This model will be used to frame my discussion of future research directions.

In the next section, previous research on career renewal is reviewed. Next, an empirically measurable definition for the phenomenon of midcareer renewal is proposed and an integrative framework for understanding midcareer renewal is developed, based on my critical analysis of past research. Finally, the challenges that face researchers studying career renewal are detailed and an agenda for future research is provided.

REVIEW OF THE
LITERATURE ON MIDCAREER RENEWAL

The literature on renewal has been multidisciplinary and relatively sporadic over the last 50 years. It has also covered not only career renewal but also the broader concept of personal renewal. In this chapter the literature related to midcareer renewal will be analyzed, divided into two major foci: studies growing out of the traditional linear career stage paradigm and studies that focus directly on the process of renewal with minimal reference to career stage theory.

The empirical study of renewal began in the context of the interest in "midlife crisis" in the 1970s and 80s (Hill & Miller, 1981; Kets de Vries, 1978; McGill, 1977; Smith, 1975). These studies combined a focus on larger personal issues as well as career issues. Midlife crisis on the whole had a relatively negative stereotype in this period (Sullivan & Crocitto, 2007), as it was often seen as a reaction to the recognition by many men that they would die and that the best years of their life had probably passed (Jaques, 1965; Tien, 1989). In this time period, few studied the positive outcomes of career change because such movements were seen as detrimental to climbing the corporate ladder (Morrison, 1977). Although not the focus of their research, there were a few scholars who identified renewal as an option during midcareer (Murphy & Burck, 1976; Schlossberg, 1985; Vaillant & Milofsky, 1980).

Most of the literature on career renewal has been published since 2000. One of the major difficulties is that there is no agreed upon, common definition of the phenomenon of career renewal. For example, Oplatka, Bargal, and Inbar (2001) reviewed the career renewal literature, summarizing four primary "points of view" about the concept of renewal. These points of view were (a) renewal as a counter-concept to professional obsolescence (Dubin, 1975); (b) renewal as a new start with new energy and a new sense of identity (Hudson, 1991); (c) renewal as a response to a lack of intellectual stimulation because daily activities have become routine (Gardner, 1964); and (d) renewal as a personal quality of great men or women (Bargal, 1982). As illustrated in the review by Oplatka and associates (2001), there are many different perspectives on what career renewal means. Even Oplatka and associates did not offer a definition of career renewal. This lack of precision or agreement about the phenomenon makes building knowledge about it difficult because scholars using different measures of renewal may be studying much different transitions. This lack of clear definition led me to read broadly, looking for studies of career transitions that resulted in positive outcomes for the individuals involved. In that reading, I discovered two additional studies (Ibarra, 2003; Sullivan, Martin, Carden, & Mainiero, 2003) which focused on career change and recycling, respectively, but included career renewal in the definition of the phenomenon they were studying. Because these studies included subjects that experienced renewal, I included them in this review.

Three studies approach career renewal within the framework of linear stage theories. The authors of two of these studies use Super's work (1957, 1990) as a basis and Riverin-Simard (1988) places her discussion of renewal within the series of stages she identified in her analysis.

Midcareer Renewal Studies Based on Career Stage Theory

Bejian and Salomone (1995) wrote a theoretical article proposing that "renewal" be considered a stage between the end of Super's establishment stage and the beginning of the maintenance stage. They defined renewal as a "transitional stage" where people ascribe meaning to past decisions, make new decisions, and plot a course of action. Specifically, they theorized that this stage is marked by the presence of "marker events triggering renewal," (a "trigger" for career renewal is an event the individual perceives as the beginning of the renewal process) and proposed these developmental tasks be performed during the stage: (a) reappraisal of career commitment and choice; (b) integration of the polarities of one's personality; and (c) modification of one's life structure.

Sullivan et al. (2003) expanded upon Super's (1984) concept of "recycling." They define recycling as a process in which individuals reexamine career choices and subsequently take action to change some aspect of their career. Sullivan et al. look specifically at this occurrence in midcareer, but note that it might happen in either the establishment or maintenance stage. Their study is included in this review of career renewal literature because the authors state "recycling can be a time of career evaluation and renewal" (pp. 34-35) and differentiate those individuals they studied from workers who readjusted their career aspirations by maintaining their occupational position and accepting that their career might not be as personally satisfying as it had been. Thus, these authors studied positive change during midcareer and their study likely included a number of people who experienced renewal.

Sullivan et al. (2003) interviewed 15 individuals and reported that the triggers for these recyclers were organizational changes (e.g., downsizings and mergers), personal career plateaus, and personal crises. Further, they found that the triggers caused personal reflection which led to career redirection. The common personal characteristics found among the interviewees were that they were risk takers and optimists. While this study identifies components that are part of the general definition of midcareer renewal (reflection, optimism, a changed direction), they stop short of making a claim that their research participants renewed and call their changes "recycling."

Riverin-Simard (1988) identified renewal as a possibility in midcareer as part of her large study of the career development and continuing education of 786 adults in Quebec. Like Super (1954, 1990), she described a linear, sequential set of phases for adult career development, although she identified nine phases, whereas Super's model had only four stages. She interviewed 91 people in each of the two age ranges referred to here (Riverin-Simard, 1988). Based on a content analysis of these interviews, she identified the age when midcareer individuals reconsidered their career trajectories and contemplated significant change to be after the stability of achieving what Super would call the maintenance stage. The age range for reconsideration was between 43 and 47. Then, between 48 and 52, individuals made the changes they had chosen. Individuals used one of two approaches during the redirection of their career. One approach was based on a biological model that suggested decline in a career was inevitable; these people's involvement in and rewards from their career declined. The second approach, taken by what she called "exceptional navigators" (approximately 15% of her sample), looked at their career as having "limitless possibilities for self actualization," with each succeeding career stage being equally important in a continuing trajectory without decline. These exceptional navigators were those who renewed their career.

These three studies all attempt to place renewal in a position within the traditional linear, sequential paradigm of career development. Each, however, places renewal in a slightly different spot. Career development theory has been moving toward a more dynamic, less sequential understanding of careers (Hall & Mirvis, 1995; Patton & McMahon, 1999). For example, Super (1990) hypothesized that his four career stages might also include minicycles. Other theorists who have modified their theory to include multiple cycles are Holland (1992) and Dawis (1994). Furthermore, Hall and Mirvis (1995) and Power (2006) make arguments for multiple cycles within midcareer based on the growing turbulence within employers. Each of these cycles could be accompanied by a sense of renewal.

Midcareer Renewal Studies Focused on the Renewal Process

A second major group of studies on midcareer renewal focused on the renewal process without connecting it to stage theory. Oplatka (2001a, 2001b, 2003, 2004, 2005a, 2005b, Oplatka et al., 2001) is the most prolific scholar studying midcareer renewal.[2] He has published a series of articles on the renewal of school principals in Israel (Oplatka, 2001a, 2001b, 2003; Oplatka et al., 2001), each focusing on a different trigger found within the group. Through purposeful and snowball sampling, he identified 25 principals who were between 43 and 52, were successful in their work, energetic, and had not experienced burnout (I. Oplatka, personal communication, May 17, 2008). Oplatka conducted a similar research project asking principals and teachers to identify teachers in mid-to-late career who were considered motivated, were not burned out, and had experienced career transitions (2005a). His interviews with a total of 20 teachers (2004) produced three additional articles on renewal, again divided on the basis of triggering events (Oplatka, 2004, 2005a, 2005b).

The triggers for renewal Oplatka identified among the principals were: sabbatical (Oplatka et al., 2001), changing schools (2001b), and seeking out innovation and implementing it (2003). His study of teachers found one similar trigger—changing schools (2005a)—and two additional triggers: forced change (2005b) and the addition of a first-time principal to a school where the teacher worked (2004). Oplatka also identified common components of the renewal process (Oplatka, 2001b; Oplatka et al., 2001).

Ibarra (2003) published a study based on 39 in-depth interviews with midcareer people who successfully changed careers. Like Sullivan et al. (2003), Ibarra did not use the word renewal, but instead referred to the reinvention process. She defined reinvention as the process by which individuals launch themselves anew. She also specified that the book describing the process was for anyone who had experience and wanted to change careers successfully. Because her focus was on reinvention and successful change, I believe her sample included many individuals who renewed.

Ibarra (2003) selected her research participants so that they represented a variety of career changers. Her research participants ranged in age from 32 to 51 and included (a) younger people leaving consulting and accounting, (b) individuals who were midlevel and leaving big companies, (c) individuals joining high tech start-ups, and (d) others who were seeking social contribution. Ibarra's focus was the process of change itself, which she saw as a learning process whereby individuals not only changed their career but also their identity. She described the process as (a) involving crafting experiments where individuals could try out their new identities, (b) shifting connections so that individuals found new role models and new peer groups to guide their behavior, and (c) making sense of their new directions by finding catalysts or triggers for change so that they could rework their story.

The next study of the renewal process is by Boyatzis and McKee (2005) and focuses on resonant leaders. Drawing on their own consulting experiences as well as previous research, they define a resonant leader as an individual who is inspirational, able to create a hopeful emotional tone, empathic, compassionate, mindful, authentic, and in tune with self, others, and the environment. Often these individuals sacrifice their own needs to fulfill the leadership role and become involved in a downward spiral resulting in the deterioration of their resonant leader qualities. In order to renew themselves, these leaders engage in a process of intentional change in order to regain their abilities as resonant leaders. Their study contributes to our understanding of renewal because it describes a process by which people with one type of career focus (i.e., resonant leadership) renew.

Three general conclusions can be gleaned from this review of the theoretical and empirical literature on midcareer renewal. First, although previous research has produced a number of different definitions of the phenomenon, there is no common definition of career renewal. A single definition would greatly aid future research by assuring that researchers are studying the same phenomenon. Second, most of the research on renewal has been qualitative. While qualitative research provides a rich store of observations to analyze, the laborious nature of the methodology usually limits sample size. Quantitative studies using larger sample sizes should now be undertaken to refine our understanding of the process as well as to determine how many midcareer people actually experience career renewal, how many experience less successful midcareer transitions, and how many remain engaged consistently throughout their career and have no need of renewal. Third, most of the research on midcareer renewal has been published in the last 7 years, suggesting that interest is growing among scholars. In order to facilitate greater empirical research on career renewal, the next two sections detail a measurable definition of midcareer renewal and offer an integrative framework for suggesting directions for future research.

A DEFINITION OF MIDCAREER RENEWAL

Although there have been a number of empirical studies that touch on the subject of midcareer renewal, the studies do not utilize a common, measurable definition of career renewal. Sullivan et al. (2003) and Ibarra (2003) studied larger phenomena (those who recycled and those who changed careers in midcareer, respectively) that included participants renewing but did not make identifying renewers a part of their analysis. Oplatka (2001b, 2003, 2004, 2005a, 2005b, Oplatka et al., 2001) operationalized renewal by studying those who were in midcareer but had not burned-out, while Boyatzis and McKee (2005) defined renewal as a process to regain the characteristics of a specific type of leadership.

Without a common definition, researchers cannot reliably identify the particular individual characteristics and process components that are crucial to renewal and that differentiate it from other, less successful career transitions (for examples see Feldman & Leana, 2000; Hanisch, 1999; Wanberg, 1995). Because of this lack of consensus about what career renewal is, I propose a common definition of midcareer renewal that is based on measuring a person's perceptions of the level of his or her positive involvement in work and/or feelings of subjective career success before and after some process or series of events.

Because the word "renew" means "to make new, or as new, again; to restore to the same condition as when new, young, fresh" (Renew, 1989), I suggest that individuals who renew must initially perceive a decrease in feelings of positive work involvement and/or subjective success from previous levels. This perceived change in level of success and/or involvement prepares the individual for the possibility of renewal. Both Oplatka (2001b, 2003; Oplatka et al., 2001), and Boyatzis and McKee (2005) mention this decline in personal perceptions of subjective success and positive involvement in work as part of their understanding of renewal. Then, for renewal to have occurred, something must have happened which led the individual to perceive his or her positive involvement with work and/or feelings of subjective career success to have reached level(s) equal to or surpassing the past level(s) of success and/or involvement.

This is only a first step in defining renewal, since it is focused on the outcomes rather than the process itself. But an agreement and measure of outcomes would allow researchers to differentiate renewal from recycling or other types of career transitions that are less positive for the individual and to test the differences between individuals and/or processes for those who do and do not renew. In previous studies of renewal (Boyatzis & McKee, 2005; Oplatka, 2001b, 2003, 2004, 2005a, 2005b; Oplatka et al., 2001), renewal is identified by individuals' self-report of personal re-energizing at work and feelings of positive involvement. These feelings would certainly be similar to what is being suggested here. But these measurements are missing in both the Ibarra (2003) and Sullivan et al. (2003) studies and their absence is a prime reason why these studies can only be partially considered as studies of career renewal.

Operationalizing this definition has yet to be attempted. A first step would be to identify the components of positive involvement in one's work and the components of subjective career success, and then to devise a scale that could measure levels of each as perceived by individuals. At this point, I believe that both positive involvement in the work and feelings of subjective career success should be measured in the scale, because it is not clear that one or the other is the sole indicator of career renewal. For example, it is conceivable that some people might still feel positive involvement in their work (e.g., they enjoy helping others through their work) but no longer consider their career to be as successful as before. Likewise, some might consider themselves to be as successful as in the past but no longer experience the same level of positive feelings from their work involvement as they once did.

A question that arises from this proposed definition is how midcareer renewal might differ from learning or achievement at any stage of career development. For example, Hall's (1996, 2002) concept of the protean career specifies that the individual is constantly moving through learning cycles. What would differentiate midcareer renewal for someone with a protean career in early career? I would suggest that individuals must first accomplish the developmental tasks of Super's (1957, 1990) establishment stage and have achieved what he or she considers career success and/or positive involvement in their work in the maintenance stage before their process could be considered midcareer renewal. The level and nature of the individual's positive involvement in his or her work and feelings of subjective career success in the maintenance stage would provide a base line for determining if he or she has experienced midcareer renewal.

AN INTEGRATIVE FRAMEWORK
FOR STUDYING MIDCAREER RENEWAL

Midcareer renewal has been studied in terms of three major components: triggers for the process, the process components themselves, and personal characteristics of those who renew. I will synthesize and discuss the commonalities and differences in the findings about each of these components using the recent empirical studies that focus directly on renewal or on processes with significant overlap with renewal. In Figure 5.1 the hypothesized components of renewal are summarized and a brief description of them is provided.

Triggers for the Renewal Process

The first component, the trigger for the renewal process, has been described as an internal change in interests or priorities and/or an external event that begins or is the articulated reason for an individual's renewal. For example, Sullivan et al. (2003) identified three major triggers for recycling: personal crisis, organizational change, and career plateau. Oplatka (2001b, 2003, 2004, 2005a, 2005b; Oplatka et al., 2001) identified a number of triggers in his studies including forced change, sabbaticals, voluntary school change, lack of stimulation, and a new boss.

Sometimes the stimulus for a major personal change process is mostly internal. For instance, this is the case when renewal is instigated by a feeling of low achievement or a lack of stimulation at work, triggers Oplatka (2003) identified. Another example of a primarily internal trigger would be adult developmental changes. With their Kaleidoscope Career Model, Mainiero and Sullivan (2006) have mapped the shifting personal priorities that people use to manage their career as they move through life and,

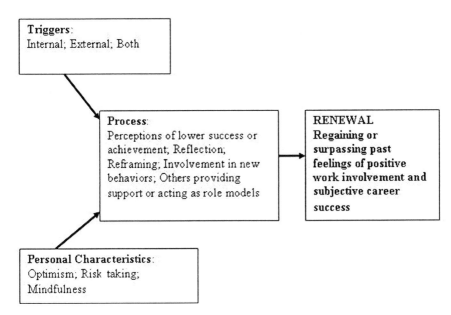

Figure 5.1.   Major components of the midcareer renewal process.

to the extent that career renewal comes as a result of transitions in reaction to these shifts, the trigger would be an internal reordering of career goals. The internal stimulus also plays an important part in the Boyatzis and McKee study (2005), because the once-resonant leader needs to perceive himself or herself to be not as effective as in the past in order to initiate the renewal process.

At other times the motivating event is primarily external: for example, downsizings (Sullivan et al., 2003), teachers or school principals changing schools (Oplatka, 2001b, 2005a), or governmental mandated changes (Oplatka, 2005b). External events might influence the renewal process in two primary ways. First, the external trigger might coincide with an internally felt need for change and lead naturally toward renewal. Second, the external trigger might come as a shock to an individual and force the individual to rework his or her feelings of career success. The psychological process that is necessary for renewal in these second, more involuntary situations has been explored to a limited extent in the psychotherapeutic literature (Jaffe, 1985).

It seems likely that renewal can be initiated by either an internal or an external trigger. An interesting research question, however, is whether the renewal process or its outcomes differ depending on whether the initiating trigger is internal or external. Another interesting research question is how a trigger that is perceived negatively by the individual affects the renewal process or outcomes—or if it diminishes the likelihood that renewal may occur.

Components of the Renewal Process

A second major component of midcareer renewal is the process itself. Ibarra's (2003) study, for example, focused on the renewal process. What she found was that the career change involved changing the individual's identity via experiments, new contacts, and reflection to make sense of the process. Sullivan et al. (2003) did not focus on the process in any detail but instead described how individuals who recycled engaged in reflection, searched for answers, and changed the patterns of their life and career. Boyatzis and McKee (2005) also focused much of their book on the renewal process of resonant leaders. This process of "intentional change" for individuals involves five major discoveries: (a) describing your ideal self, (b) recognizing how you behave and are viewed by others (i.e., your real self), (c) comparing your ideal and real selves and developing a learning agenda to come closer to your ideal self, (d) experimenting with and practicing new habits, and (e) developing and maintaining close relationships that help you move through the learning agenda. A unique variation in Boyatzis and McKee's process is that they added an assessment of what others believe about the individual at the beginning of the renewal process. This might be a function of the particular type of career (i.e., resonant leadership) they studied.

Oplatka's (2001b, 2003, 2004, 2005a, 2005b; Oplatka et al., 2001) studies identified three major variations in the renewal process. The general components of the process that most of his research subjects used were (a) a recognition of low personal achievement or stagnation, (b) reflection, (c) reframing at the level of the individual's basic assumptions and beliefs along the lines of the work done by Mezirow (1991), (d) involvement in new opportunities and tasks, and (e) the achievement of renewed energy (Oplatka, 2001b; Oplatka et al., 2001). A major variation occurred, however, in the group of principals whose renewal process was a constant cycle, such that they felt anxiety at not innovating, found and implemented an innovation, and experienced renewal only to begin the process again (Oplatka, 2003). Participants in this group saw innovation as a crucial part of their professional role as educators, so they did not reframe their basic assumptions or beliefs to achieve renewal (Oplatka, 2003). Another major variation occurred in the group of teachers for whom the trigger for renewal was involuntary change. Oplatka found that they needed to go through a period of fear and anger at the forced nature of the change before they began the general renewal process he had seen in other groups (Oplatka, 2005).

These various analyses of the process of renewal reveal some common-alities as well as some interesting variations. Most processes began with a perceived lessening of personal career success and/or achievement. The one exception may be the Ibarra study (2003), because she does not include attitudinal precursors to embarking on career change in her anal-ysis. Common to all the described processes except one process occurring with one of Oplatka's subgroups (2003) was the need for serious reflection on and reframing of basic assumptions and beliefs about self and work.

Another empirical commonality in the renewal processes described is taking on new activities as a part of the renewal process. Each of the researchers, however, differed in the timing of these activities. The research of Ibarra (2003) and some of Oplatka's (2001b, 2003, 2005a) studies suggest that these activities occur early in the renewal process, whereas Boyatzis and McKee (2005) suggest the new behaviors occur after a period of purposeful assessment and goal setting. What causes the dif-ference in the sequencing of action and reflection? Is this apparent differ-ence an artifact of the research methodology or the researchers' descriptions of the processes? This question of sequence seems very closely related to the question of trigger sequence discussed earlier. These are questions that would benefit from future study.

Finally, all the studies except Sullivan et al. (2003) made note of the importance of other people supporting the process. Ibarra (2003) identi-fied the need for people changing careers to seek out new contacts, Boy-atzis and McKee (2005) suggested that others' perceptions were important to establishing goals for renewal and to supporting the process, and Oplatka (2001a, 2001b, 2003, 2004, 2005a, 2005b, Oplatka et al., 2001) identified both general support from others as well as support through offering opportunities for change as important to the renewal process. The role of other individuals in the renewal process deserves more systematic study as it may vary based on other variables.

Personal Characteristics of Those Who Renew

The third component of midcareer renewal is the role personal charac-teristics play in the process. Are certain people destined to renew while others are not (Gardner, 1990; Bargal, 1982)? Sullivan et al. (2003) identi-fied two main characteristics of those who recycled: optimism and risk taking. Furthermore, Sullivan et al. (2003) described the recycling process as involving reflection and so the characteristic of mindfulness (i.e., the capacity for being aware of one's self) is implied. Boyatzis and McKee

(2005) identified three characteristics in their resonant leaders who renewed: mindfulness, hope, and compassion. Oplatka's (2003) comments about personal characteristics were more specific to the context in which the renewal occurred. For example, he noted that those who renewed via innovation were positively predisposed toward change. Ibarra (2003) did not explore personal characteristics in relation to the process of changing careers.

In sum, only two out of the eight studies examined focused on personal characteristics. Mindfulness and optimism were the only common characteristics in these studies. Risk taking might also be considered as a common characteristic, although only mentioned by Sullivan et al. (2003), because change appears to be characteristic of the renewal process and change typically involves some level of risk.

In Table 5.1 there is a summary of what these studies about midcareer renewal have found with regard to the three major components of the process. All of these studies have involved relatively few research participants and have been exploratory studies. What is needed now is more data to answer the research questions suggested by this chapter and to describe the components and sequence of the renewal process in more detail. Thus, these results set the stage for moving to more quantitative studies. In the last two sections of this chapter, I will describe the challenges and promise of further quantitative study on this topic.

THE CHALLENGES OF RESEARCHING MIDCAREER RENEWAL

Although renewal has been studied within a variety of academic fields, until recently there has been relatively little empirical work done on it. There are a number of possible reasons for lack of focus on this topic. In this section the focus is on one general reason followed by discussion of some of the methodological challenges.

A general explanation for the lack of studies on midcareer renewal is that the phenomenon has been less prevalent in the past. Now, the increased turbulence within organizations and greater number of individuals planning to stay in the workforce longer (Groeneman & Pope, 2008) are increasing the number and scope of midcareer transitions. This situation is similar to that of the newer career models that have generated little empirical attention (Arthur & Rousseau, 1996; Arthur, Khapova, & Wilderom, 2005; Briscoe, Hall, & Frautschy DeMuth, 2006) but have become more prevalent due to the organizational turbulence. It can be argued that midcareer renewal is related to these new career models because the new models generally encourage career transitions of all kinds and midcareer renewal is one outcome of such transitions. Possible reasons for less

Table 5.1.   Major Findings on Midcareer Process by Investigator

Investigators	Focus: Triggers	Focus: Personal Char	Focus: Process
Oplatka (2001b, 2003, 2004, 2005a, 2005b, Oplatka et al., 2001)	• School change • Sabbatical • New supervisor • Innovation • Forced change	Situation specific observations	• Recognition of low achievement/stagnation • Reflection • Reframing • Involvement in new opportunities and tasks • Renewed energy
Boyatzis & McKee (2005)	• Sacrifice syndrome	• Mindfulness • Hope • Compassion	(Intentional Learning) • Comparing ideal and real self • Experimenting with and practicing new habits • Developing support
*Sullivan, Martin, Cardin, & Mainiero (2003)	• Organizational change • Personal crisis • Career plateaus	• Risk takers • Optimists	• Reflection • Search for new answers • Changed patterns in life and career
*Ibarra (2003)	• Aid in sense making	N.A.	• Experiments with new identities • Development of new networks for guidance and support • Reflection and sense making

Note: *These studies were on processes which appeared to have significant conceptual overlap with renewal.

empirical research in these newer areas of study are that graduate students follow the research interests of their advisors and/or scholars choose to refine subjects that have already been defined and in which journal interest has already been shown.

There are also a number of methodological challenges to doing research specifically on midcareer career renewal. First, it is often difficult to find willing midcareer research participants; second, people in midcareer are busy and have many responsibilities, such as providing primary support for a family and working to better their career; and finally, work

organizations are often unwilling to help identify possible research participants because participation in a research project could take workers' time
away from their job responsibilities and might set precedent for permit-
ting more studies in the future. Luckily, the studies highlighted here provide some ideas to meet the methodological challenges.

Oplatka's (2001a) method of finding research participants may be a
guide for some. Rather than looking directly for people who had experienced renewal (something that is often a private happening and not
shared widely), he asked others to identify workers in his target population who were middle aged, viewed as active, successful workers, and were
not burned out. Also, this approach to finding research participants may
take advantage of an organization's desire to know more about renewal in
the hopes of nurturing this experience for its workers. Ideally, in the
future, researchers would identify not just those who are likely to have
already renewed their career but also individuals who are demographi-
cally similar and have experienced similar triggers in their working life
but have not experienced career renewal. It is only by comparing renewers with similar nonrenewers that we can begin to identify differences
between the two groups.

Another method for finding research participants is to use the various
triggers identified in these early studies to identify a group of individuals
to be questioned about career renewal. These pools of research participants are likely to include people who have not experienced renewal so,
as a result, this approach would also provide data concerning how common the phenomenon is, as well as what individual characteristics are correlated with renewal. Such triggers include sabbaticals (while sabbaticals
may not be common in business in the United States, some European
countries have sabbaticals or periods away from employers that are available for a wide range of employees and academics), employer changes,
occupational changes, or changes in supervisors. Asking individuals
directly whether they have experienced a particular type of trigger would
be more neutral than asking them if they have renewed.

Other methods to recruit midcareer research participants include
recruiting in part-time undergraduate and MBA classes, in public workshops on issues surrounding midcareer management, and/or on Web sites
devoted to midcareer issues. Researchers should consider the potential
biases in using these sources to recruit research participants, however. For
example, those in educational programs may privilege education as a
source of renewal and/or success, or internet users who are currently in
midlife may be more open to change and thus more likely to renew.

A second methodological challenge has been the lack of consensus
regarding a definition of renewal and how to measure it. Earlier in this
chapter, I proposed a definition of midcareer renewal. Using this defini-

tion as a basis, future researchers should be able to develop a scale to measure midcareer renewal. Developing such a scale will be crucial to building a strong research stream. Ease of measurement is the bridge that will allow surveys to be administered to larger samples and thus provide researchers with a greater understanding of the phenomenon, including how many individuals are experiencing midcareer renewal and what personal characteristics and external conditions are most associated with positive outcomes.

A third methodological challenge is that while longitudinal studies provide many benefits over cross-sectional designs when studying career transitions, both prospective and retrospective longitudinal designs have serious drawbacks (Giele & Elder, 1998). Attrition of subjects is a major obstacle in prospective longitudinal designs (Farrington, Gallagher, Morley, St. Ledger, & West, 1990). Prospective longitudinal designs would permit scholars to collect measurements of work involvement and subjective career success across different time periods so that within-person changes could be examined more objectively. However, measuring career involvement and subjective career success for a large number of people and then hoping that a reasonable number of these participants experience a dip in these measurements and subsequently renew their career would likely be very labor intensive. Riverin-Simard's study (1988) suggested that only 15% of her sample were "exceptional navigators" who were likely to experience midcareer renewal. The other more well-known difficulties of finding people 5 or 10 years after initial data gathering would also be present. Another view of the renewal process is that it is a totally subjective phenomenon that can be measured at any point after it has occurred. Retrospective longitudinal research studies, however, also have limitations including the difficulties of obtaining attitudinal data and data about gradual changes using this method (Janson, 1990).

The challenges that face researchers interested in midcareer renewal are numerous and one methodology is unlikely to meet all the requirements. Different combinations of answers to these methodological questions will provide different perspectives on the phenomenon and increase our overall knowledge about it over time.

THE PROMISE OF THE STUDY
OF MIDCAREER RENEWAL IN THE TWENTY-FIRST CENTURY

In the twenty-first century, the study of midcareer renewal holds great future promise not only because it may increase individuals' career fulfillment but also because, if organizations heed the information and manage in ways that encourage career renewal, their workers' productivity and

124 S. J. POWER

contributions may also increase. If people who experience midcareer renewal become more energized in their work (Ibarra, 2003; Oplatka, 2001b, 2003, 2004, 2005a, 2005b, Oplatka et al., 2001) and regain past levels of effectiveness (Boyatzis & McKee, 2005), they should perform better on the job. I hope these potential positive organizational outcomes associated with midcareer renewal will encourage more researchers to address the challenges examined in this chapter and to conduct more empirical research on this increasingly important subject. This section will further describe why research on midcareer renewal is more important now than ever before.

The studies on midcareer renewal indicate that external change can trigger the possibility of renewal (Oplatka, 2001b, 2004, 2005a, 2005b, Oplatka et al., 2001; Sullivan et al., 2003). An increase in inter-organizational and occupational mobility as well as movement in and out of the earning workforce and between different types of employment status could certainly all be considered external changes and can be seen in many employee groups. There has been a marked increase in interorganizational movement among midcareer white-collar men (Farber, 2008). Women are staying longer in the workforce (National Research Council, 1999) and this longer tenure and the turbulent business environment means that they, too, are experiencing more transitions in midcareer. For instance, there have been reports of many high-performing women moving out of corporate environments and going into business for themselves. Entrepreneurship is only one of the many potential transitions that working women may experience (Gordon, Beatty, & Whelan-Berry, 2002; Gordon & Whelan, 1998; Mainiero & Sullivan, 2006).

Many baby boomers are planning to continue working into what has traditionally been their retirement years (for a detailed discussion, see Wang et al., this volume). This extended work life makes sense given the lengthening of human life (National Center for Health Statistics, 2007). In the spring of 2007, AARP (formerly the American Association of Retired People, now AARP; the largest organization of people over 50 years old in the United States) sponsored a national survey of workers aged 45-78; 70% of those surveyed expected to work in retirement (Groeneman & Pope, 2008). The primary reason for working in retirement was the need for money (76%), followed by the desire to work for enjoyment (70%). This lengthening of individuals' working life could well extend the maintenance stage or midcareer for many. For individuals at traditional retirement age career transitions are likely as they attempt to move from traditional employment to more flexible employment or to pursue other kinds of work (see Gentry, Griggs, Deal, & Mondore, this volume). Twenty-seven percent of baby boomers (i.e., those born between

1946 and 1964) surveyed by AARP in 2002 said they wanted to change careers (Brown, 2003).

These increases in career transitions in midcareer mean more opportunities for renewal or decline. Much popular literature as well as some academic studies have indicated that many transitions are not positive (Baumol et al., 2005; Cappelli, 2001; Farber, 2005; Herzenberg, Alic, & Wial, 1998; Morton, 2002; Osterman, 1996; Sullivan, Carden, & Martin, 1998; Wanberg, 1995). In fact, many men of working age have dropped out of the workforce in disappointment because they can not find jobs that they believe are worthy of their efforts or that they enjoy (Uchitelle & Leonhardt, 2006). Furthermore, men have experienced serious income loss, except for the highest earners (Mishel, Bernstein, & Allegretto, 2005) and other negative results from job loss (Sullivan, Forret, & Mainiero, 2008). Discovering why and how renewal occurs in some cases and not in others promises to help more individuals remain happy and engaged through the many transitions they can now expect in their working life.

Another promise for the study of midcareer renewal can be seen in a historical overview of classic U.S. motivation and leadership theories (Flippo, 1984). Such a review shows a progression up Maslow's (1943) hierarchy of needs when motivating employees. Preferred managerial practices have moved from dictatorial leadership styles that focus on survival needs to leadership styles and motivational approaches that are more respectful and interactive and that are aimed at meeting employees' social and esteem needs (Flippo, 1984). This new era of employment dynamics opens the possibility that a growing number of employees may use their increased mobility to more actively shape their career to their unique and changing interests throughout their career and thus become more self-actualized (Arthur et al., 1999; Power, 2006).

The studies reviewed in depth in this chapter suggest a series of important research areas that promise to add significantly to our body of knowledge about midcareer renewal. I have already mentioned some research questions during the analysis of what is currently known about the components of midcareer renewal. Now I will highlight a number of other, broader research questions.

Forced external change as a trigger for midcareer renewal has not attracted much attention (see Oplatka, 2005b; Sullivan et al., 2003). With the exception of these two studies, however, the recent studies of renewal have focused on triggers that did not include a compulsory change. With the number of involuntary, external changes being forced on individuals by continuing downsizing, identifying what factors allow some of those transitions to lead to renewal could be very helpful. Although "career growth" is not the same as career renewal, Latack and Dozier's (1986) model describing the factors that generate career growth after job loss may provide a useful beginning point for future studies on career renewal that follows involuntary employment changes.

To date, we really know very little about the process of career renewal and how it differs from other transitions. The data in Figure 5.1 is a beginning; we need to go even further by studying not just those who have renewed but also those who have not renewed or who have tried and failed. We also need to have much more data on the renewal process before we can really identify the most important variables in midcareer renewal or determine the importance of sequence within the process (e.g., internal vs. external triggers occurring first).

Another source of information to illuminate the variations in the process might be to compare the renewal of those who stay within their occupation and/or with their employer with those whose career renewal involves changing occupation or employers. Oplatka's renewal studies (2001b, 2003, 2004, 2005a, 2005b, Oplatka et al., 2001) were of people who remained in their occupation, although some changed schools, and the Boyatzis and McKee study (2005) was of leaders who remained leaders. By contrast, the studies by Ibarra (2003) and Sullivan et al. (2003) involved changes of occupation and/or employer. Does the added risk, including the public nature of the process for those who change work focus or employer, change the nature of the renewal process and/or increase its likelihood of success?

One thing that the current studies do not touch on is the impact that nationality and/or culture may have on the phenomenon of midcareer renewal. Super, Super, and Sverko's Work Importance Study (1995) found that personal development and using abilities were the most important life values for both students and adults in the countries they studied, although this finding has been called into question, particularly in developing cultures (Thomas & Inkson, 2008). To the extent that personal development and using abilities are important life values and cultural and national structures allow it, midcareer workers all over the world may seek renewal if they do not find their current work fulfilling. Does the process or frequency of midcareer renewal vary in different cultures and/or nations? For example, a number of European countries provide employees with the opportunity for sabbatical-like periods away from their job. Does this practice lead to a greater likelihood of career renewal? Does the role of work in individuals' lives affect the likelihood that they will experience career renewal? What role does the relative affluence of the country play in the frequency of renewal, if any? What roles do different cultural dimensions (see for instance, Hofstede, 2001; Schwartz, 1999) play in the frequency or likelihood of midcareer renewal? These are research questions that have not yet been addressed.

Another area of great promise is the potential connections between career renewal and improved performance on the job. There are likely to be a number of moderating factors related to managerial behaviors and employee-organization fit that will affect the connection between personal career renewal and organizational performance (see Feldman & Vogel, this volume). Assuming those moderating factors can be aligned to encourage career renewal, many midcareer adults have knowledge and experience in the working world that can be of great use to employers if they are motivated to contribute. An employee whose career has been renewed is more likely to be motivated to perform at higher levels than those who have not experienced renewal, because career renewal leads to more positive involvement with work and/or more subjective feelings of success, which could also lead to more involvement with work.

CONCLUSION

The focus in this chapter has been on the under-studied phenomenon of midcareer renewal. The argument is made that the study of renewal promises to provide us with important information because of the increased number of career transitions within midcareer, because employees seem to be calling for it, and because a good deal of qualitative work has already been done as a foundation.

I have reviewed both the theoretical and empirical work that has focused either on midcareer renewal or on processes very closely related. While studies on the renewal process have been done over the last 50 years, there has been a cluster of work since 2000 that indicates a building of interest in this subject. The recent empirical studies have described the major components of the phenomenon and provided qualitative observations on which to build hypotheses. There are a number of research challenges, not the least of which is building a scale to measure the achievement of career renewal. Another challenge is finding midcareer research participants. Ideas for meeting these challenges were discussed.

The promise of the study of midcareer renewal in the twenty-first century appears to be great. Knowledge about how to encourage career renewal would allow more personal development for many who have less than positive career transitions. In addition, the potential of improved performance by midcareer individuals whose positive involvement with their work has been regained will allow well-managed organizations to utilize their experience and knowledge more effectively.

There is much to be learned about the process of midcareer renewal. It is hoped the definition of midcareer renewal and the integrative model of renewal offered in this chapter encourages future research on this relatively unexplored topic.

NOTES

1.   Midcareer is a difficult concept to define, just as middle-class has been (Leigh, 1994). For my purposes, however, it makes sense to define midcareer in a period similar to Super's (1957, 1990) maintenance stage. Specifically, I define midcareer as time after establishment in the working world (establishment being defined as assimilating to the culture of the full-time working world and consolidating one's position by showing positive work attitudes, productive work habits, and getting along with co-workers) and before disengagement begins. This is based on Super's career stages (1957, 1990) but I have broadened the concepts so that they apply to experience in the full-time working world generally, rather than being applied to a single "career" or employer. This will allow the use of the concepts to apply to workers whether they have followed a post-WW II, one-employer career pattern or whether they have been through more significant career changes as is the case for many in today's working world.
2.   The author wishes to thank Professor Oplatka for his comments on earlier drafts of this chapter.

REFERENCES

Anand, N., & Daft, R. L. (2007). What is the right organization design? *Organizational Dynamics, 36*, 329-344.

Arthur, M. B., Inkson, K., & Pringle, J. K. (1999). *The new careers: Individual action and economic change*. London: SAGE.

Arthur, M. B., Khapova, S. N., & Wilderom, C. P. M. (2005). Career success in a boundaryless career world. *Journal of Organizational Behavior, 26*, 177-202.

Arthur, M. B., & Rousseau, D. M. (1996). Introduction: The boundaryless career as a new employment principle. In M. B. Arthur & D. M. Rousseau (Eds.), *The boundaryless career* (pp. 3-20). New York: Oxford University Press.

Bargal, D. (1982). Obsolescence and renewal in the career of the professional social worker. *Comparative Social Work Education, 51*, 32-42.

Barley, S. B., & Kunda, G. (2003). *Gurus, hired guns, and warm bodies*. Princeton, NJ.: Princeton University Press.

Baumol, W. J., Blinder, A. S., & Wolff, E. N. (2003). *Downsizing in America: Reality, causes, and consequences*. New York: Russell Sage Foundation.

Bejian, D. V., & Salomone, P. R. (1995). Understanding midlife career renewal: Implications for counseling. *Career Development Quarterly, 44*, 52-64.

Boyatzis, R., & McKee, A. (2005). *Resonant leadership*. Boston: Harvard Business School Press.

Briscoe, J. P., Hall, D. T., & Frautschy DeMuth, R. L. (2006). Protean and bound-aryless careers: An empirical exploration. *Journal of Vocational Behavior, 69,* 30-47.

Brown, S. K. (2003). *Staying ahead of the curve 2003: The AARP working in retirement study.* Retrieved June 5, 2005, from www.aarp.org/research/

Cabrera, E. F. (in press) Protean organizations: Reshaping work and careers to retain female talent. *Career Development International.*

Cappelli, P. (2001). Assessing the decline of internal labor markets. In I. Berg & A. L. Kalleberg (Eds.), *Sourcebook of labor markets: Evolving structures and processes* (pp. 207-245). New York: Kluwer Academic/Plenum.

Cascio, W. F. (2000). New workplaces. In J. M. Kummerow (Ed.), *New directions in career planning and the workplace* (2nd ed., pp. 3-32). Palo Alto, CA: Davies-Black.

Dawis, R. V. (1994). The theory of work adjustment as convergent theory. In M. L. Savickas & R. W. Lent (Eds.), *Convergence in career development theories* (pp. 33-43). Palo Alto, CA: Consulting Psychologist.

Dubin, S. S. (1975). The psychology of keeping up-to-date. In H. G. Kaufman (Ed.), *Career management: A guide to combating obsolescence* (pp. 44-48). New York: JEEG.

Farber, H. S. (2005). *What do we know about job loss in the United States? Evidence from the displaced workers survey, 1984-2004.* Working Paper No. 498, January 5 edition. Unpublished manuscript. Retrieved March 10, 2006, from http://www.irs.princeton.edu/pubs/working_papers.html

Farber, H. S. (2008). Employment insecurity: The decline in worker-firm attachment in the United States. Working Paper No.530, July 2008. Unpublished manuscript. Retrieved on December 6, 2008 from http://www.irs.princeton.edu/pubs/pdfs/530.pdf

Farrington, D. P., Gallagher, B., Morley, L., St. Ledger, R. J., & West, D. J. (1990). Minimizing attrition in longitudinal research: Methods for tracing and securing cooperation in a 24-year follow-up study. In D. Magnusson & L. R. Bergman (Eds.), *Data quality in longitudinal research* (pp. 121-147). Cambridge, England: Cambridge University Press.

Feldman, D. C., & Leana, C. R. (2000). What ever happed to laid-off executives? A study of reemployment challenges after downsizing. *Organizational Dynamics, 29,* 64-75.

Feldman, D. C., & Vogel, R. M. (2009). The aging process and person-environment fit. In S. G. Baugh & S. E. Sullivan (Eds.), *Research in careers: Vol. 1. Maintaining focus, energy, and options over the career* (pp. 1-26). Charlotte, NC: Information Age.

Flippo, E. B. (1984). *Personnel management.* New York: McGraw-Hill.

Gardner, J. W. (1964). *Self renewal.* New York: Harper Colophon Books.

Gardner, J. W. (1991). Personal renewal. *McKinsey Quarterly, 2,* 71-81.

Gentry, W. A., Griggs, T. L., Deal, J. J., & Mondore, S. P. (2009). Generational differences in attitudes, beliefs, and preferences about development and learning at work. In S. G. Baugh & S. E. Sullivan, *Research in careers: Vol. 1. Maintaining focus, energy, and options over the career* (pp. 51-74). Charlotte, NC: Information Age.

Giele, J. Z., & Elder, G. H. (1998). *Methods of life course research: Qualitative and quantitative approaches.* Thousand Oaks, CA: SAGE.

Gordon, J. R., Beatty, J. E., & Whelan-Berry, K. S. (2002). The midlife transition of professional women with children. *Women in Management Review, 17,* 328-341.

Gordon, J. R., & Whelan, K. S. (1998). Successful professional women in midlife: How organizations can more effectively understand and respond to the challenges. *Academy of Management Executive, 12*(1), 8-24.

Gould, R. L. (1978). *Transformations: Growth and change in adult life.* New York: Simon & Schuster.

Groeneman, S., & Pope, E. (2008). *Staying ahead of the curve, 2007, the AARP work and career study.* Arlington, VA: AARP. Retrieved October 25, 2008, from www.aarp.org

Hall, D. T. (2002). *Careers in and out of organizations.* Thousand Oaks, CA: SAGE.

Hall, D. T., & Associates. (1996). *The careeer is dead—Long live the career.* San Francisco: Jossey-Bass.

Hall, D. T., & Mirvis, P. H. (1995). The new career contract: Developing the whole person at midlife and beyond. *Journal of Vocational Behavior, 47,* 269-289.

Hanisch, K. A. (1999). Job loss and unemployment research from 1994 to 1998: A review and recommendations for research and intervention. *Journal of Vocational Behavior, 55,* 188-220.

Herr, E. (1996). Toward the convergence of career theory and practice. In M. L. Savickas & W. B. Walsh (Eds.), *Handbook of career counseling theory and practice* (pp. 13-36). Palo Alto, CA: Davies-Black.

Herzenberg, S. A., Alic, J. A., & Wial, H. (1998). *New rules for a new economy: Employment and opportunity in postindustrial America.* Ithaca, NY: Cornell University Press.

Hill, R. E., & Miller, E. L. (1981). Job change and the middle seasons of a man's life. *Academy of Management Journal, 24,* 114-127.

Hofstede, G. H. (2001). *Culture's consequences: Comparing values, behaviors, institutions, and organizations across nations* (2nd ed.). Thousand Oaks, CA: SAGE.

Holland, J. L. (1992). *Making vocational choices* (2nd ed.). Odessa, FL: Psychological Assessment Resources.

Hudson, F. M. (1991). *The adult years: Mastering the art of self-renewal.* San Francisco: Jossey-Bass.

Ibarra, H. (2003). *Working identity. Unconventional strategies for reinventing your career.* Boston: Harvard Business School Press.

Jaques, E. (1965). Death and the mid-life crisis. *International Journal of Psychoanalysis, 46,* 502-514.

Jaffe, D. T. (1985). Self-renewal: Personal transformation following extreme trauma. *Journal of Humanistic Psychology, 25,* 99-124.

Janson, C.-G. (1990). Retrospective data, undesirable behavior, and the longitudinal perspective. In D. Magnusson & L. R. Bergman (Eds.), *Data quality in longitudinal research* (pp. 100-121). Cambridge, England: Cambridge University Press.

Jones, L. K. (1996). A harsh and challenging world of work: Implications for counselors. *Journal of Counseling & Development, 74,* 453-459.

Kets de Vries, M. F. R. (1978). The midcareer conundrum. *Organizational Dynamics, 7*(2), 45-62.

Latack, J. C., & Dozier, J. B. (1986). After the ax falls: Job loss as a career transition. *Academy of Management Review, 11*, 375-392.

Lawrence, B. (1980). The myth of the midlife crisis. *Sloan Management Review, 21*(4), 35-49.

Levinson, D. J., Darrow, C. M., Klein, E. B., Levinson, M. H., & McKee, B. (1978). *Seasons of a man's life.* New York: Knopf.

Leigh, N. G. (1994) *Stemming middle-class decline.* New Brunswick, NJ: Center for Urban Policy Research.

Mainiero, L. A., & Sullivan, S. E. (2006). *The opt-out revolt: Why people are leaving companies to create kaleidoscope careers.* Mountain View, CA: Davies-Black.

Maslow, A. H. (1943). A theory of human motivation. *Psychological Review, 50*, 370-396.

McGill, M. E. (1977). Facing the mid-life crisis. *Business Horizons, 20*(6), 5.

Mezirow, J. (1991) *Transformative dimensions in adult learning.* San Francisco: Jossey-Bass.

Mishel, L. R., Bernstein, J., & Allegretto, S. A. (2005). *The state of working America, 2004/2005.* Ithaca, NY: ILR.

Morison, R., Erickson, T., & Dychtwald, K. (2006). Managing middlescence. *Harvard Business Review, 84*(3), 79-86.

Morrison, R. (1977). Career adaptivity: The effective adaptation of managers to changing role demands. *Journal of Applied Psychology, 62*, 549-558.

Morton, L. P. (2002). Targeting mid-life men. *Public Relations Quarterly, 47*(4), 43.

Murphy, P. P., & Burck, H. D. (1976). Career development of men at mid-life. *Journal of Vocational Behavior, 9*, 337-343.

National Center for Health Statistics. (2007). *Health, United States, 2007.* Washington, DC: United States Printing Office. Retrieved October 27, 2008, from www.cdc.gov/nchs/fastats/lifexpec.htm

National Research Council. (1999). *The changing nature of work: Implications for occupational analysis.* Washington D.C.: National Academic Press.

Oplatka, I. (2001a). Building a typology of self-renewal: Reflection upon life story research. *The Qualitative Report, 6*(4), Retrieved April 24, 2008, from http://www.nova.edu/ssss/QR/QR6-4/oplatka.html

Oplatka, I. (2001b). Self-renewal and inter-organizational transition among women principals. *Journal of Career Development, 28*, 59-75.

Oplatka, I. (2003). School change and self-renewal: Some reflections from life stories of women principals. *Journal of Educational Change, 4*, 25-43.

Oplatka, I. (2004). The arrival of a new woman principal and teachers' self-renewal: Reflections from life stories of mid-career teachers. *Planning and Changing, 35*, 55-68.

Oplatka, I. (2005a). Breaking the routine: Voluntary inter-school transition and women teachers' self-renewal. *Teachers and Teaching: Theory and Practice, 11*, 465-480.

Oplatka, I. (2005b). Imposed school change and women teachers' self-renewal: A new insight on successful implementation of changes in schools. *School Leadership and Management, 25*, 171-190.

Oplatka, I., Bargal, D., & Inbar, D. (2001). The process of self-renewal among women headteachers in mid-career. *Journal of Educational Administration, 39,* 77-94.

Osterman, P. (1996). *Broken ladders: Managerial careers in the new economy.* New York: Oxford University Press.

Patton, W., & McMahon, M. (1999). *Career development and systems theory: A new relationship.* Pacific Grove, CA: Brooks/Cole.

Power, S. J. (2006). *The mid-career success guide: Planning for the second half of your working life.* Westport, CT: Greenwood.

Power, S. J., & Rothausen, T. J. (2003). The work-oriented midcareer development model: An extension of Super's maintenance stage. *The Counseling Psychologist, 31,* 157-197.

Reitman, F., & Schneer, J. A. (2003). The promised path: A longitudinal study of managerial careers. *Journal of Managerial Psychology, 18,* 60-75.

Renew. (1989). In J. Simpson (Ed.), *Oxford English dictionary online.* Retrieved October 20, 2008, from http://dictionary.oed.com

Riverin-Simard, D. (1988). *Phases of working life* (J. McElhone, Trans.). Montreal, Qúebec, Canada: Meridian.

Schlossberg, N. K. (1985). Adult career development theories: Ways to illuminate the adult experience. In L. Leibowitz & H. D. Lea (Eds.), *Adult career development* (pp. 2-16). Alexandria, VA: National Career Development Association.

Schwartz, S. H. (1999). A theory of cultural values and some implications for work. *Applied Psychology: An International Review, 48*(1), 23-47.

Smith, L. (1975). Executives and the mid-life crisis. *Management Review, 64*(9), 55.

Sullivan, S. E. (1999). The changing nature of careers: A review and research agenda. *Journal of Management, 25,* 457-483.

Sullivan, S. E., Carden, W. A., & Martin, D. F. (1998). Careers in the next millennium: Directions for future research. *Human Resource Management Review, 8,* 165.

Sullivan, S. E., & Crocitto, M. (2007). The developmental theories: A critical examination of their continuing impact on careers research. In H. Gunz & M. Peiperl (Eds.), *Handbook of career studies* (pp. 283-309). Los Angeles: SAGE.

Sullivan, S. E., Forret, M. L., & Mainiero, L. A. (2008). *Gender differences in psychological reactions to unemployment in the boundaryless career era.* Unpublished manuscript.

Sullivan, S. E., Martin, D. F., Carden, W. A., & Mainiero, L. A. (2003). The road less traveled: How to manage the recycling career stage. *Journal of Leadership and Organizational Studies, 10,* 34-42.

Super, D. E. (1957). *The psychology of careers.* New York: Harper & Row.

Super, D. E. (1984). Career and life development. In D. Brown, L. Brown & Associates (Eds.), *Career choice and development* (pp. 192-234). San Francisco: Jossey-Bass.

Super, D. E. (1990). A life-span, life-space approach to career development. In D. Brown & L. Brooks (Eds.), *Career choice and development* (2nd ed., pp. 197-261). San Francisco: Jossey-Bass.

Super, D. E., Super, C. M., & Sverko, B. (1995). *Life roles, values and careers: International findings of the work importance study* (1st ed.). San Francisco: Jossey-Bass.

Thomas, D. C., & Inkson, K. (2008). Careers across cultures. In H. Gunz & M. Peiperl (Eds.), *Handbook of career studies* (pp. 451-470). Thousand Oaks, CA: SAGE.

Tien, S. S. (1989). The phases of renewal: Steps to integration of the self in psychotherapy. *Journal of Contemporary Psychotherapy, 19*, 171-186.

Uchitelle, L. (2006). *The disposable American: Layoffs and their consequences* (1st ed.). New York: Knopf.

Uchitelle, L., & Leonhardt, D. (2006, July 31). Men not working, and not wanting just any job. *New York Times*, pp. 1-14.

Vaillant, G. E. (1977). *Adaption to life*. Boston: Little Brown.

Vaillant, G. E., & Milofsky, E. (1980). Natural history of male psychological health: Empirical evidence for Erickson's model of the life cycle. *American Journal of Psychiatry, 137*, 1348-1359.

Wanberg, C. R. (1995). A longitudinal study of the effects of unemployment and the quality of reemployment. *Journal of Vocational Behavior, 46*, 40-54.

Wang, M., Adams, G. A., Beehr, T. A., & Shultz, K. S. (2009). Bridge employment and retirement: Issues and opportunities during the latter part of one's career. In S. G. Baugh & S. E. Sullivan (Eds.), *Research in careers: Vol. 1. Maintaining focus, energy, and options over the career* (pp. 135-162). Charlotte, NC: Information Age.

Watts, A. G. (1996). Toward a policy for lifelong career development: A transatlantic perspective. *Career Development Quarterly, 45*, 41-53.

CHAPTER 6

BRIDGE EMPLOYMENT
AND RETIREMENT

Issues and Opportunities
During the Latter Part of One's Career

Mo Wang, Gary A. Adams, Terry A. Beehr, and Kenneth S. Shultz

The major focus of this chapter is the transitions that older workers in their late career make from work to retirement. In particular, we discuss the unique role that bridge employment can play as a strategy for older workers to implement career growth and/or change toward the end of their career. Bridge employment is typically defined as the pattern of labor force participation exhibited by older workers as they transition from late career jobs toward complete labor force withdrawal (Shultz, 2003). As such, bridge employment can take many forms, including part-time, full-time, seasonal, temporary work, and even self-employment, depending on the needs and desires of the older worker/retiree. However, we extend the existing literature by examining bridge employment from a dynamic perspective, in order to better understand its antecedents, outcomes, and general utility for older workers as a strategy for making the transition from career employment to full time retirement.

Maintaining Focus, Energy, and Options Over the Career
pp. 135–162

We begin with a brief overview of the literature on late career issues. Next we discuss contextual issues in late career at the individual, organizational, and societal levels. We then provide a concise review of the literature on the retirement decision-making process and discuss the various transitions possible from work to retirement, with a particular focus on bridge employment. We conclude our chapter by addressing the antecedents and outcomes associated with various forms of bridge employment that have been reported in the empirical and theoretical literature, and expand on what has been found to date by applying a dynamic perspective in order to better understand career change, renewal, and termination patterns as workers approach retirement and ultimately exit the workforce completely.

BRIEF OVERVIEW OF LATE CAREER ISSUES

Shultz and Wang (2008) recently detailed the changing nature of mid and late careers of older workers. They note that mid and late career issues have been largely ignored, but that they are beginning to receive some attention due to both a demographic shift to an older workforce and the changing nature of careers in general. No longer is midcareer simply seen as a time of maintenance and late career as a time of decline and obsolescence pushing one toward retirement. Instead the proliferation of the concept of the protean (or self directed) career (e.g., Hall, 2004) and the life span developmental model of careers (e.g., Sterns & Subich, 2002) in recent years has made each career stage a viable area of inquiry, including late careers. Shultz and Wang (2008) go on to note that the protean and life span developmental models of careers "have a much greater appreciation for the continued potential for growth and renewal of workers in their mid to late careers" (p. 131).

These changes in late career are occurring in a workplace where the nature of work and the workforce are also rapidly changing. The work itself is becoming less physically demanding but with increasing cognitive and psychosocial demands. In addition, the workforce is aging and becoming more ethnically and gender diverse. As a result, older workers approaching the later stages of their career are faced with a wide variety of individual level factors (e.g., physical aging, cognitive aging, experience and expertise, work-family balance), job level factors (e.g., job characteristics and stressors, job satisfaction), as well as organizational level factors (e.g., organizational climate, declines for certain types of labor) influencing their decisions to continue with some form of work or exit the workforce completely. As Greller and Simpson (1999) note, "A successful late career is the most likely prelude to a successful retirement. A frustrat-

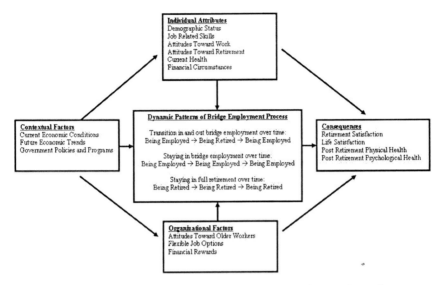

Figure 6.1.   Bridge employment and retirement process from a dynamic perspective.

ing, disrupted, and personally diminishing late career from which one was compelled to exit provides a poor basis for what is to come next" (p. 328). Therefore, we next outline a variety of contextual issues that older workers face in late career and how such factors may affect the decisions they make with regard to possible continued employment or complete retirement. These issues are illustrated in Figure 6.1, which visually presents the bridge employment process from a dynamic perspective.

CONTEXTUAL ISSUES IN LATE CAREER

The careers of older employees are different in several important ways from the careers of younger employees (see Gentry, Griggs, Deal, & Mondore, this volume, for a discussion of generational differences and Feldman & Vogel, this volume, for a discussion of aging and fit). In addition, their work lives are affected by variables at three levels (Beehr & Bennett, 2007): (1) their own *individual* situation, (2) the situation that is part of their employing *organization* (if they are not self-employed), and (3) the surrounding context provided by the *society* in which they live and work. Their individual situations include their own health, their family situation, and their work-related abilities and attitudes. Organizational influences on the older employees can include the type of job, any organizational structural changes such as downsizing or restructuring, and the organization's official and unofficial policies and practices, including age discrimination. The society in which older employees live and work also can affect their work and life experiences. Governments can pass laws influencing workplace situations and retirement policies, for example, and the society in which one lives is comprised of a specific proportion of people of different ages and of different attitudes toward older people. Conditions at these three levels define the context of workers as they age and as they consider retirement. Examples of these conditions at all three levels are seen in Figure 6.1.

Individual. Several factors in workers' own life situations affect their work and movement toward retirement as they age. There are aging related changes in abilities and affect that could be related to work, including declines in general physical health and physical abilities (e.g., Costa & Sartori, 2007), perhaps small declines in some kinds of cognitive ability (e.g., Singer, Verhaegen, Ghisletta, Lindenberger, & Baltes, 2003) and declines in sensory functions (e.g., Costa & Sartori, 2007). These declines among older workers, however, are relatively small (Jex, Wang, & Zarubin, 2007). Perhaps older people whose declines are largest are more likely to retire, and therefore older *workers'* ability declines are not very strong. This would be particularly true for blue collar jobs that are more physical in nature. In addition, and contrary to a theme of decline being associated with aging, older employees often have more skills and knowledge related to their specific job. Overall, the net effect of these factors seems to be that there is little meaningful effect of aging on job performance (Beehr & Bowling, 2002; Ng & Feldman, 2008) or on the tendency to engage in extra-role performance or organizational citizenship behaviors (Cleveland & Lim, 2007). In addition, age is positively but weakly associated with job satisfaction (e.g., reviews by Rhodes, 1983; Shultz & Wang, 2008; Warr, 1994).

Age has a well-known negative relationship with employee turnover (e.g., reviews by Rhodes, 1983; Warr, 1994). When older people become unemployed, however, it takes them longer to find new work (e.g., Couch, 1998; Shultz & Wang, 2008). Retirement may be an option for some older people who have trouble finding adequate employment, but many people recently report that they expect to work longer than was the case in the past, probably increasing the average retirement age (Mermin, Johnson, & Murphy, 2007); it is possible that retirement is not the preferred or viable alternative for many older people finding themselves unemployed.

Individuals' family factors, such as the marital state of older workers, seem to influence their relationship to work and retirement as well. For example, there is a tendency for couples to retire at about the same time (e.g., Kim & Feldman, 1998; Talaga & Beehr, 1995), and doing so may be less stressful (e.g., Moen, Kim, & Hofmeister, 2001). Thus, individual factors related to workers' aging include potential declines in health and various abilities, relatively positive work-related affect, a tendency to stay on the job (except at very late ages), and family situations.

Organizational. The situation in the older worker's employing organization also is important. It is likely that older workers in some organizations encounter very different circumstances, opportunities, and constraints than in other organizations. Across most organizations, older employees are likely to have different types of jobs, on average, compared with younger, newer workers. If they have been in the organization for any length of time, they no longer have entry level jobs, for example. Instead, older workers' jobs are likely to entail more responsibility, more autonomy, and more pay than newer workers' jobs. Related to taking on more responsibility, older workers might also take on more emergent tasks than less experienced younger workers (Beehr & Bowling, 2002).

Organizations can have different age-related climates, which would be correlated with various types of age equity versus age discrimination policies and/or practices (Klug & Krings, 2008). Age discrimination might explain, for example, situations where age is not as strongly related to objective job performance as it is to more subjective performance ratings (Waldman & Avolio, 1986). Age discrimination can be involved in many personnel practices, including hiring decisions (e.g., Gringart, Helmes, & Speelman, 2008), age typing of jobs (e.g., Cleveland & Landy, 1983; 1986), and fewer training opportunities for older workers (e.g., Gentry, Griggs, Deal, & Mondore, this volume; Maurer, 2007). However, more subtle forms of age discrimination may also be present. For example, instead of fewer training opportunities for older workers, there may be socially conveyed lower expectations for success in training of older workers. Furthermore, as a result of age discrimination, older workers may avoid those individuals perpetrating the discrimination, thereby reducing the flow of information and subsequent responsiveness to requests for information. Thus, in both of these more subtle cases of age discrimination, objective decreases in job performance may be observed.

Fortunately, some of the relationships between age and potentially discriminatory activities are not strong or consistent, and they may be weakening over time (Beehr & Bowling, 2002; Finkelstein & Farrell, 2007). Shultz and Wang (2008) suggest the following as organizational policies that are friendly to mid and late career employees: flexible time schedules, job sharing programs, cafeteria benefit choices, family-leave programs, educational programs for retirement transitions, employee assistance programs with services for workers with age-correlated issues, early and phased retirement programs, partnerships among public and private organizations, and advocacy groups to enhance training opportunities of older workers. Some of these programs (e.g., early or phased retirement programs) have been used by employers to induce older workers to leave the organization and potentially the workforce, but they can also serve as the impetus to engaging in bridge employment.

Society. In addition to the individual and organizational contexts, the context of the larger society in which both individuals and organizations are embedded is relevant for understanding the experiences of older workers. Societal variables that can affect older workers, along their decisions to retire, include the changing nature of work, the aging of the workforce, retirement and labor laws, and societal norms about older people in general and older workers in particular.

In many countries, people are living longer and staying healthy longer. Without an accompanying increase in birth rates, the net effect is an aging society and an aging workforce (e.g., Alley & Crimmins, 2007; Hatcher, 2003). Thus, older workers are likely to be more plentiful in the future, even if they were to retire at the same average age as in the past. There are laws regarding how old people can be and still continue working (i.e., not retire from the workforce) in some countries; even in countries where mandatory retirement ages are largely banned (e.g., the U.S.; Beehr & Bennett, 2008), societal norms can influence people's decisions to continue working or to retire (Beehr & Adams, 2003).

In addition to societal norms, of course finances play a key role in older workers' decisions to remain in the workforce or not. If the older employee's financial situation would be uncertain in retirement, he or she may decide to continue working until an older age. This can happen if the economy is poor (e.g., one has invested in the stock market but it is performing poorly), if the employer's pension plan is financed poorly or is unstable, or if the government's retirement system is seen as unreliable. Finances, and in particular the perceived adequacy of retirement income, are one of the most reliable predictors of an older worker's decision to stay in the workforce or to retire (Barnes-Farrell & Matthews, 2007; Beehr, 1986; Talaga & Beehr, 1989).

The age-typing of jobs (e.g., Cleveland & Landy, 1983, 1986) noted earlier as an organizational level phenomenon is almost certainly due in part to the society or culture in which the organization is embedded (Finkelstein & Farrell, 2007). It is even legal and seen as appropriate in some countries (e.g., China and India) to advertise and hire for certain jobs based at least in part on age (Finkelstein & Farrell, 2007). Societal norms have a downward influence, affecting organizations' practices and individuals' opinions and actions.

Overall, contextual issues at the individual, organizational, and societal levels influence the careers of older members of the workforce. They are related to the types of jobs older workers have, the way they are treated in those jobs, the way they perform their jobs, and whether they stay in the workforce at all. Therefore, we next discuss research and theorizing specific to the retirement decision-making process.

RESEARCH ON THE RETIREMENT DECISION-MAKING PROCESS

Over the past 50 years a number of empirical and theoretical models from across the social science literature have been applied to retirement decision making (see Adams & Beehr, 2003). In this section we provide an overview of the empirical literature examining the decision to retire. Then, we briefly review some of the more prominent theoretical models that focus on the retirement decision (see Smith-Ruig and also Power, this volume, for a discussion of career stage models and late career issues). These include rational choice theory, role theory, continuity theory, and the life course-ecological perspective. Because a complete review of each of these models is beyond the scope of this chapter, only the main themes, implications, and results are described.

Empirical Predictors of Retirement

Predictors of the decision to retire can be categorized as falling into at least two broad categories (1) microlevel personal factors and (2) mesolevel work-related factors, which occur in a larger macrolevel social, economic, and political context (Beehr, 1986; Feldman, 1994; Talaga & Beehr, 1989). The variables within these categories can be seen as "push" or "pull" factors that influence the decision to retire by making either work or retirement to be perceived as more or less attractive options (Shultz, Morton, & Weckerle, 1998). Next, we briefly review some of these personal and work-related predictors.

Personal Predictors. Some of the most important predictors of retirement are at the individual level. DeVaney and Kim (2003) suggest that personal level predictors are related to the decision to retire owing to the opportunity structure they create for the individual. This opportunity structure consists of a person's ascribed and attained statuses (Ekerdt, Kosloski, & DeViney, 2000). Ascribed status refers to family background, age, gender, and race. Attained status refers to education, experience, health, wealth, and income. In general, variables reflecting attained status have consistent relationships with the decision to retire. For instance, those with more accumulated financial resources and higher perceptions of their adequacy (Gruber & Wise, 1999; Quinn, Burkhauser, & Myers, 1990) are more likely to retire, as are those with poor actual and perceived health (Mutchler, Burr, Massagli, & Pienta, 1999), and specifically more serious health conditions (Shultz & Wang, 2007). The results for other attained status predictors, such as education and occupation, tend to be somewhat more complex, perhaps because they are often related to each other as well as other personal and work-related variables such as finances and specific working conditions (i.e., physically demanding jobs).

Work-related Predictors. Work-related predictors refer to characteristics of the work role and a person's thoughts and attitudes about work. Empirical results for the relationship between one's occupation and the decision to retire are mixed, and this is likely because occupation is a broad proxy for specific work characteristics. Evidence for this can be found in a study of occupational characteristics by Hayward, Grady, Hardy, and Sommers (1989). They found that people in jobs with higher substantive complexity were less likely to retire while people in jobs with greater physical demands were more likely to retire. Along these same lines, Lin and Hsieh (2001) reported that those who perceived their job as being stressful and having a higher workload intended to retire early. Several interesting studies have reported that those who report simply "being tired of work" are likely to decide to retire (Beehr, Glazer, Nielson, & Farmer, 2000; Bidwell, Griffin, & Hesketh, 2006). On the other hand, a sense of attachment or commitment to various facets of work, such as the organization where one is employed and one's career, have been shown to be negatively related to the decision to retire (Adams, 1999; Adams & Beehr, 1998; Adams, Beehr, Prescher, & Lepisto, 2002). Next we discuss three prominent models used in the retirement decision-making literature.

Theoretical Models of Retirement

Rational Choice Theory. Rational choice theory has a long history in the area of economics. Drawing from the theory of rational decision making that focuses on how to allocate one's time (Becker, 1965) this approach frames the retirement decision in terms of a choice between work and leisure. It also adopts what is known as the life-cycle model of savings (Ando & Modigliani, 1963), which recognizes that the decision takes place over time, and that it involves considering when to accumulate financial resources (from paid work) as well as when to consume them on leisure (retirement; Gustman & Steinmeier, 1986). Research in this area has contributed to our understanding of retirement decisions by clarifying the impact of various means of accumulating financial resources (e.g., social security and pension plan features), various plans for the consumption of resources, and the interplay between the two affecting the retirement decision-making process (Hatcher, 2003; Quinn et al., 1990). One of the main implications of this approach to understanding retirement decision making is that finances matter greatly. Accumulated wealth and preferences for consumption help determine when people can retire. They also help determine how a person will eventually define retirement in terms of a complete, continuous exit from paid work or, owing to a shortfall in financial resources, a partial exit that may include ongoing or sporadic periods of paid work (Kim & DeVaney, 2005; Mutchler et al., 1997).

Role Theory. Role theory focuses on both the roles people occupy and the manner in which people transition between roles (Ashforth, 2001). A role is a position and its accompanying expectations and behaviors situated within a particular social system. Throughout our lives and at any particular point in time people engage in a number of different roles which are embedded in larger social contexts and networks. For instance, the role of parent within a family, worker within an organization, and retiree within society are just some of the roles people might occupy. For the individual, role memberships are important because they structure a person's life and can be a source of meaning and self-identity. In addition, roles played in one part of our life (caretaker) may influence other roles (worker). Role transitions occur as people move between two roles held at the same time (micro role transitions) and as they move between roles held at different times in their lives (macro role transitions). The decision to retire can be seen as a macro role transition in which a person negotiates the overlapping processes of role exit and role entry (Ashforth, 2001). An implication of role theory is that when people view their work role membership positively, have strong attachments to it, and derive a strong sense of meaning and self-identity from it, they are also more likely to delay retirement (Adams et al., 2002; Taylor et al., 2007; Wang, 2007). This is believed to be particularly true when the new role is still undefined, because it may lead to a perception of "rolelessness." On the other hand, it could be expected that when people view their work role negatively, they are more likely to decide to exit that role through retirement (Beehr et al., 2000; Bidwell et al., 2006; Lin & Hsieh, 2001; Taylor et al., 2007; Wang, 2007).

Continuity Theory. Continuity refers to the idea that people maintain consistent patterns of psychological characteristics as well as social and physical environments over time (Atchley, 1989, 1999). Atchley used the term internal continuity when referring to patterns of psychological characteristics such as a person's self concept, ideas, attitudes, interests, preferences, and behaviors. He used the term external continuity when referring to a person's social and physical environments. These include maintaining consistent patterns of behavior and activity as one interacts in the social and physical environment. The basic premise of this theory is that people adapt to change via internal and external continuity when confronted with challenges in their lives such as those brought about by aging. This theory would reject the notion that retirement leads to a sense of rolelessness (Richardson & Kilty, 1991), except in those cases when the individual cannot maintain continuity. When applied to retirement decision making, this theory would predict a normatively timed retirement that might be defined by continued paid or unpaid work, or the substitution of work with other activities that the person has been engaged in, such as hobbies and other leisure pursuits (Kim & Feldman, 2000).

Life Course Perspective. The life course perspective (Elder & Johnson, 2003; Kim & Moen, 2002; Szinovacz, 2003) is a broad approach to understanding people's behavior that subsumes these other theories. This model suggests that transitions over the course of the life span can best be understood by considering a person's individual history and the contexts in which that history and the transition itself are embedded (Quick & Moen, 1998). Together history and context create pathways into the transition, determine the meaning ascribed to the transition, and set up trajectories through and beyond the transition. In applying this model to the retirement decision, Szinovacz (2003) described contexts at the micro-, meso- and macrolevels. The microlevel context includes personological variables such as health, financial wealth, human capital and family, as well as psychological characteristics such as personality, attitudes, and behavior patterns. The mesolevel context refers to employers, labor unions, and the conditions in the community (e.g., transportation, housing, opportunities for leisure and volunteering). The macrolevel context refers to government policies, labor market conditions, and population structure and norms, many of which we discussed previously. All of these jointly influence the path into the decision to retire and help determine how that retirement will be defined and experienced (Kim & Moen, 2002). From this perspective, because of the variability in people's history and contexts, there will be variability in when they retire and what they will do during retirement. Therefore, in the next section we describe some of the more prominent options for transitioning between work and complete retirement.

Transition Options From Work to Retirement

Retirement was once commonly considered a permanent and complete exit from the workforce after a long-term career to a shorter period of nonwork or "leisure" financed by personal savings and/or public and private pensions. However, as noted earlier, in both the popular press

(Block, 2007) and the research literature (Bennett & Beehr, 2007), the concept of retirement has been undergoing a significant amount of "redefinition." As a result, the decision to retire now involves *when* to retire as well as *what* one will do in retirement. Those approaching retirement have a diverse set of choices about how they can define what they will do in retirement. These range from a complete and continuous withdrawal from work to the initiation and pursuit of another full time career, with innumerable options in between. Although variously defined by authors across the literature, the most general term used to describe continued work in retirement is *bridge employment*. As we defined at the beginning of this chapter, bridge employment is work in positions or careers taken by older workers after exiting positions or career paths of considerable duration and before complete and continuous withdrawal from paid and unpaid work (Shultz, 2003). Note that this definition is similar to others in the literature (e.g., Feldman, 1994) in that it refers to a period of work between one's long-term career and complete workforce exit. However, it also differs in that it does not imply a certain amount of work (full-time vs. part-time), status, salary, or reason for engaging in the work. It also does not imply an ongoing status. In this way, our definition is intentionally broader and better able to capture the various forms of bridge employment that older workers and retirees may engage in. Further, it recognizes people may have multiple exits and entries using any of these forms of bridge employment.

The various forms of bridge employment can be described along three dimensions: (1) the employer, (2) the workload, and (3) the function it serves for the individual. The first of these is the degree to which a person is working for his/her preretirement employer. This dimension can range from working solely for one's previous employer through working for one's previous employer and other employers (e.g., consulting), to working solely for some other employer or oneself. In addition, the individual's preretirement role, occupation, and industry could also be incorporated under the employer dimension. The second dimension addresses the issue of both quantitative and qualitative workload. It can range from working just a few hours each week and/or having fairly low levels of responsibility to full-time work and/or having high levels of responsibility. The function dimension addresses the reasons why a person might be engaging in bridge employment. As such, it references the needs people are trying to meet (Loi & Shultz, 2007). This dimension can range from those jobs taken in order to meet basic financial needs through those taken to meet needs for maintaining stable self-identity, time structure, and social contacts, to those taken as opportunities for significant new growth and the development of new knowledge, skills, and abilities (KSAs). It should be noted that we do not expect each of the various bridge employment options to differ from the others on all three dimensions, rather each person can choose a unique mix of conditions in order to meet his/her needs and desires.

Phased Retirement. Phased retirement is characterized by ongoing employment with one's preretirement employer but with a reduced number of hours/workload. As such, it is a formal or informal human resources management practice that can vary from employer to employer. Phased retirement is typically accomplished by reducing the number of hours worked each day, the number of days worked each week, or the number of weeks worked each year. Using data from the 2002 Health and Retirement Study (HRS; adults aged 61 to 71), Chen and Scott (2005) estimated that of those who provided data, 4% were engaged in phased retirement. In a study by the Brown (2005), when asked about their interest in phased retirement, 38% of workers between the ages of 50-65 indicated they would be very or somewhat interested in such an arrangement. In two national surveys of work organizations it has been found that approximately 26% - 28% of employers offered phased retirement (Bond, Galinsky, Kim, & Brownfield, 2005). Thus, phased retirement is a growing, and increasingly desirable, possibility for a significant minority of older workers making the transition from work to retirement at the end of their career.

Full- and Part-time Work. Work after retirement can range from part-time to full-time working hours. Although not consistently defined or distinguished from phased retirement, the term *partial retirement* is often used to describe work involving reduced hours and/or workload with an employer other than one's preretirement employer. Still others choose to work full-time. Brown (2005) reported that 25% of those aged 50 and older who worked or planned to work after age 65 ($n = 722$), planned to work part-time for a different employer and another 5% planned to work full-time for a different employer. Using data from the Health and Retirement Study, Chen and Scott (2005) estimated that of those ($n = 3,269$) who provided data in 2002, 23% were engaged in partial retirement and 28% were working full-time.

There are a variety of forms that bridge employment might take. The first of these are positions in the secondary labor market. These generally offer lower wages and require few high level KSAs. Examples of these types of positions are lower level jobs found in the retail and service industries. They are likely to fall on the low end of function dimension. This outcome would be most consistent with the tenets of role theory. A second form of bridge employment is a *continuing career* in one's preretirement career field. In these positions, while the employer is different from preretirement, the context and/or nature of the work are largely unchanged. These positions involve using established KSAs on familiar tasks and are likely help meet basic needs as well as maintain a stable self identity, thus supporting the tenets of continuity theory.

A third form is a *tangential career*, which involves work in a position loosely related to one's preretirement career or interests and hobbies. Here the context and/or nature of the work are different, but many of KSAs needed to perform the work are similar. Examples of this type of retirement would be when a person whose preretirement career was in the area of corporate sales takes a position as a fund-raiser for a local not-for-profit organization or an avid gardener starts a small greenhouse business. These allow one to apply existing expertise to new types of tasks. This outcome would support the tenets of the life course perspective. Finally, a worker may engage in an altogether new career—a so called *encore career* (Freedman, 2007). An example of this form of bridge employment is the case of a person who had a preretirement career as a counseling psychologist but retrains to become a high school Spanish teacher. These second careers are characterized by contexts and/or work tasks that may be substantially different from preretirement and bring about the need to develop new KSAs. This outcome would also be consistent with the life course perspective. Thus, bridge employment can take a wide variety of forms, as well as serve a wide variety of functions for older individuals. Therefore, we next we discuss the antecedents and outcomes of bridge employment.

ANTECEDENTS AND OUTCOMES OF BRIDGE EMPLOYMENT

Although the bridge employment definition we adopted earlier is broader and recognizes multiple forms of workforce exits and entries, in empirical studies bridge employment is often categorized into two primary types: career bridge employment (i.e., individuals accept bridge employment in the same industry/field as their so-called career jobs) and bridge employment in a different field (Davis, 2003; Gobeski & Beehr, 2008; Kim & Feldman, 2000; Wang, Zhan, Liu, & Shultz, 2008). This type of categorization emphasizes bridge employment as a temporary career stage that links career jobs and leisure retirement, and thus contains a longitudinal life adjustment component that is inherently consistent with several of the theoretical perspectives discussed earlier, such as role theory, continuity theory, and the life course perspective. As such, when reviewing the antecedents and outcomes of bridge employment, we rely on these theoretical perspectives in explaining the empirical findings.

Antecedents of Bridge Employment

After reviewing the existing literature, we summarize the antecedents of bridge employment into four major categories (see Figure 6.1). They are individual attributes, job-related psychological variables, family-related variables, and retirement-specific variables.

Individual Attributes. Age has been repeatedly demonstrated to be negatively associated with individuals' decisions to pursue bridge employment: the older the retiree is, the less likely that the retiree would engage in bridge employment (e.g., Adams & Rau, 2004; Kim & Feldman, 2000; Wang et al., 2008). Consistent with the life course perspective's emphasis on the developmental trajectory, as older workers are facing the decline of both physical energy and cognitive abilities, their engagements in further employment after retiring from career jobs are likely to be limited (Adams & Rau, 2004; Jex et al., 2007). Furthermore, they may be less likely to achieve continuity through work because of their age-related declines in health.

Education has also been demonstrated to be related to bridge employment decisions. For example, Kim and DeVaney (2005) found that retirees with college or above degrees were more likely to engage in full- or part-time work than full-time retirement. Wang et al. (2008) found that retirees who had higher education levels were more likely to take career bridge employment and bridge employment in another field than to fully retire. Consistent with continuity theory, educated individuals have more capacity in maintaining their life patterns because of their professional knowledge and/or skills. Thus, they may have more opportunities to continue to work in their career field by engaging in consulting roles. This is supported by Gobeski and Beehr (2008) who found that having job-relevant skills is related to taking career bridge jobs. General education may, however, also lead to more opportunities to be hired in different career fields after retiring from one's career jobs (e.g., Greller & Stroh, 2004). Specifically, retirees who have higher levels of education are likely to have more choices in choosing a bridge job. It might also be easier for them to switch and adjust to a new career field.

A retiree's health is another major factor to consider when making bridge retirement decisions (Jex et al., 2007). Health problems might lead to constraints on retirees' ability to perform effectively or achieve continuity of life structure through further participation in the workforce. Previous studies have examined the predictive effect of health and consistently found that healthy retirees were more likely to accept bridge employment in the same career field or in a different field (e.g., Kim & Feldman, 2000; Wang et al., 2008).

Financial status affects bridge employment decisions, as well. According to Shultz (2003), financial constraint works as a stimulus for the retirees to take bridge employment. Nevertheless, the relationship is rather complicated. Previous studies have found that some financial components are more related to bridge employment than others. For example, Kim and DeVaney (2005) found that investment assets and debt but not regular income, liquid assets, or real assets were significantly related to the odds for people to engage in bridge employment over full retirement. In addition, viewing financial constraint as a push factor for bridge employment may only tell part of the story. For example, Wang et al. (2008) found that retirees' total wealth was not able to predict the odds for retirees to take career bridge employment against full retirement. This suggests that financial motivation may not be a primary driving force for people to engage in career bridge employment against full retirement. In other words, retirees may engage in career bridge employment because they are satisfied with and attached to their career job (e.g., Shultz, 2003), and committed to their organization (e.g., Adams & Beehr, 1998), but not because they are in relatively bad financial shape.

Job-related psychological variables. According to role theory, the nature of the preretirement job may affect retirees' decisions with regard to bridge employment. Specifically, empirical studies have shown that retirees' experience and feelings regarding their preretirement job roles, such as work stress, job satisfaction, commitment, and age-related fairness perception, all contribute to their bridge employment decisions. First, if an individual considers the career job role to be highly stressful, he/she is more likely to view career job exit as an escape from the bad situation. For example, Wang et al. (2008) and Gobeski and Beehr (2008) found that individuals who retired from highly stressful jobs were more likely to fully retire. In addition, if they did engage in a bridge job, it was more likely for them to accept bridge employment in a different field. Similar to the impact of work stress, dissatisfaction with one's career job sometimes appears to function as a push factor in the retirement decision (Shultz et al., 1998). If individuals are not satisfied with their career job, they are more likely to be motivated to escape the dissatisfying status and move toward a more satisfying situation (i.e., either take bridge employment in a different field or fully retire). This notion has been supported by empirical findings from Wang et al. (2008), as well. Other studies have found, however, that job satisfaction is not related to full retirement (e.g., Beehr, et al. 2000; Gobeski & Beehr, 2008; McCune & Schmitt, 1981), although it is related to taking a bridge job in a noncareer field (Gobeski & Beehr, 2008).

Individual differences in commitment to one's career or organization also lead to different bridge employment decisions. For example, organizational commitment (Heindel, Adams, & Lepisto, 1999) and career commitment (Gobeski & Beehr, 2008; Heindel, Adams, & Lepisto, 1999) both predict older workers' plans for bridge employment in their current career field. In addition, Davis (2003) found that older workers' commitment to pursue a new career accounted for the overall participation in bridge employment. These findings are consistent with both role theory and continuity theory, as making bridge employment decisions in accordance to their identity pursuit would benefit retirees in maintaining their life patterns and social values.

Finally, older workers' age-related fairness perception about the job could also influence their bridge employment decisions. For example, Weckerle and Shultz (1999) found that when older workers perceived their employer as preferring younger workers for promotion, they were less likely to consider bridge employment as an option. Rau and Adams (2005) found that a targeted equal employment opportunity statement positively influenced older workers' attraction to a bridge employment position. These findings are consistent with the life course perspective, as retirees are likely to perceive that they are approaching the normative end of their career development, and thus are more sensitive to factors that may put them at a disadvantage in their career pursuit.

Family-related variables. According to the life course perspective, family is an important life sphere that may influence the sphere of employment status (Szinovacz, 2003). Specifically, family-related variables, such as spouse's working status and dependent status, have been shown to be related to bridge employment decisions. For example, Kim and Feldman (2000) found that if the spouse was still in the workforce, retirees were more likely to engage in some type of bridge employment. They also found that having dependents to support was positively related to retirees' decision to take bridge employment against full retirement. These findings suggest that family variables could potentially impact retirees' motivation to engage in bridge employment by imposing situational constraints (i.e., undermining the positive qualities associated with full retirement, such as having more leisure time and not having to work for pay).

Nevertheless, there are studies (e.g., Wang et al., 2008) that have shown other family-related variables, such as marital status and marital quality, were not related to bridge employment. Because there have been relatively fewer studies investigating this type of antecedent, it is still too early to draw conclusions on these variables.

Retirement-specific variables. The final antecedent category discussed in the current chapter is with regard to retirement itself. According to the life course perspective, specific characteristics of the retirement transition may impact retirees' workforce participation in the postretirement trajectory (Szinovacz, 2003). These retirement-specific variables include retirement planning, retirement voluntariness, and retirement negativity. First, the extent to which retirees have planned, formally or informally, for their retirement has been shown to predict their bridge employment decisions (Kim & DeVaney, 2005; Wang et al., 2008). Consistent with continuity theory, retirement planning may smooth the retirement transition process because it allows people to form realistic expectations about the social and financial aspects of retirement, and clarify goals after leaving the career job (Spiegel & Shultz, 2003; Wang, 2007).

Second, the extent to which retirees feel that their decision to retire is voluntary has been shown to relate to their willingness to continue the same job. Specifically, Weckerle and Shultz (1999) found that older workers who felt the decision to retire was voluntary were less likely to take either career bridge employment or a bridge employment in a different field. This is consistent with the notion that involuntary retirement can be viewed as a type of interruption of one's career continuity (Feldman, 1994). Hence, taking bridge employment could be conceptualized as manifesting and channeling one's motivation to recover the continuity in one's life style.

Finally, the negativity (i.e., negative feelings) retirees experience about retirement has been shown to be positively related to bridge employment seeking behaviors (Adams & Rau, 2004). Similar to involuntary retirement, retirement negativity experienced during the retirement transition may also signify interruption of one's role continuity (Adams & Rau, 2004). Therefore, retirees who experience this negativity are more likely to engage in bridge employment to smooth this adjustment process.

Outcomes of Bridge Employment

Compared to the number of studies that have focused on examining the antecedents of bridge employment, there have been significantly fewer studies examining outcomes of bridge employment. Further, although most of the previous development on bridge employment has suggested that bridge employment is beneficial in terms of addressing the projected growing labor shortages due to the retirement of the baby boomers and helping organizations in maintaining their talent pools (Alley & Crimmins, 2007; Shultz, 2003), there has been little empirical data to test these macrolevel premises. Therefore, we focus on reviewing microlevel individual outcomes of bridge employment (see Figure 6.1). Specifically, these outcomes include retirees' adjustment quality to their retirement life and retirees' health postretirement.

Retirement adjustment outcomes. According to continuity theory, engagement in bridge employment is an efficient way to maintain continuity of personal goals and life styles (Atchley, 1999; Kim & Feldman, 2000; Quick & Moen, 1998). This may ease the potentially disruptive transition out of the labor force and provide retirees extra time to accommodate the life-style changes caused by retirement. Therefore, if retirees continue to hold bridge employment jobs during their retirement transitions, they may not experience significant changes in psychological well-being and may actually experience higher levels of retirement satisfaction and life satisfaction.

For example, Wang (2007) found that retirees who held bridge employment jobs were more likely to experience minimum changes of psychological well-being during the retirement transition than retirees who directly took full retirement. In addition, Kim and Feldman (2000) found positive associations between taking bridge employment jobs and higher levels of retirement satisfaction and life satisfaction among retirees. Further, Kim and Feldman (2000) found that career bridge employment had stronger positive associations with retirement satisfaction and life satisfaction than bridge employment in a different field. This is probably because retirees who engage in career bridge employment are more likely to experience greater continuity of work structure, valued activities, career identification, and social contact than their counterparts who engage in bridge employment in a different field.

Health outcomes. Health is one of the most important attributes for older adults. Among the elderly, major diseases and decline in daily functions are two salient indicators of deteriorating physical health (Siegler, Bosworth, & Elias, 2003). First, older adults are more susceptible to heart disease and cancer, and are more likely to have multiple disorders as they age. Second, because of the general physical and cognitive decline in capabilities as we age, older people have a higher risk of experiencing functional limitations. They may sometimes find it difficult to carry on with daily life independently (e.g., have difficulty in walking across a room, dressing, or bathing). Psychologically, for older adults, deteriorating mental health usually includes symptoms of depression or anxiety (Cavanaugh & Blanchard-Fields, 2002).

An empirical study conducted by Zhan, Wang, Lie, and Shultz (in press), found that retirees who engage in bridge employment after their career job (either career bridge employment or bridge employment in a different field) experienced fewer major diseases than those who retire completely, even after controlling for preretirement health. This is probably because active life styles associated with bridge employment decrease risks of major diseases by increasing vital activity and attenuating sympathetic hyperactivity (Keller & Lemberg, 2002). The same study also found that retirees who took either form of bridge employment, compared to retirees who chose full retirement, reported fewer functional limitations.

It suggests that maintaining a working status might be beneficial in terms of slowing down the declines in daily functions. This is because working requires certain levels of cognitive and physical involvement and, in turn, is likely to help retirees to maintain their daily function levels.

Finally, Zhan et al. (in press) found that only the career bridge employment, but not the bridge employment in a different field, was positively related to retirees' mental health. On the one hand, it is consistent with role theory in that career bridge employment provides the most similar role identity to the retiree's previous role at work. Therefore, retirees who engage in career bridge employment might be least influenced by role transition or role loss, in turn, leading to better mental health than those who directly take full retirement. On the other hand, the lack of beneficial effect of bridge employment in a different field on retirees' mental health may be due to the fact that retirees in this situation need to face the stress coming from role change and adapting to the new work environment. Specifically, they may have to adjust to a new role identity, and the continuity of their life style might be disrupted. In terms of its impact on mental well-being, this may not differ that much from what retirees who choose to fully retire have to experience: work role exit, disruption of life style, and a loss of social support from their work environment. Therefore, it is conceivable that retirees who engaged in bridge employment in a different field did not differ from their fully retired counterparts in terms of mental health.

Taking a Dynamic Perspective to Understand Bridge Employment

Earlier in this chapter we adopted a broad definition for bridge employment, which encompasses the various forms of bridge employment and recognizes that people may have multiple exits and entries using any of these forms. However, in the existing literature—both theoretical development and empirical examination—bridge employment choice is often conceptualized as a one-time decision-making event (e.g., Davis, 2003; Feldman, 1994; Kim & DeVaney, 2005). There are certain advantages in doing so. For example, this conceptualization puts the study of bridge employment into the background of career related decision-making literature, which helps guide the search for both predictors and outcomes of bridge employment (Wang et al., 2008). Further, it lowers the requirement for the empirical operationalization, only involving one snap-shot measurement of retirees' bridge employment status.

Nevertheless, it is our position that this one-time decision-making conceptualization may be better replaced by a dynamic perspective in understanding bridge employment. Specifically, this dynamic perspective emphasizes that bridge employment is a *longitudinal workforce participation process* between one's retirement decision and entering full retirement. Therefore, instead of focusing on retirees' bridge employment status at one time point, we should pay more attention to retirees' longitudinal change patterns in bridge employment status (i.e., the whole process of entering bridge employment, switching from one bridge employment status to another, and eventually exiting bridge employment into full retirement; see the central box in Figure 6.1). There are several advantages for endorsing this dynamic perspective.

First of all, this dynamic conceptualization of bridge employment gets closer in reflecting the reality of bridge employment. Using nationally representative data from the Health and Retirement Study (HRS), we found that among retirees who retired between 1992 and 1996, about 50% took at least one bridge employment job in the 8 years following their retirement. Among these retirees who took bridge employment jobs, only about 33% always had bridge employment jobs over the 8 years, whereas the majority of them (about 66%) transferred in and out bridge employment jobs (i.e., from "employed" to "not employed" or from "not employed" to "employed") during the eight year time period. This finding suggests that retirees often have to make bridge employment decisions in different time periods during their postretirement lives. Therefore, adopting the dynamic perspective helps comprehensively capture the reality in retirees' bridge employment decision making.

Second, endorsing this dynamic perspective in conceptualizing bridge employment phenomena provides opportunities for capturing the retirement adjustment component embedded in the bridge employment process. Unlike retirement decision making, which is often normative and dominated by health and financial reasons (Barnes-Farrell, 2003), bridge employment decisions are often implicitly driven by the motivation to adjust to retirement life (Wang, 2007; Wang et al., 2008). Therefore, studying the dynamic patterns of retirees' longitudinal changes in bridge employment provides another way for us to understand the retirement adjustment process. For example, using the HRS data to estimate the bridge employment transition probabilities in latent transition models, it seems that over time, retirees who did not engage in bridge employment at the beginning of their retirement were more and more likely to stay not employed. Specifically, the probabilities for staying in the "not employed" status were increasing (i.e., 65.95%, 78.65%, and 86.76%) over the three successive 2-year time periods. On the other hand, the probabilities for retirees who were employed at a previous time point to stay employed were quite stable (i.e., 62.95%, 63.02%, and 61.68%) over the same successive time periods. These findings suggest that both initial bridge employment status and the subsequent status change may have an impact on retirees' adjustment patterns over the postretirement years. It should also be noted that this process is not passive, but active. Hence, studying it with the dynamic perspective is likely to provide important practical implications for promoting a smoother retirement transition and better retirement life quality.

Third, endorsing this dynamic perspective in conceptualizing bridge employment phenomena also provides methodological opportunities for better evaluating more distal antecedents and outcomes of bridge employment. As noted earlier, the central premise of the life course perspective is that the variability in people's developmental history and context will influence people's retirement transition and bridge employment status. However, tests of this premise often yield inconsistent findings in empirical studies. As Barnes-Farrell (2003) pointed out, although a number of individual and contextual factors, such as individual dispositions (e.g., locus of control and self-image orientation), psycho-social variables (e.g., social support and organizational climate), and family-related variables (e.g., marital status and marital quality), may have the potential to influence retirees' preferences and intentions for bridge employment, these variables do not always play out in terms of actual decision making at one specific time point. Instead, their predictive effects may be overshadowed by other more proximal predictors at that time point (e.g., financial pressure or health considerations; Barnes-Farrell, 2003; Wang et al., 2008). Therefore, although these individual and contextual variables may be theoretically relevant to bridge employment decision at each specific time point, their effects may be better tested in a model that predicts the overall dynamic characteristics of bridge employment (e.g., frequency or average level of involvement in engaging in bridge employment during a long period of retirement life). In other words, these distal variables can be viewed as background variables that shape the decision-making contingencies, thus predicting the longitudinal bridge employment change patterns better than the one snap-shot measure of bridge employment status.

Similar logic applies to examining outcomes of bridge employment, as well. We should recognize that it is not the one-time bridge employment decision that shapes retirees' adjustment patterns, retirement life quality, or health, but the overall length and quality of bridge employment. Therefore, the current operationalization of bridge employment in the literature (i.e., one snap-shot status measure) tends to provide unreliable estimates for beneficial effects of bridge employment on retirement adjustment outcomes and health outcomes (e.g., Zhan et al., in press). Further, applying the dynamic conceptualization of bridge employment may also help us to clarify the underlying mechanism for bridge employment to have beneficial effects on these outcomes. It is conceivable that at the beginning of the retirement transition, bridge employment is beneficial in maintaining the continuity of life patterns and styles, thus leading to salient positive psychological outcomes. With the retirement adjustment approaching a desirable state, the beneficial effect of bridge employment may become more physical and activity-based, thus leading to more salient physical and functional benefits on retirees' health.

Implications for Future Research and Practice

The dynamic model of the bridge employment process that we present here has several important implications for research and practice. We hope that our discussion will spur future researchers to more broadly define bridge employment than has been done in the past.

Given that research on the reasons for bridge employment is still relatively new, there is much left to be done. Three issues in particular stand out: the need to examine (1) bridge employment experiences over time, (2) predictors of types of bridge employment, and (3) effects of bridge employment on the person. The need to examine bridge employment over time is inherent in the dynamic model of retirement and bridge employment. Future research issues include the potentially changing importance of individual, organizational, and contextual factors in bridge employment activities. That is, the factors predicting types of bridge employment at earlier stages of one's postcareer life may be less important at later stages. Regarding types of bridge employment, the examination of this important issue is only in its infancy. There have been a few studies of career versus noncareer bridge employment, but there is still much to be learned about the differences in their predictors and nature. In addition, there are probably other typologies of bridge employment that make sense and that we still do not fully understand, including intrinsically and extrinsically motivated employment and full versus part-time bridge employment. Finally, we also need more information about the outcomes of bridge employment, especially the effects it has upon the person employed. This includes the mental, physical, financial, and social consequences of being employed in various capacities after leaving one's career job.

Knowledge about older employees' preferences, tendencies, and decisions regarding retirement and bridge employment is valuable in several applied ways. Governments need to understand and predict such behaviors if they are to provide for their citizens as a whole, including both older citizens and younger ones. There are implications for government retirement plans (e.g., the social security system in the United States). For example, knowing what choices older employees will make helps the law-makers decide issues regarding financial neediness of older citizens, which has implications for both benefits and taxes. Such knowledge is also important for employers, who can make bridge employment opportunities more or less available, and for social service professions that deal with older workers and retirees.

In conclusion, we have discussed a wide variety of issues in this chapter with regard to the late career transition from career employment to full-time leisure retirement. Because our focus was on bridge employment in particular, we presented a dynamic model of the bridge employment process early in the chapter. We next provided a brief overview of late career issues and summarized the key contextual variables in this area. Next, we summarized the retirement decision-making literature, including the empirical predictors of retirement, the major theoretical models of retirement, and the transition options with regard to the transitions from work to retirement. This led into our discussion of bridge employment, specifically with regard to what we know about its antecedents and outcomes. We then provided a more detailed discussion of the dynamic nature of bridge employment and presented new analyses in order to support our contentions regarding the ubiquitous and dynamic nature of bridge employment, with regard to both its antecedents and outcomes. Finally, we concluded the chapter with a discussion of the implications for research and practice that our proposed dynamic model of bridge employment has for both the literature on late careers and retirement.

REFERENCES

Adams, G. A. (1999). Career-related variables and planned retirement age: An extension of Beehr's model. *Journal of Vocational Behavior, 55*, 221-235.

Adams, G. A., & Beehr, T. A. (1998). Turnover and retirement: A comparison of their similarities and differences. *Personnel Psychology, 51*, 643-665.

Adams, G. A., & Beehr, T. A. (2003). *Turnover and retirement: Reasons, processes, and results.* New York: Springer.

Adams, G. A., Beehr, T. A., Prescher, J., & Lepisto, L. (2002). Applying work-role attachment theory to retirement decision-making. *International Journal of Aging and Human Development, 54*, 125-137.

Adams, G., & Rau, B. (2004). Job seeking among retirees seeking bridge employment. *Personnel Psychology, 57*, 719-744.

Alley, D., & Crimmins, E. M. (2007). The demography of aging and work. In K. S. Shultz & G. A. Adams (Eds.), *Aging and work in the 21st century* (pp. 7-23). New York: Psychology Press/Routledge.

Ando, A., & Modigliani, F. (1963). The life-cycle hypothesis of savings: Aggregate implications and tests. *American Economic Review, 53*(1), 55-84.

Ashforth, B. E. (2001). *Role transitions in organizational life: An identity-based perspective*. Mahwah, NJ: Erlbaum.

Atchley, R. C. (1989). A continuity theory of normal aging. *The Gerontologist, 29,* 1989.

Atchley, R. C. (1999). Continuity theory, self and social structures. In C. Ryff & V. Marshall (Eds.), *Families and retirement* (pp. 145-158) Newbury Park, CA: SAGE.

Barnes-Farrell, J. L. (2003). Beyond health and wealth: Attitudinal and other influences on retirement decision-making. In G. A. Adams & T. A. Beehr (Eds.), *Retirement: Reasons, processes, and results* (pp. 159-187). New York: Springer.

Barnes-Farrell, J. L., & Matthews, R. A. (2007). Age and work attitudes. In K. S. Shultz & G. A. Adams (Eds.), *Aging and work in the 21st century* (pp. 139-162). New York: Psychology Press/Routledge.

Becker, G. (1965). A theory of the allocation of time. *Economic Journal, 75,* 493-517.

Beehr, T. A. (1986). The process of retirement: A review and recommendations for future investigation. *Personnel Psychology, 39,* 31-56.

Beehr, T. A., & Adams, G. A. (2003). Concluding observations and future endeavors. In G. A. Adams & T. A. Beehr (Eds.), *Retirement: Reasons, processes, and results* (pp. 293-298). New York: Springer.

Beehr, T. A., & Bennett, M. M. (2007). Examining retirement from a multi-level perspective. In K. S. Shultz & G. A. Adams (Eds.), *Aging and work in the 21st century* (pp. 277-302). New York: Psychology Press/Routledge.

Beehr, T. A., & Bennett, M. M. (2008). Unemployment and retirement. In J. Barling & C. L. Cooper (Eds.), *The Sage handbook of organizational behavior, Vol. 1* (pp. 217-232). Los Angeles: SAGE.

Beehr, T. A., & Bowling, N. A. (2002). Career issues facing older workers. In D. C. Feldman (Ed.), *Work careers: A developmental perspective* (pp. 214-241). San Francisco: Jossey-Bass.

Beehr, T. A., Glazer, S., Nielson, N. L., & Farmer, S. J. (2000). Work and nonwork predictors of employees' retirement ages. *Journal of Vocational Behavior, 57,* 206-225.

Bidwell, J., Griffin, B., & Hesketh, B. (2006). Timing of retirement: Including delay discounting perspective in retirement model. *Journal of Vocational Behavior, 68,* 368-387.

Block, S. (2007, August 31). Off to work they go, even after retirement age; Many people don't want to quit, even if they can afford it. *USA Today,* p. B. 1.

Bond, J. T., Galinsky, E., Kim, S. S., & Brownfield, E. (2005). *National study of employers.* New York: Families and Work Institute. Retrieved May 8, 2008 from http://familiesandwork.org/eproducts/2005nse

Brown, K. S. (2005). Attitudes of individuals 50 and older toward phased retirement. *AARP Knowledge Management,* 1-30.

Cavanaugh, J. C., & Blanchard-Fields, F. (2002). *Adult development and aging.* Belmont, CA: Wadsworth Group.

Chen, Y. P., & Scott, J. (2005). *Phased retirement: Who opts for it and towards what end?* Washington, DC: AARP. Retrieved May 6, 2008, from http: //assets.aarp.org/ rgcenter/econ/2006_01_retire.pdf

Cleveland, J. N., & Landy, F. J. (1983). The effects of person and job stereotypes on two personnel decisions. *Journal of Applied Psychology, 68,* 609-619.

Cleveland, J. N., & Landy, F. J. (1986). Age perceptions of jobs: Convergence of two questionnaires. *Psychological Reports, 60,* 1075-1081.

Cleveland, J. N., & Lim, A. S. (2007). Employee age and performance in organizations. In K. S. Shultz & G. A. Adams (Eds.), *Aging and work in the 21st century* (pp. 109-138). New York: Psychology Press/Routledge.

Costa, G., & Sartori, S. (2007). Ageing, working hours and work ability. *Ergonomics, 50,* 1914-1930.

Couch, K. A. (1998). Late life job displacement. *The Gerontologist, 38,* 7-17.

Davis, M. A. (2003). Factors related to bridge employment participation among private sector early retirees. *Journal of Vocational Behavior, 63,* 55-71.

DeVaney, S. A., & Kim, H. (2003). Older self-employed workers and planning for the future. *The Journal of Consumer Affairs, 37,* 123-142.

Elder, G. H., Jr., & Johnson, M. K. (2003). The life course and aging: Challenges, lessons and new directions. In R. Settersten (Ed.), *Invitation to the life course: Toward a new understanding of later life* (pp. 49-81). Amityville, NY: Baywood.

Ekerdt, D. J., Kosloski, K., & DeViney, S. (2000). The normative anticipation of retirement by older workers. *Research on Aging, 22,* 3-22.

Feldman, D. C. (1994). The decision to retire early: A review and conceptualization. *Academy of Management Review, 19,* 285-311.

Feldman, D. C., & Vogel, R. M. (2009). The aging process and person-environment fit. In S. G. Baugh & S. E. Sullivan (Eds.), *Research in careers: Vol. 1. Maintaining focus, energy, and options over the career* (pp. 1-26). Charlotte, NC: Information Age.

Finkelstein, L. M., & Farrell, S. K. (2007). An expanded view of age bias in the workplace. In K. S. Shultz & G. A. Adams (Eds.), *Aging and work in the 21st century* (pp. 73-108). New York: Psychology Press/Routledge.

Freedman, M. (2007). *Encore: Finding work that matters in the second half of life.* New York: Public Affairs.

Gentry, W. A., Griggs, T. L., Deal, J. J., & Mondore, S. P. (2009). Generational differences in attitudes, beliefs, and preferences about development and learning at work. In S. G. Baugh & S. E. Sullivan (Eds.), *Research in careers: Vol. 1. Maintaining focus, energy, and options over the career* (pp. 51-74). Charlotte, NC: Information Age.

Gobeski, K. T., & Beehr, T. A. (2008). How retirees work: Predictors of different types of bridge employment. *Journal of Organizational Behavior, 30,* 401-425.

Greller, M. M., & Simpson, P. (1999). In search of late career: A review of contemporary social science research applicable to the understanding of late career. *Human Resources Management Review, 9,* 309-347.

Greller, M. M., & Stroh, L. K. (2004). Making the most of "later-career" for employers and workers themselves: Becoming elders not relics. *Organizational Dynamics, 33,* 202-214.

Gringart, E., Helmes, E., & Speelman, C. (2008). Harnessing cognitive dissonance to promote positive attitudes toward older workers in Australia. *Journal of Applied Social Psychology, 38,* 751-778.

Gruber, J., & Wise, D. A. (1999). Social security and retirement around the world. *Research in Labor Economics, 18,* 1-40.

Gustman, A. L., & Steinmeier, T. L. (1986). A structural retirement model. *Econometrica, 54,* 555-584.

Hall, D. T. (2004). The protean career: A quarter century journey. *Journal of Vocational Behavior, 47,* 232-247.

Hatcher, C. B. (2003). The economics of the retirement decision. In G. A. Adams & T. A. Beehr (Eds.), *Retirement: Reasons, processes, and results* (pp. 136-158). New York: Springer.

Hayward, M. D., Grady, W. R., Hardy, M. A., & Sommers, D. (1989). Occupational influences on retirement, disability, and death. *Demography, 26,* 393-409.

Heindel, R. A., Adams, G. A., & Lepisto, L. (1999, April). *Predicting bridge employment: A test of Feldman's (1994) hypotheses.* Paper presented at the 14th annual conference of the Society for Industrial and Organizational Psychology, Atlanta, Georgia.

Jex, S. M., Wang, M., & Zarubin, A. (2007). Aging and occupational health. In K. S. Shultz & G. A. Adams (Eds.), *Aging and work in the 21st century* (pp. 199-223). New York: Psychology Press/Routledge.

Keller, K. B., & Lemberg, L. (2002). Retirement is no excuse for physical inactivity or isolation. *American Journal of Critical Care, 11,* 270-272.

Kim, H., & DeVaney, S. (2005). The selection of partial or full retirement by older workers. *Journal of Family and Economic Issues, 26,* 371-394.

Kim, J. E., & Moen, P. (2002). Retirement transitions, gender, and psychological well-being: A life-course model. *Journals of Gerontology: Series B: Psychology Science and Social Sciences, 57B,* 212-222.

Kim, S., & Feldman, D. C. (1998). Healthy, wealthy, or wise: Predicting actual acceptance of early retirement incentives at three points in time. *Personnel Psychology, 51,* 623-642.

Kim, S., & Feldman, D. C. (2000). Working in retirement: The antecedents of bridge employment and its consequences for quality of life in retirement. *Academy of Management Journal, 43,* 1195-1210.

Klug, A., & Krings, F. (2008). Attitudes toward older workers and human resource practices. *Swiss Journal of Psychology, 67,* 61-64.

Lin, T., & Hsieh, A. (2001). Impact of job stress on early retirement intention. *International Journal of Stress Management, 8,* 243-247.

Loi, J. L. P., & Shultz, K. S. (2007). Why older adults seek employment: Differing motivations among subgroups. *Journal of Applied Gerontology, 26,* 274-289.

Maurer, T. J. (2007). Employee development and training issues related to the aging workforce. In K. S. Shultz & G. A. Adams (Eds.), *Aging and work in the 21st century* (pp. 163-178). New York: Psychology Press/Routledge.

McCune, J. T., & Schmitt, N. (1981). The relationship between job attitudes and the decision to retire. *Academy of Management Journal, 24,* 795-802.

Mermin, G. B. T., Johnson, R. W., & Murphy, D. P. (2007). Why do boomers plan to work longer? *Journals of Gerontology: Series B: Psychological Sciences and Social Sciences, 62B,* S286-294.

Moen, P., Kim, J. E., & Hofmeister, H. (2001). Couples' work/retirement transition, gender, and marital quality. *Social Psychology Quarterly, 64,* 55-71.

Mutchler, J. E., Burr, J. A., Pienta, A., & Massagli, M. P. (1997). Pathways to labor force exit: Work transitions and work instability. *Journals of Gerontology: Series B. Psychological Science and Social Science,* 52B, S4-S12.

Ng, T. W. H., & Feldman, D. C. (2008). The relationship of age to ten dimensions of job performance. *Journal of Applied Psychology, 93,* 392-523.

Power, S. J. (2009). Midcareer renewal: A research agenda for the twenty-first century. In S. G. Baugh & S. E. Sullivan (Eds.), *Research in careers: Vol. 1. Maintaining focus, energy, and options over the career* (pp. 107-133). Charlotte, NC: Information Age.

Quick, H. E., & Moen, P. (1998). Gender, employment, and retirement quality: A life course approach to the differential experiences of men and women. *Journal of Occupational Health Psychology, 1,* 44-64.

Quinn, J. F., Burkhauser, R. V., & Myers, D. A. (1990). *Passing the torch: The influence of economic incentives on work and retirement.* Kalamazoo, MI: W. E. Upjohn.

Rau, B. L., & Adams, G. A. (2005). Attracting retirees to apply: Desired organizational characteristics of bridge employment. *Journal of Organizational Behavior, 26,* 649-660.

Rhodes, S. R. (1983). Age-related differences in work attitudes and behavior: A review and conceptual analysis. *Psychological Bulletin, 93,* 328-367.

Richardson, V., & Kilty, K. M. (1991). Adjustment to retirement: Continuity vs. discontinuity. *International Journal of Aging & Human Development, 33,* 151-169.

Shultz, K. S. (2003). Bridge employment: Work after retirement. In G. A. Adams and T. A. Beehr (Eds.), *Retirement: Reasons, processes, and results* (pp. 214-241). New York: Springer.

Shultz, K. S., Morton, K. R., & Weckerle, J. R. (1998). The influence of push and pull factors on voluntary and involuntary early retirees' retirement decision and adjustment. *Journal of Vocational Behavior, 53,* 45-57

Shultz, K. S., & Wang, M. (2007). The influence of specific physical health conditions on retirement decisions. *International Journal of Aging & Human Development, 65,* 749-161

Shultz, K. S., & Wang, M. (2008). The changing nature of mid- and late careers. In C. Wankel (Ed.), *21st century management: A reference handbook* (Vol. 2, pp. 130-138). Thousand Oaks, CA: SAGE.

Siegler, I. C., Bosworth, H. B., & Elias, M. F. (2003). Adult development and aging. In I. B. Weiner (Ed.), *Handbook of psychology: Vol. 9. Health psychology* (pp. 487-512). Hoboken, NJ: Wiley.

Singer, T., Verhaegen, P., Ghisletta, P., Lindenberger, U., & Baltes, P. B. (2003). The fate of cognition in very old age: Six-year longitudinal findings in the Berlin Aging Study (BASE). *Psychology and Aging, 38,* 318-331.

Smith-Ruig, T. (2009). Mapping the career journey of accountants in Australia. In S. G. Baugh & S. E. Sullivan (Eds.), *Research in careers: Vol. 1. Maintaining focus, energy, and options over the career* (pp. 163-196). Charlotte, NC: Information Age.

Spiegel, P. E., & Shultz, K. S. (2003). The influence of pre-retirement planning and transferability of skills on naval officers' retirement satisfaction and adjustment. *Military Psychology, 15*, 284-306.

Sterns, H. L., & Subich, L. M. (2002). Career development in midcareer. In D. C. Feldman (Ed.), *Work careers: A developmental perspective* (pp. 186-213). San Francisco: Jossey-Bass/John Wiley & Sons.

Szinovacz, M. E. (2003). Context and pathways: Retirement as institution, process and experience. In G. A. Adams & T. A. Beehr (Eds.), *Retirement: Reasons, processes, and results* (pp. 6-52). New York: Springer.

Talaga, J. A., & Beehr, T. A. (1989). Retirement: A psychological perspective. In C. L. Copper & I. T. Robertson (Eds.), *International review of industrial and organizational psychology* (pp. 185-211). Chichester, England: Wiley.

Talaga, J. A., & Beehr, T. A. (1995). Are there gender differences in predicting retirement? *Journal of Applied Psychology, 80*, 16-28.

Taylor, M. A., Shultz, K. S., Morrison, R. F., Spiegel, P. E., & Greene, J. (2007). Occupational attachment and met expectations as predictors of retirement adjustment of naval officers. *Journal of Applied Social Psychology, 37*, 1697-1725.

Waldman, D. A., & Avolio, B. J. (1986). A meta-analysis of age differences in job performance. *Journal of Applied Psychology, 71*, 33-38.

Wang, M. (2007). Profiling retirees in the retirement transition and adjustment process: Examining the longitudinal change patters of retirees' psychological well-being. *Journal of Applied Psychology, 92*, 455-474.

Wang, M., Zhan, Y., Liu, S., & Shultz, K. (2008). Antecedents of bridge employment: A longitudinal investigation. *Journal of Applied Psychology, 93*, 818-830.

Warr, P. (1994). Age and employment. In H. C. Triandis, M. D., Dunnette, & L. M. Hough (Eds.), *Handbook of industrial and organizational psychology* (2nd ed., Vol. 4, pp. 485-550). Palo Alto, CA: Consulting Psychologists Press.

Weckerle, J. R., & Shultz, K. S. (1999). Influences on the bridge employment decision among older U.S.A. workers. *Journal of Occupational and Organizational Psychology, 72*, 317-330.

Zhan, Y., Wang, M., Liu, S., Shultz, K. (in press). Bridge employment and retirees' health: A longitudinal investigation. *Journal of Occupational Health Psychology.*

CHAPTER 7

MAPPING THE CAREER JOURNEY OF ACCOUNTANTS IN AUSTRALIA

Theresa Smith-Ruig

"Career is not a destination, it is a journey."

—participant David
(accountant with a large IT company, age 43).

This quote encapsulates how many individuals conceptualize their career history. Like any journey, there are a myriad of factors that can influence how careers are enacted, including the speed of career progression, the hazards that may be encountered along the way, or the various pathways available to travelers. The challenge for career researchers today is to develop a model that depicts or maps the career experiences of men and women. There are a number of research questions, however, that confront scholars in the field of career theory. (1) Do men and women enact similar careers? (2) Do individuals follow a more traditional, linear career path or

Maintaining Focus, Energy, and Options Over the Career
pp. 163–196
Copyright © 2009 by Information Age Publishing

a boundaryless career as outlined by Arthur and Rousseau (1996)? (3) How do changing definitions of career and career success influence the nature of an individual's career journey? Finally, (4) What factors influence an individual's career journey?

The purpose of this chapter is to explore some of these questions by outlining the results of a qualitative study into the career experiences of 59 men and women employed in the accounting profession in Australia. Through semi-structured interviews, participants were asked to define what a career and career success meant to them, and to explore how a range of personal, interpersonal and organizational factors were perceived to have an influence on their career history. Results revealed that the men and women passed through three main career or age-related stages: (a) early career, which entailed *exploration* (early 20s); (b) midcareer, which included *establishment* (late 20s to late 30s) and *maintenance* (late 30s to late 40s); and (c) late career, which involved *preretirement* (early 50s onwards). The career stories of the participants demonstrated that the men and women had similar career experiences during the exploration and preretirement stages, and only differed during the establishment and maintenance stages, as women tried to balance work and family. The study showed that the participants followed either traditional or boundaryless career paths, depending on their age, stage in life, family commitments, or definitions of career and success.

The chapter begins with a brief review of the existing theories on career development, emphasizing the shift from traditional to boundaryless career theories. The distinction between objective and subjective career success is also discussed. Super's (1957) career stage theory is used as a framework to analyze and present the research discussed in this chapter. The results are also compared to Sullivan and Mainiero's (2007) theory, as this is one of the more recent cross-gender models. The design of the qualitative study, including methodology and sample selection, is then outlined in this chapter. The results of the research are then presented. The implications for further research and the practical implications for HR professionals are discussed in the final section of the chapter.

BACKGROUND ON CAREER THEORY AS A FRAMEWORK FOR ANALYSIS

In traditional career development individuals progressed through roles typically within one organization, achieving greater pay, power, position, and responsibility (Levinson, Darrow, Klein, Levinson, & McKee, 1978; Super, 1957). One of these earlier theorists was Super (1957), who described the dynamics of how people chose and implemented a self-concept through their work. By self-concept Super (1957) was referring to an individual's self-identity. He proposed that people experienced four different psychological states as they progressed through their career—level of interest; satisfaction; motivation; and commitment. A career stage was determined by a person's perceptions and circumstances in relation to his or her career (main determinants), with age as a secondary determinant. The other variables included biological, societal, and psychological variables (Super, 1957).

Super (1957) proposed five main stages: (a) the growth stage (0-15 years); (b) exploration (15-25); (c) establishment (25-45); (d) maintenance (45 to retirement); and finally (e) the disengagement stage (retirement to death). This career stage theory was used in the research as a means to analyze and present the data. It should be noted that the growth and disengagement stage were not featured in this research, given the age and on-going employment of the participants.

In her review of career theory, Sullivan (1999) noted that two major issues have arisen regarding Super's (1957) model: is his theory generalizable to women and is his theory applicable, given the changing work environment? She argued that researchers have often used Super's theory as a post hoc explanation for their findings, rather than for hypothesis testing (Sullivan, 1999). The latter is a valid criticism, given that it reflects the process of data analysis adopted for the research discussed in this chapter (this is explained later in the chapter). Sullivan (1999) found that research that supports Super's notion of implementing the self-concept through one's career included research by Osipow (1983); while research that focused on the differences in attitudes and behaviors across the career stages included Cohen (1991) and Lynn, Cao, and Horn (1996).

There are few studies that have tested the generalizability of Super's (1957) theory to women. Ornstein and Isabella (1990), for example, found little support for the applicability of Super's model to women. Sullivan (1999) concluded that Super's (1957) theory does not adequately capture the complex lives of women.

By the late 1980s and 1990s, Arthur and Rousseau (1996) believed a shift was occurring toward boundaryless careers. They argued that careers in the 21st century would no longer be automatic or linear, they would be boundaryless. The career would be directed by the individual, not the organization, and driven by changes in the person and in the environment. Arthur and Rousseau (1996) believed that employment would progress across roles, organizations, and occupations. They argued that there would be a focus on continuous learning and development and that an individual's skills would create career opportunities (Arthur & Rousseau, 1996). As Adamson, Doherty, and Viney (1998) stated, employees will want to ensure that even if they do not progress within their organization, their job will provide them with professional challenge so that they remain engaged, skillful in their profession, and marketable. Wise and Millward (2005) explained that the structure, definition, and evaluation of career is highly personalized and represents how an individual values a career.

Thus, a main focus among contemporary career theorists has been on exploring what role personalized definitions of career and career success play in analyzing an individual's career history (Gunz & Heslin, 2005; Hall, 1996a, 1996b; Heslin, 2005). Success can be measured in both objective and subjective terms. Objective success refers to extrinsic measures, such as salary or position, whereas subjective success is measured in relation to intrinsic variables, such as job satisfaction, personal development, or achievement (Heslin, 2005; Knabi, 1999; McColl-Kennedy & Dann, 2000; Melamed, 1996). Success is derived from individuals' own perceptions of what they value as important (McColl-Kennedy & Dann, 2000). The boundaryless and protean career theories, for example, emphasize subjective success, such as a work-life balance, rather than objective success, such as vertical progression (Arthur & Rousseau, 1996; Hall, 1996b).

Heslin (2005) believes that greater emphasis needs to be placed on the individual and contextual factors that influence conceptualizations of success. For example, subjective career success may encompass reactions to both the objective (e.g., pay) and subjective (e.g., fulfillment) aspects of one's career and the definition of success can change as careers unfold. An important point that Heslin (2005) makes is that an individual may reach an objective plateau in his or her career (i.e., where career progression has ceased), but he or she may still feel satisfied and successful if career or life goals are being met (i.e. the individual has a good work-life balance). The attitude towards one's career journey will, therefore, be positive or negative depending on how an individual defines success. Arthur, Khapova, and Wilderom (2005, p. 180) similarly note that:

> Observing career success through either a purely objective lens or a purely subjective lens offers a limited picture. The depth of the career success construct can be better seen from looking through both lenses at the same time.

ALPHA VERSUS BETA CAREERS

There has been little research to date that has tried to compare the career patterns of men and women. Recently, however, Sullivan and Mainiero (2007) identified two major career patterns: an *alpha* career pattern, which was displayed by individuals who were strongly focused on their career; and a *beta* career pattern, which was displayed by individuals who had made adjustments in their career to enable a greater work-life or work-family balance. The researchers proposed three parameters that influenced the career trajectories of participants: authenticity, balance, and challenge. Sullivan and Mainiero (2007) argued that at any point in time all three parameters are active in an individual's career or life, but one tends to dominate over the others.

- *Authenticity*; defined as being true to oneself by aligning personal values and behaviors.
- *Balance;* defined as efforts designed to achieve equilibrium between work and nonwork aspects of one's life.
- *Challenge*; defined as engaging in activities that permit the individual to demonstrate responsibility, control, and autonomy while learning and growing.

The researchers described the alpha career pattern for men as challenge, authenticity, and balance; that is, their careers tended to be linear or sequential, with a focus on challenge, followed by personal development, and then a focus on concerns of balancing work and lifestyle (Sullivan & Mainiero, 2007). During the challenge phase, men were devoted to family, but expressed this commitment through a need to provide financially for the family via their career. As the men's careers plateaued in the latter part of midcareer, the men started to question their life and, thus, authenticity became the focus. Then, in late career men wanted to spend more time with the family and think about life beyond their workplace (Sullivan & Mainiero, 2007).

The beta career pattern for women was described by Sullivan and Mainiero (2007) as challenge, balance, and authenticity. The focus was on ambition and advancement in early career, but the need to balance work and family commitments featured in the later portion of early career and in midcareer. The researchers found that issues of authenticity were featured in late career, such as starting one's own business or following leisure or spiritual pursuits.

Cabrera's (2007) research tested the applicability of Mainiero and Sullivan's (2005) Kaleidoscope Career Model (KCM) with a survey of female graduates of an international business school in the United States. The research supported the KCM by revealing that midcareer women were most interested in finding balance in their lives and the desire for authenticity increased across the life span.

The researchers noted that there were men who followed the beta career pattern and women who followed an alpha career (Sullivan & Mainiero, 2007). The women who followed an alpha career tended to have a husband who worked from home or did not work at all. They also found that there were some younger men who followed a beta career path, believing that the level of responsibility, travel demands, and the demands of work were not worth the sacrifice of family or nonwork interests. Similar to women, these beta career men tended to forgo their career ambitions in midcareer to follow a more relaxed and family centered lifestyle (Sullivan & Mainiero, 2007).

A common theme among these theories (Arthur & Rousseau, 1996; Hall, 1996a, 1996b; Sullivan & Mainiero, 2007; Super, 1957) is an emphasis on understanding how an individual defines career and how this influences his or her career experiences. For this reason, these theories are used as the foundation for analyzing and presenting the career histories of the men and women in this research. The research will demonstrate that the career patterns of men and women tend to be influenced by their changing views of how they value career versus family or versus personal growth or development.

The extant literature also discusses a range of personal, interpersonal, and organizational factors that can influence an individual's career (Burke & Vinnicombe, 2006; Lyness & Thompson, 2000; Powell & Mainiero, 1992; Richardson, 1996; Sullivan, 1999; Tharenou, Latimer, & Conroy, 1994; White, Cox, & Cooper, 1992). These factors were explored in the research to compare and contrast their influence on both men's and women's careers and are briefly discussed in this chapter.

The results presented in this chapter therefore seek to answer the following three key research questions:

1.   Are there gender differences in how careers are enacted?
2.   Do men and women follow traditional or nontraditional careers or both types of careers at different points in time?
3.   Are there gender differences in the factors that may constrain or enable career enactment?

RESEARCH DESIGN

Semi-structured interviews were used in this study to explore the career enactment of 59 accountants in Australia, in line with previous researchers who successfully employed interviews to examine careers (Arthur, Inkson, & Pringle, 1999; Cochran, 1990; Cohen & Mallon, 2001; Levinson et al., 1978; Levinson & Levinson, 1996; Marshall, 1989, 1995; Sullivan & Mainiero, 2007; White et al., 1992). The use of this qualitative methodology permitted me to explore and understand the range of feelings, attitudes, and motivations expressed by each participant, creating an individualized account of his/her career history.   The findings presented in this chapter, which focus on gender differences and careers, are part of a larger project on careers in accounting (Smith-Ruig, 2008).

Twelve face-to-face interviews were conducted and 47 via the telephone, lasting from 30 to 90 minutes. The interviews were conducted until saturation was reached—that is, no new themes emerged (Flick, 1998). Participants were all asked a similar range of questions, the first of which was to describe their career history. Participants were asked to define what a career and career success meant to them. They were also asked to outline whether the following factors had an influence on their career experiences: (a) personal factors, such as family commitments; (b) interpersonal factors, such as mentors and networks; and (c) organizational factors, such as opportunities for work experience, training and development, organizational culture, and organizational career management practices.

The sample included 30 men and 29 women employed in a range of organizations, including education ($n = 5$ men and $n = 5$ women), chartered accounting firms ($n = 11$ men and $n = 13$ women), the corporate sector ($n = 11$ men and $n = 5$ women), the not-for-profit sector ($n = 1$ man), and self-employed ($n = 2$ men and $n = 7$ women).

The following information includes details on the job and organizational tenure of participants. Nine men and three women had remained employed with the same organization during their entire career (to the point of the interview). An additional 29 participants ($n = 13$ men and $n = 16$ women) moved to one organization after one or two job changes and intended to remain employed there. The average position tenure of participants was 4.6 years and the average organizational tenure was 9.5 years. Twenty-nine participants reported working for their current organization for 5 years or longer.

The men were aged from 23 to 66 (with an average age of 41) and the women were aged 28 to 72 (with an average age of 43). Fifty-two of the participants were aged 30 and older, while one man and one woman were over the age of 65. One participant was born in Canada, one in Poland, and two in the United Kingdom, but all four had migrated to Australia. The remaining participants were all permanent Australians of Caucasian descent.

Participants were asked a number of demographic questions about their marital status and family commitments. Six men and 3 women were single; 23 men and 21 women were married; one man and one woman indicated they were living with a partner; one woman was divorced; and 3 women reported being divorced and living with a new partner. Twenty-two men and 19 women had children; however, the children were no longer living at home with 8 of the participants. Five of the women that did not have children stated that they consciously chose not to have them. The reasons included (a) feeling as though they were not maternal; (b) the timing of relationships prevented having children; and (c) actively choosing not to have a child. In terms of their career, these women had progressed to senior positions, including associate professor, senior partner, vice president of a business unit, chief financial officer, and self-employment. They were all over 38 years of age. The remaining 5 women without children were planning to have a family at some stage in the future. Of the 8 men that did not have children, 6 were single and the other two were planning to have a family.

A number of sampling techniques were used during the data collection. First, purposive sampling was used, where a number of organizations were specifically chosen in an attempt to obtain a variety of sizes and types, as well as by targeting participants through a national accounting association. Second, convenience sampling, where some organizations were chosen based on close geographic location to the researcher, was utilized. Third, snowball sampling, where participants were asked to help identify other potential participants in the study, was also employed. For those organizations that were approached directly to participate in the study, a human resource representative was asked to nominate individuals to participate in the research. It is recognized that the latter issue does raise questions of bias; however, the participants sampled appeared to express both positive and negative attitudes about their career and organization, thereby suggesting limited bias. I limited the research to the accounting profession so that more valid comparisons could be made between the career experiences of the participants. Most existing cross-gender studies of career development have involved samples from a wide range of occupational backgrounds (Arthur et al., 1999; Levinson et al., 1978; Levinson & Levinson, 1996; Sullivan & Mainiero, 2007). The value of this research is that the professional similarity of the participants meant that it was easier to make realistic comparisons regarding the career experiences among the participants and, in particular, to explore whether gender influences how careers are enacted.

There were several key steps in the data analysis phase. First, each interview was audio taped and then transcribed into Microsoft Word. Second, the career history of each participant was then summarized. *Career history* was defined as the events in an individual's work and personal life that influenced his or her career experiences. From there, Strauss and Corbin's (1998) techniques for grounded theory analysis were used to analyze the transcripts and career histories. That is, each interview was content analyzed and coded based on the research objectives. Analysis involved looking for themes that confirmed existing research, as well as for emerging themes relating to the three key research objectives. For example, all the participants' responses to the same question (i.e., how they defined career and success, or what influence family commitments had on their career) were compared and contrasted. The researcher was the sole person responsible for coding the data.

The summary of the career history of each participant was developed from the interview transcript and then compared and contrasted with all other participants' histories. The data revealed that there were similar issues that participants faced during various stages in their life and career. It was determined that Super's (1957) age and career-related stage theory could be used as a framework to analyze and present the results.

RESULTS AND DISCUSSION

Research Question 1:
Career Enactment—A Career Stage Framework

The results of the research revealed that the men and women tended to enact similar careers during the early career stage and during the preretirement stage. The key area of difference occurred during the establishment and maintenance phases, when women placed greater emphasis on balancing work and family. The following discussion illustrates how the men and women in the study enacted their career as they passed through three main career or age-related stages: (a) early career (b) midcareer, including establishment and maintenance; and (c) late career.

Early Career or Exploratory Stage

The early career stage represented a period in which the majority of participants ($n = 26$ men and $n = 26$ women) entered the accounting profession at the bottom rung. Only 4 men and 3 women embarked on an accounting-related career later in life. Participants either completed study before entering the workforce or combined work and study. Some were quite clear about their ambitions, while others progressed through a series of jobs before having a fixed direction. The early career stage was characterized by the participants progressing through a series of roles in one or multiple organizations, slowly progressing up the organizational hierarchy. This model is in line with the traditional notion of a career.

For example, 9 men entered an organization following graduation from the university and remained there to date. A further 13 men worked for one or more organizations before settling down to a particular firm for the longer term by their late 20s. Of these, 8 participants all initially worked in a professional services firm (during their early 20s) before moving on (late 20s onwards) to the corporate sector ($n = 4$ men), to a smaller firm ($n = 1$), to establish his own practice ($n = 1$), or to pursue an academic career ($n = 2$). Only one man changed his career path during the early career phase, leaving the "aggressive culture" of the professional services firm (i.e., one of "big four" consulting firms of PricewaterhouseCoopers, Deloitte, KPMG, and Arthur Anderson) to pursue an academic career at the age of 24.

Similar to the men, many women ($n = 16$) worked in one or more organizations before settling down (late 20s onwards) to a particular firm for the longer term. Nine of these participants worked in a professional services firm before moving on to the corporate sector or to a smaller accounting firm. A further 6 participants had a number of roles in various sized accounting firms or the corporate sector before settling down to a particular organization by their late 20s to early 30s.

A common detour off the career path during the early 20s for some participants (10 men and 4 women) was to travel and work overseas for a short period of time to broaden their skills and experience (see Tharenou, this volume). Some worked in their field of training, while others engaged in the popular "back packing" style of employment (casual and unskilled).

The exploratory phase of the participants' career provided a critical foundation to their career, during which they acquired the skills and experience to progress. The reasons for early career changes were to have more job variety, more challenging and rewarding work, or to seek out more concrete career opportunities. Participants reported being energized and enthusiastic toward attaining career goals. This attitude is similar to the "challenge" parameter suggested by Sullivan and Mainiero (2007). The reasons for job change also demonstrate that the participants' conceptualization of career and success was measured in both objective terms (wanting other career opportunities or more senior positions) and subjective terms (rewarding and challenging work).

The following comment by Greg highlights how many of the men viewed the early years of their career as a time of continuous learning and acquiring the skills they needed to help advance their career. Greg viewed his time in an accounting firm as providing the critical skills that enabled him to pursue a more senior position in a large multinational firm.

> Coming out of the university, the chartered firm was definitely the right move as it rounded you out in the technical side of things. I firmly believe doing the professional year and getting the charter qualification was very useful in cementing and embedding the technical capabilities for the rest of my career. (Greg, senior manager in a large multinational, age 34)

Midcareer Stage for Men

The second stage classified as middle adulthood (late 20s to late 40s) or midcareer was characterized by two sub-categories of establishment and maintenance as noted by Super (1984). During these phases, the men enacted their career on two different paths, depending on their definitions of career and success. There were two categories of men: work-devoted men and men who combined both work and family. The work-devoted men continued to experience traditional career progression, believing that they had to be more committed to their career journey, as they were now responsible for providing for their family. These men enacted a career pattern similar to Sullivan and Mainiero's (2007) alpha career.

For example, during the establishment phase, all of the men pursued a traditional career. The emphasis was on cementing their career within the profession and pursuing senior positions. Fourteen of the men experienced a traditional linear career, slowly progressing through roles within one organization and pursuing more senior positions. A further 8 men had a series of roles in different organizations, all focused on upward progression.

As part of the *establishment* phase, some of the men focused on *settling down* in order to provide "financial security" and "stability" in their career and family. In the following comment, Doug explains how he felt it was necessary to actively pursue promotions in his late 20s in order to gain greater financial and job security as he started a family.

> I only moved on when I started a family when I started to think I should better myself and provide a secure financial base and that's when I started thinking about the money. If I didn't have a family I would be on the north coast with one of those small councils earning $40,000 and enjoying myself. (Doug, senior accountant with an accounting firm, age 57)

The *establishment* phase was followed by a *maintenance* phase. Here the participants (aged from mid 30s onward) focused on *stabilizing* their position (typically within one organization). By this stage in their career, the participants had reached senior positions in their organization, such as partner or senior manager. Since no further upward progression was possible in their own organization, they tended to "coast" along in their career.

It was during the maintenance phase that the men who wanted a greater family focus ($n = 6$) began to change their career path. These men were less intent on pursuing rapid career progression or senior positions, as they wanted a greater work-life and work-family balance. These men mirrored the group of men who followed a beta career pattern in Sullivan and Mainiero's (2007) research. For example, Adrian began his career climbing the ladder in a professional services firm. Following the birth of his daughter, who became seriously ill, he moved to a second-tier firm in order to seek greater flexibility. After deciding not to pursue a partner position in that firm, he chose to establish his own business, believing that this situation would provide the greatest work-family balance.

There were some men ($n = 5$) in the study who experienced a traditional career, but admitted they wanted to spend more time with their family. However, they were unwilling or unsure about doing so, due to stereotypes and organizational expectations about careers.

For example, Michael was a senior accountant in a regionally based accounting firm aged in his mid 30s. He left a large professional services firm in a metropolitan city to move back to the small country town where he and his wife grew up. Michael was unsure about further career progression, as he wanted to spend more time with his family; however he was reluctant to tell his employer, as he was worried that the senior partners would be disapproving of his lack of career ambition. Michael felt that the organization would be resentful of his unwillingness to progress upward, given all the time and resources the firm had invested in him, because he lacked that drive.

One of the participants (Adam, aged 35) expressed considerable frustration and uncertainty about his career. He had achieved the senior position of a chief financial officer in a large organization, but was feeling depressed about the lack of a good work-family balance. He did not know how to address this career dilemma.

> When I came back to Australia and started this job (as chief financial officer), it was all about this was pay off time; the big opportunity; the chance to really push myself and take on a position of responsibility and the conventional career thing. I did it quickly for my age. Then perhaps I did it too quickly, because I became overworked and dropped all my outside interests and hobbies. I lost my health, fitness and I got depressed … (I've had a child now and it's all of a sudden, well hang on having done this career thing, it's not all that great). Perhaps I don't regret any of this because it all made sense at the time, the steps I have taken were the right steps. But having gone through it all, it's probably time to take new steps. (Adam, chief financial officer in a medium sized multinational company, age 35)

It is interesting to note that Super (1957) in his theory indicated that individuals did not reach the maintenance stage until 45; however, in this study of accountants it was demonstrated that individuals actually entered the maintenance stage as early as the mid to late 30s. A possible explanation for this difference is due to the fact that many of the accountants reached partner or senior positions by their early 30s, and thus had nowhere else to progress in the firm, due to the absence of additional hierarchical levels, or because they had attained all the objective success they sought.

Some of the men (n = 6) during this part of the journey reached what they referred to as a *crossroads* or plateau. These men admitted feeling discontented, bored with their job, vulnerable, and unsure over their future direction. The participants reached one of three types of plateaus: a structural plateau, where they did not have access to further hierarchical levels or structures within the organization; a content plateau, where they became bored with the job; and a life plateau, where they began to feel unsuccessful in life and career (Bardwick, 1986; Bown-Wilson & Parry, this volume). As a result, the participants began to re-evaluate their career. These participants were in their 30s and 40s. Some chose to leave their organization to establish their own business (n = 2) or to pursue an academic career (n = 4). The motivation for the career change was to obtain greater flexibility and more control over the job and to perform more fulfilling and stimulating work. They were looking for what Sullivan and Mainiero (2007) referred to as "authenticity" and "balance."

For example, Chris discussed his crossroads in terms of reaching a senior position in his career, after which he changed direction in his 40s in order to obtain a greater work-life balance, as well as to pursue more fulfilling work in academia.

> This period is a new life for me. I have satisfied my desire as far as achievement goes in the area of senior management ... I got quite senior in my previous roles ... I wanted to get away from working 70 hours a week. I had enough of that. I needed a little more family life. Also [I have a] desire to do a PhD. (Chris, accounting lecturer, age 53)

Midcareer Stage for Women

The midcareer stage for the women also comprised an establishment and maintenance phase. In the establishment phase (late 20s or early 30s), the career path was characterized by two alternatives. First, a minority of women (n = 5) experienced a traditional career, continuing to climb the corporate ladder and achieving increasing remuneration, responsibility, and promotions. These individuals tended to be women who did not have a family or who had a husband that assumed the major share of family commitments. They are similar to the women in Sullivan and Mainiero's (2007) study who enacted an alpha career pattern. While some of these women did not have children, some indicated that their career experiences were constrained by employer assumptions that they still may have children, by a male-dominated culture, by a lack of equal access to career paths, or simply because they were female. The following quote from Christine indicates how she believed her husband's assistance with family commitments assisted her career journey.

> From that point of view it's been quite easy.... So if the kids are sick he [husband] goes and picks them up. It's flexible. If he was employed it would have been a lot more difficult. But that's the way we've done it, purposefully, so that I could come back to work. (Christine, senior associate in a regional accounting firm, age 37)

The majority of women ($n = 19$) during this stage took a short break (less than 12 months per child) from their career path to have children. Only one woman in the study took a break from the workforce for an extended period (greater than 2 years) to have children. The remaining women all returned to work within 12 months. The focus was on what Sullivan and Mainiero (2007) termed "balance." All of the women with children indicated that they worked part-time at various stages during their career. Of the 19 women with children, 8 were working part time at the time of the interview. A common feature among the careers of the working mothers ($n = 5$) was to structure their part-time hours around children's school times. The women agreed that part-time work offered greater flexibility.

In order to better balance work and family commitments, a number of the working mothers changed their type of employment. These shifts included moving into the education field ($n = 5$), working as a consultant or contractor ($n = 4$), or establishing their own practice ($n = 6$). Some women made multiple changes. These job changes were often temporary. It allowed the working mothers flexibility over working hours and the type of work they undertook. One participant even left the accounting profession altogether and retrained as a primary (elementary) school teacher because the latter job offered greater flexibility in working hours. It enabled her to be employed on a casual basis, thereby choosing what hours and days of work suited her. This participant would switch back to being an accountant during peak accounting periods (i.e., the end of the financial year). The latter tended to coincide with school holidays when she was not employed as a teacher.

For example, the following career history of Louise illustrates the age-related stages that she has progressed through during her career. While she was young and single, Louise worked as an accountant for a large multinational IT company, where she experienced progression up the ladder. However, she left the firm when she married. Louise initially undertook temporary work while she made plans for the wedding. She then worked for a manufacturing company until her first child was born. Louise moved in an out of the workforce while she had three children. During this time, Louise worked for her husband's business as the accountant. This position enabled her to work flexible hours. Her longest break from the workforce was one of 3 years after the birth of her third child. Louise then returned to the workforce part time to work in a second-tier accounting firm. The following statement by Louise illustrates how her career changed as her personal motivations and circumstances in life changed:

> I think I used to define it very differently. I think previously when I first started in commercial accounting it was to go and be a financial controller of an organization and that was where you set your sights. But now it's what makes you feel happy and fulfilled, and what works for you. Priorities change and your situation changes. Even getting married you rethink things. I used to work long hours at [IT company], such as coming in at 7 am and leaving for home at 9 pm on a regular basis. Originally that was only month end but it grew to be nearly all the time. At that point in time I thought, "Hang on, what's the point?" I was earning good money for my age, and I had a car. You think what is the point if you are exhausted all the time. It was a very interesting and stimulating job. You just take stock. (Louise, senior accountant in an accounting firm, age 39)

Some of the women ($n = 5$) encountered a number of hazards and speed bumps during this phase, representing the organizational factors that restrained their career journey. These obstacles included negative attitudes by their employers toward part-time work, lack of flexible work practices, an "old boys' culture," organizational politics, and negative attitudes about women. For example, Tracey, who was a director in a professional services firm, believed that "a lot of time is spent trying to understand or deal with the politics," given that the firm was quite male dominated.

By their late 30s (maintenance phase) many of the women reached a plateau in their career journey. Like men, this group included those women who reached senior positions within their organization and those who did not wish to progress any further in their career. Some women continued to coast along in their career, while five women also reported reaching a crossroads, similar to what the men discussed. These women redirected their career journey to pursue more fulfilling work, such as self-employment or work in academia. Their focus moved to "authenticity" (Sullivan & Mainiero, 2007). For example, Cathryn, age 39, was an accounting academic at university and indicated she was at a crossroads in her career.

> I suppose that's where I am struggling now, in terms of which direction do I go in.... I haven't really thought it out in any great detail, I have just glided along. (Cathryn, accounting lecturer, age 39)

Late Career or Preretirement Stage

As noted in the previous section, Super (1957) suggested that the maintenance stage lasted from 45 until retirement. In contrast, this research found that there was an additional phase prior to retirement (preretirement). One of the reasons for this additional phase was that participants in this research tended to reach a career plateau much earlier (and hence reach the maintenance phase), compared to the timing proposed by Super (1957). It was noted earlier that men and women actually reached the maintenance stage by their mid 30s onwards, at which point they just coasted along in their careers. It was not until their early 50s that the participants started discussing the issue of retirement, thus signaling a new phase in their career journey.

Given Australia's legislation surrounding the official age of retirement (the age at which individuals can access their superannuation and other retirement benefits), how men and women view retirement is changing. The financial issues around retirement also influence how men and women work in the lead up to retirement. For example, in Australia some individuals are eligible to access part of their superannuation early (prior to the official retirement age) if they have adopted a "transition to retirement plan." The aging of Australia's population has meant that the official age for retirement has been extended.

During the preretirement stage, the men and women followed one of two career paths. Either they continued to coast along in their career, with no fixed direction or age for retirement, or they began the decline journey; that is, moved into phased retirement by working part time or engaging in more volunteer work. A number of the participants ($n = 6$) were interested in spending more time on hobbies or leisure interests or performing unpaid work, representing an emphasis on "authenticity." Two women and two men expressed interest in becoming directors of charitable or nonprofit organizations. Two women indicated they needed to continue working part-time beyond formal retirement for financial reasons.

Research Question 2:
Traditional Versus Nontraditional Careers

The career histories of the participants were analyzed in order to determine whether they followed a traditional or a boundaryless career path. The research demonstrated that there were both men and women who still followed a traditional career model—that is, progressing through an organization to achieve increasing pay, position, and responsibility. However, it should be noted that this finding might be due to the professional structure of an accounting career. For example, for those individuals interested in becoming a partner in a firm, there was a particular linear career path they were required to follow. Individuals tended to commence as a trainee or graduate (refers to a position title for an individual recently graduated from university) and progress up the organizational hierarchy to senior accountant, associate, director, and partner. If the individual did not commence as a graduate in the firm, he or she typically had to spend time in a senior role before being considered for or admitted to the partnership. The number of hierarchical levels might have differed depending on the size of the firm, but there was a distinct "sequential path."

Of the 24 participants who were employed in an accounting firm, 12 (n = 8 men and n = 4 women) had reached partner position, while a further 2 participants were interested in becoming a partner. All of these individuals followed a traditional path, including the women. Two of these women did not have children and one had a husband who assumed the major share of household and family commitments.

Participants employed in the corporate sector or in the education field also exhibited a traditional structure to their career history. For example, 7 out of the 10 participants employed in the education sector experienced a traditional career journey, remaining at the same academic institution and slowly progressing through roles from lecturer, to senior lecturer, to associate professor. Similarly, the majority of participants in the corporate sector progressed through roles from graduate in the organization, to manager, and to senior manager. While some participants had changed organizations early in their career, they tended in time to find an organization where they were interested in remaining until retirement.

In line with the boundaryless and protean career concepts proposed by Arthur and Rousseau (1996) and Hall (1996a, 1996b), there were some participants in the study who discussed proactively seeking out their own career path in order to satisfy their own personal motivations and circumstances. The emphasis was on achieving a greater work-life balance or personal development. For example, some of the women enacted boundaryless careers, as they sought out work that would enable a better work-family balance. There were other participants who indicated that they did not have traditional views of a career; that is, climbing the ladder and achieving increasing power, position, or status.

For example, there were 2 men and 3 women in the study who followed a boundaryless or protean career path as they had varied careers early in life before pursuing an accounting career. Peter, for example, began his career as a truck driver, followed by a sales clerk in the motor spare parts industry, before pursuing an accounting career with a professional services firm at the age of 22.

> I don't think there has been any grand strategy in my career. It's been more a series of tactical responses, I think. It was almost by accident that I ended up being a chartered accountant.... I started in the motor spare parts industry driving a truck during school holidays and continued that after school. There was nothing I really wanted to do at university. That eventually led to managing the place until it went into liquidation. I worked with the liquidators for a couple of months and they offered me a job. That's when I started in the chartered accounting game and I started my degree. (Peter, partner at a professional services firm, age 51)

The pursuit of on-going skills development and knowledge acquisition is a further feature of boundaryless careers as outlined by Arthur and Rousseau (1996). Participants in the study were asked how they would define a career and their definitions included: (a) rewarding and challenging work, identified by 19 participants ($n = 7$ men and $n = 12$ women); (b) continued development ($n = 6$ men and $n = 2$ women); and (c) continued learning ($n = 6$ men and $n = 5$ women).

In the following comment, Margaret discusses that the opportunities for challenging roles and continued development are important in maintaining a passion and interest in the job. Margaret (age 54) was one of the early women to be admitted to partnership at her professional services firm. She strongly emphasized the importance of continued development throughout her career.

> The best opportunity I got was to run an office. That was an autonomous office so we were responsible for the top and bottom line and the people within it. I learnt a tremendous amount, a huge amount. I think that was really useful for me. That was really the first time in my career when I started to flap my wings, I think. I think it's really about having an opportunity to do something. I think if people spend their entire careers in these professional firms just as line partners as we call them, I'm surprised they haven't slashed their wrists. You need something to absolutely challenge you or what's the point? (Margaret, partner at a professional services firm, age 54)

Research Question 3:
Constraining and Enabling Influences on Career

Considerable research over the decades has explored the range of factors that can influence an individual's career history (Lyness & Thompson, 2000; Powell & Mainiero, 1992; Richardson, 1996; Sullivan, 1999; Tharenou et al., 1994; White et al., 1992). Few studies however, have examined the influence of these factors for both women and men employed in a similar professional context. In the following section, I report briefly on the constraining or enabling influence that a range of factors had on career, including (a) personal factors, such as family commitments; (b) interpersonal factors, such as mentors and networks; and (c) organizational factors such as opportunities for work experience, training and development, organizational culture, and the provision of organization-based career management practices. The role of family commitments has been covered in the previous section of the results, so in this section I will focus on discussing interpersonal and organizational factors.

The links between mentoring and career development have long been discussed in the literature (Kanter, 1977; Kram, 1985; Terjesen, 2005). The research revealed that the majority of the participants ($n = 48$, $n = 25$ men and $n = 23$ women) had experiences with some form of mentor or sponsor throughout their career, both on a formal and an informal basis. Only 11 participants ($n = 5$ men and $n = 6$ women) indicated that they did not receive any form of mentoring during their career. In general, the participants believed that both formal and informal mentoring programs were useful in providing career encouragement by (a) exposing them to a variety of situations; (b) providing career advice; (c) providing role models; (d) explaining organizational rules, practices, culture, and appropriate conduct; (e) providing performance feedback; and (f) providing a variety of viewpoints. Twenty-six of the participants ($n = 15$ men and $n = 11$ women) also reported acting as a mentor, either formally or informally.

There were two major emerging themes to arise from this research with regard to mentoring. The first theme related to the link between age and the use and purpose of mentoring. For example, in the early stages of career, participants found mentors useful in providing career advice and guidance and easing their induction into the organization. At later stages in their career, participants used mentors to help their admission into the senior ranks of the organization or to deal with organizational dynamics. Three of the participants (all women), for example, relayed stories of how their mentor was crucial in pushing them out of their "comfort zone" and helping them to move into senior positions. Twelve participants ($n = 7$ men and $n = 5$ women) revealed that they approached their mentor at crucial stages in their career in order to seek advice and direction. These findings are in line with Keller (2008), who explained that, traditionally, mentoring in a professional service firm meant helping others learn business-related lessons quickly with less risk. She believed that the mentor was a power figure who would arrange for career-building assignments and introductions to influential or senior people within the firm.

Among the more senior or older participants there was also a common theme that they all wanted to "leave a legacy." Eleven of the participants ($n = 5$ men and $n = 6$ women) identified that leaving a legacy or influencing the careers of others were important measures of success for them. For this reason, they were interested in being mentors. For example, many of the women were interested in leaving a legacy ($n = 6$) or helping others progress through the organization ($n = 7$). This attitude was expressed mainly by the older participants in the final stages of their career. At this point, they had themselves reached senior positions and so were keen to help others have successful and positive career experiences. The women specifically mentioned the desire to help mentor other women in their organization. In contrast to this finding, van Emmerik, Baugh, and Euwema (2005) found that high career aspirations were more strongly associated with serving as a mentor for men than for women. They explained that perhaps women do not expect mentoring to provide as great a career "payoff" for their investment in mentoring than men do. The difference in the two findings could be due to the fact that the women in my research had reached senior positions in their career, thus mentoring was not focused on furthering their career aspirations.

It was interesting to note that while many participants relayed stories of how mentors had influenced their life throughout their early and midcareer, some participants noted the paucity of effective mentoring once they had reached senior positions, or during the latter stages of their career. For example, 3 participants ($n = 1$ man and $n = 2$ women), who had all reached partner in two of the top four professional services firms in Australia, believed that while their organizations did a lot for younger partners and other employees, little attention was focused on partners once they reached their 40s and 50s.

The second major emerging theme to arise from the research was that some of the more senior or older participants wanted access to mentors and, as a result, approached external coaching programs. It should be noted that when referring to these programs, the participants interchanged the terms *mentors* and *coaches*. Technically, the word "coach" or "coaching" should be used, as the programs used by participants involved a fee for services. In contrast, mentors typically, whether formal or informal, do not get paid for this service. This is an important distinction to make, since 5 of the participants ($n = 2$ men and $n = 3$ women) reported using external coaching, as opposed to the remainder of participants, who simply used the mentoring relationships developed in their organization. The fact that coaches are paid for their services and mentors are not may create different types of relationships and these potential differences should be examined in the future.

These 5 participants explained that their organizations had encouraged them as senior members of staff to participate in external coaching programs. One other man admitted seeking out external coaching without the organization's encouragement, while one woman, who was self-employed, also saw a business coach. The coaching helped participants learn more about themselves and their career goals and concerns. It also helped to identify their "strengths and weaknesses" as well as their "passions." Coaching was an important means by which participants sought career and business guidance. There was a key gender difference in the purpose of using the external coaches; that is, while men used external coaches to crystallize career goals, women sought external coaches to act as role models in their career.

The other major interpersonal factor identified in the literature review as influencing career experience is that of networking (Burke, Rothstein, & Bristor, 1995; Cross & Linehan, 2006; Marshall, 1995; Powell & Mainiero, 1992; Travers & Pemberton, 2000). The research showed that most participants believed that access to formal and informal networks could have an influence on an individual's career, but not all participants reported using them. Forty-four participants ($n = 22$ men and $n = 22$ women) reported using networks, including both internal and external networks. Fifteen of the participants ($n = 8$ men and $n = 7$ women) reported that networks were not a relevant feature of their career; however some of these participants discussed using informal mentors. Eleven of these participants were employed in smaller organizations in regional areas where the opportunities for networking internally were limited due to the smaller number of employees. However, some of these employees indicated they mixed socially with their colleagues outside of the workplace.

While none of the men mentioned joining specific men's networks, 10 of the women discussed formal and informal women's networks. They viewed these as important in (a) counteracting their male-dominated workplaces, (b) identifying career opportunities, (c) networking with women in similar situations as themselves, (d) role modeling and mutual support, and (e) attracting business.

With regard to organizational factors, opportunities for training and development were identified from the extant literature (Tharenou et al., 1994) as a potential influence on career. The research demonstrated that a number of participants who began their career in smaller or regionally based accounting firms did not stay long in that situation due to the lack of further training and career opportunities. The smaller firms were viewed as an initial training ground before moving on to larger metropolitan-based organizations. Ten of the participants ($n = 4$ men and $n = 6$ women) actually admitted that one of the reasons for their job change was to move to an organization that offered more opportunities for training and development. This finding is in line with the protean career emphasis on a self-directed career move to further one's skills and experience (Hall, 1996b).

The importance that participants placed on training and development was also highlighted by 11 participants ($n = 6$ men and $n = 5$ women), who listed continued learning, and 8 participants ($n = 6$ men and $n = 2$ women), who listed continued development, when conceptualizing career and success. Thus, it is clear that both the men and women agreed that training and education played an important role in their career experience. Without it, they believed that they would not have had the skills or abilities to perform their work or pursue other career opportunities. Undertaking such learning also suggests a degree of career commitment on behalf of the participants, as they were prepared to invest time and resources into such career management strategies. The question arising from these findings is whether the regulatory framework of the accounting profession, which demands a certain level of educational qualifications and continued training and development, results in greater career investment in training compared to other professions.

Gaining work experience is another human capital attribute that can influence career experiences (Kanter, 1977; Larwood & Gattiker, 1987; Melamed, 1996; Powell & Mainiero, 1992; Tharenou et al., 1994). Participants were asked if they had any key challenges or particular work experiences that they felt had influenced their career experience. Work experience refers to undertaking particular projects or tasks during their working life. Fifteen participants ($n = 8$ men and $n = 7$ women) cited key challenges or particular work experience that they believed had an influence on their career experience, including obtaining site or operational experience; an overseas posting; or being given significant responsibilities, such as managing an office or business unit. Both the men and women agreed that such challenges provided them with the opportunity to demonstrate their skills to others, increase their knowledge and experience, and increase their confidence; in addition, the challenges opened other career opportunities to them. These opportunities are reflected in the following comment by Adrian, a partner in a professional services firm.

> Most people when they look back no matter how old or young they are, or whatever they have done, and someone says what is your best moment, they usually pick a moment where someone threw them in the deep end. There is nothing to get you out of your comfort zone like a secondment [posting] to a foreign country.... The turning point for me is my secondment to Africa, which is ironic. It was so far out of the comfort zone. In my case there were very few expatriates around and so that made me the international expert in an area that I was just learning about. I was way out of my comfort zone, but I learnt a lot very quickly in an environment that was conducive to all that. Funnily enough, that was where my career propelled forward, even

though that's not why I had gone to Africa. (Adrian, partner at a professional services firm, age 38)

An important theme to emerge from the research was that many participants believed that undertaking a variety of work experiences and challenging work were critical in maintaining an interest in their career and keeping them "energized" (as highlighted by the following comment).

It's a real re-invigorater for me in terms of wanting to stay and seeing how I can contribute. I would probably not be having the same energized conversation with you if I was only doing audit work. I learned long ago in reflecting on this that I thrive on doing different things, and the things I have learned the most from have not necessarily been the things I trained for. For what has been important is being prepared to have a go at different things and that might be as small as different clients, and finding out through that process what I am not really suited for.... So rather than changing jobs and thinking "oops wrong job for me, for my personality type," I've done that by taking on different experiences. I sometimes wonder whether people take that time to reflect about their experiences when they move jobs. (Susan, partner at a professional services firm, age 43)

The culture of an organization has an influence on the work environment, performance, staff morale and satisfaction and, ultimately, the career experience of individuals (Kanter, 1977; Marshall, 1995; Powell & Mainiero, 1992; Tharenou et al., 1994). An important theme that emerged from this research is that participants conceptualized organizational culture in terms of the social fabric of their organization and the nature of the work environment. Fifteen participants ($n = 9$ men and $n = 6$ women) conceptualized career in relation to a good work environment. The cultures of the professional services firms, for example, were described by participants in both positive and negative terms. The positive aspects related to the young, supportive peer culture that characterized the top four firms. Participants reported that this atmosphere had a positive influence on their career. The culture encouraged and promoted extensive training, experience, and career progression, particularly among the younger employees.

In contrast, however, the participants also described the professional services firms as having an aggressive, high performance-focused culture with long working hours. In fact, 3 men indicated that this culture was a reason for them to make a career change into academia ($n = 2$) and to a smaller firm ($n = 1$).

I just wanted to get out. I was tired of the pressure, the culture, and I didn't want to spend the rest of my life with those people. They didn't understand why I felt a need to move. (Gary, accounting lecturer, age 42)

The age of the participants appeared to influence their willingness to tolerate the organizational culture in the professional services firm. While they were young, the participants found the culture supportive. Their age also meant it was easier to work the longer hours, since they tended not to have family commitments. In contrast, as participants got older, married, and had children, the long working hours made it difficult for them to balance work and family; thus, their willingness to tolerate such a culture decreased.

When participants in this research were asked about organizational culture, 10 of the women referred to an "old boys' club" existing within their organization. They believed that this culture had a negative influence on their career experience, including (a) decreased job satisfaction, (b) inhibited progression within the organization, (c) decreased levels of career encouragement, and (d) negative attitudes towards balancing work and family. Ironically, some of the firms where the participants believed an old boys' culture existed promote themselves as "Employers of Choice" and "family friendly." Van Vianen and Fischer (2002) and Marshall (1995) similarly found that many women are uncomfortable working in such male-dominated organizations because they feel pressure to adopt behaviors that are incongruent with their own values.

One of the most significant findings to emerge from the research was that, in contrast to theorists such as Allred, Snow, and Miles (1996), Arthur and Rousseau (1996), and Hall (1996a), the overwhelming majority of participants ($n = 27$ men and $n = 28$ women) believed organizations should play a proactive role in career management. They believed organizational career management helped to provide them with career encouragement, identify career opportunities, and crystallize their own career goals. Where it was not provided, participants were left feeling isolated from the organization, vulnerable, and unsure of their future career path. Those individuals wanting greater organizational career management tended to be the participants who experienced more traditional careers. Most participants believed that organizational career management had an important influence on their early career experience, when they were not always certain of their future career direction. For example, the organization can help identify career paths for employees when their knowledge of the organization's hierarchy is limited. The participants also wanted greater organizational career management during their midcareer as their career started to plateau or as they became bored in the job. The real concern for organizations is that many of the participants in the research who indicated anxiety and dissatisfaction were the most valued, highly skilled, and senior employees in the organization. The organization risks losing these highly valued individuals if it fails to acknowledge their need for proactive career management.

CONCLUSION

The research discussed in this chapter provides an illustration of how men and women enact their careers. The results demonstrate that men and women enact similar careers in their early adulthood stage, when they are focused on pursuing career ambitions. Both genders also experience similar careers in the preretirement stage, as they begin to move toward phased retirement, part-time work, or pursuing personal goals. The main area of difference in their career histories centered on the midcareer stages, when women's careers are characterized by balance; that is, a focus on balancing work and family commitments, as compared to those of men, which are primarily focused on challenge, i.e. pursuing promotions and also providing financial security for their families. This key difference was noted by Powell and Mainiero (1992) in their seminal work *Cross currents in the river of time*.

An emerging theme of the research is that the majority of men and women tended to reach a maintenance stage in their career by their early to mid 30s, when their career progression plateaued. This timing contrasts with the stage theory proposed by Super (1957), who believed that the maintenance phase began around 45. Is this difference due to participants in the current research experiencing a much more rapid career progression in the early career and establishment phases? If so, why are individuals reaching a plateau at a much younger age? There could be a number of reasons to explain this trend.

First, many of the participants interviewed for this research began employment with their organization as part of a graduate development program. Programs for recent university graduates are a feature of Australian organizations (both public and private). The purpose is to recruit high-performing graduates immediately after they have completed their university studies and involves the graduates rotating through various sections of an organization over a 12-24 month period. The graduate receives considerable training and development. It is a highly competitive process to be recruited for such a program. It is a form of talent management by the organization. Perhaps one of the reasons for participants reaching a plateau quite early is that they have been fast tracked as graduates. The second main reason relates back again to the professional nature of accounting firms and the desire of participants to become partners, which causes the individuals to be focused on rapid career progression.

With regard to the career plateau, it was demonstrated in this study that a number of participants ($n = 6$ men and $n = 5$ women) viewed this as a "crossroads" in their career. They had attained objective success, but were still interested in further challenges or development (subjective success). Some of the participants believed that the organization should be playing a better role in helping them to navigate this stage of their career. Armstrong-Stassen (2008) similarly found that older managerial and professional employees with high work centrality, and who believed that they had the ability to learn and develop new skills, were significantly less likely to experience job content plateauing than those with lower levels of work centrality and learning self-efficacy. Furthermore, employees who perceived greater support from their organization reported significantly less job content plateauing than those who lacked such support (Armstrong-Stassen, 2008).

In further contrast to Super's (1957) stage theory, in this research it was identified that there was an additional stage prior to retirement that participants experienced. While the maintenance phase lasted from the 30s to the late 40s, the preretirement stage commenced from the early 50s onwards. It was in the preretirement stage that participants began to discuss the issue of retirement. Some individuals were content to continue working full time up until retirement; others mentioned reducing their work to part time, while still others hoped to continue some form of paid or unpaid work post retirement. There could be a number of reasons for this trend, including (a) financial reasons around retirement planning; (b) increased life expectancy and hence better health of individuals, which means they can work longer; and (c) increased desire to remain part of a community (i.e., via work).

In relation to the findings of Sullivan and Mainiero (2007), the study confirms that the majority of men followed an alpha career pattern, that is, challenge, authenticity, and balance. The majority of women in the research followed the beta career path of challenge, balance, and authenticity. Like Sullivan and Mainiero (2007), this study also found that there was a minority of men who followed the beta career as well as women who followed an alpha career. It was typically the younger men in the research who pursued a beta career, with many of the alpha pattern men also expressing a desire for greater work-life balance. This desire may be a feature of the younger generations, X and Y, whose definitions of career and success reflect more subjective conceptualizations (see Gentry, Griggs, Deal, & Mondore, this volume, for a discussion of generational differences).

In this study it was also revealed that many participants enacted traditional careers. It should be noted here, however, that this result may be due to the sample chosen for the study. To achieve partner status in an accounting firm requires following a structured linear career path. Furthermore, the very nature of the accounting profession requires individuals to undertake continuous training and professional education throughout their career. Many women noted that they chose not to take an extended break from the workforce to have children as it would be difficult to maintain their professional qualifications (as expressed by the participant below).

> Yes, that's purposely why I kept working and could do it part time. It was a conscious decision that if you were out of the workforce too long, then things change too quickly.... Not if you want to maintain a certain level. (Christine, senior associate at a regional accounting firm, age 37).

The structured nature of an academic career or university environment also led some participants to follow a more traditional career. The question for future researchers is whether Australian organizations are more suited to traditional careers. McDonald, Brown, and Bradley (2005), for example, in their study of managers in the Australian public service, found that a traditional career based on length of service, geographic mobility, and a steady climb up the corporate hierarchy is still the dominant model in some organizations. However, the trend toward protean careers is evident and is more pronounced for women than for men.

Also demonstrated in this research was that an individual's career history was strongly linked to his or her definitions of career and success. Early on in the career, the emphasis tended to be on objective definitions of success (i.e., linear progression). However, as individuals progressed through life and career, their conceptualization of success shifted to more subjective definitions, such as seeking out personal fulfillment and development or a greater work-life balance. Interestingly, both men and women often shared similar conceptualizations of career and success. This similarity was evidenced by the fact that both men and women in the study re-evaluated their career during their 30s and 40s when they got to a crossroads or plateau in their career. Pringle and McCulloch-Dixon (2003) referred to this re-evaluation as "reassessment" and found that it was a feature of women's careers. The findings also supported the work of Baruch (2004), whose model of multidirectional career paths suggests that there was no one way or means of defining success. Nash and Stevenson (2004) also recognized how important it was for each person to understand and develop his or her unique definition of success over time.

The results relating to the third research question, whether there were gender differences in the factors that constrained or enabled career enactment, showed that both men and women had many similar experiences and attitudes toward the role of interpersonal and organizational factors in their career, however, there were a number of noteworthy emerging themes. First, both the men and women highlighted the paucity of access to mentors during the maintenance phase of their career or when they had reached senior levels in their organization. The paucity resulted in 5 men and women seeking out the assistance of external coaches. While the men used external coaches to crystallize career goals, the women sought external coaches to act as role models in their career.

Linked to this theme was the finding that the majority of participants also believed that the organization should play a greater role in providing career management. Barnett and Bradley (2007) similarly found that in a study of 90 Australian employees, organizational support for career development activities and employee participation in career management behaviors were positively related to employee career satisfaction.

Implications for Future Research

Given that this study was based on a small sample size and limited only to the accounting profession, there are a number of issues needing further research. First, research needs to explore the career histories of a much larger sample of men and women to determine whether the alpha and beta career patterns are applicable. Such research could investigate whether younger generations (particularly men) are more interested in a beta career so that they can have more time with the family.

Second, this research suggests that the traditional career is far from "dead," as proposed by Arthur and Rousseau (1996). It has been demonstrated in this study that traditional careers are still alive in accounting firms, the corporate sector, and in academia. The careers of many of the participants were still focused on progressing up the organizational hierarchy, whether to partner, to senior manager or chief financial officer, or to senior lecturer or associate professor. The question for future researchers to explore is whether such a structured career path is unique to accounting professionals or is common across a range of occupations. Do some professions lend themselves better to a traditional career? Participants in this research who worked in smaller firms or were self-employed tended to follow more boundaryless careers, so does organization size also influence the nature of career enactment?

Given that the majority of participants in this research were employed on a permanent basis, perhaps the boundaryless career is only relevant for casual or contract-based individuals. For example, the woman mentioned earlier in this chapter, who enacted a boundaryless career, was actually employed on a casual basis as both an elementary teacher and an accountant.

Third, in this research it has been emphasized that an individual's career history was often influenced by how he or she viewed career and success. More in-depth research is needed that explores what men and women want out of a career. If they have specific career ambitions, such as achieving partner status, then this goal may influence whether they pursue a traditional or nontraditional career. The majority of men and women in the study reported that an important definition of career and success was to have a good work-life balance. This goal obviously influenced the career path of many of the women, but only a few of the men. Will the changing attitudes of generations X and Y influence how career and success is defined? Will this change in attitudes, in turn, influence the way careers are enacted? What happens to individuals once they have attained their own idea of career success and what does this attainment mean for any future career paths? For example, it was noted in this chapter that once some participants reached partner status (their original objective view of success), they discussed pursuing more subjective types of career success, such as charitable work. Career and success are, therefore, reconceptualized again once individuals reach a certain point. This finding leads to the next implication regarding crossroads.

Fourth, further research needs to uncover what happens to individuals when they reach a crossroads in their career. What causes the men and women to reconceptualize their definitions of career and success? Have personal circumstances (such as having a family) changed their view of success or is their changed view due to achieving initial career goals? What role may mentors, networks, or the organization have in helping individuals navigate this crossroads in their career? As this research demonstrated, some individuals sought out external coaches to help them navigate the crossroads, while others wanted greater career management from the organization.

Fifth, the role of coaches is an area that needs further research. Is there a role for external coaches to assist employees as they navigate a difficult stage in their career? Who should provide such coaching and assume responsibility for the cost? What qualifications do these external coaches possess? Although there has been a great deal of research on mentoring (see Baugh & Sullivan, this volume), relatively little research has examined career coaches.

Finally, given that the majority of participants believed the organization should play a greater role in providing career management, future research needs to explore the expectations of individuals. What types of career management practices do employees believe organizations should provide? Do organizations feel it is beneficial to provide such career management practices? What impact would such practices have on an individual's career, and is that impact different for men and women?

Implications for Practice

One of the key themes to emerge from this research is the emphasis many participants placed on "authenticity," or subjective definitions of career and success. Both men and women expressed the desire for personal growth, continued challenge, and development. This emphasis tended to occur when the individuals reached a crossroads or plateau in their career. The message for organizations is that just because individuals may reach a physical plateau in their career, they may still be interested in continuing active development of their identity and career. As Super's (1984) theory of the self-concept suggests, an individual's identity development is a lifelong, rather than just an early career phenomenon. The lesson for organizations that wish to retain senior employees is that they will need to understand how to enhance the commitment and satisfaction of their senior employees by ensuring ongoing learning and development.

Given that a number of participants identified that "leaving a legacy" was important to them, organizations need to harness this desire among the senior employees. They could be used as mentors to help foster the career growth of the younger employees, who identified a need for career direction and advice in their early career.

In this research it was demonstrated that many individuals believe organizations should provide greater career management strategies in order to help foster their career commitment and provide future career direction. One method may be to ensure that a section on career planning is included as part of any performance appraisal process. Organizations may also assist employees by identifying career opportunities or providing them with the training and development they require to progress to roles that meet their needs. Employees who plan their career tend to know what positions they are striving for, but need the organization's help in facilitating their progress. Career management strategies, such as talent programs or high performer fast tracks, may assist the latter in achieving their goals. Given the focus and determination of those with a planned career, their goals need to be acknowledged and accommodated by the organization, or they may be quick to leave the organization in order to fulfill their career plan elsewhere.

Given that a number of participants chose to leave their organization to establish their own business or to seek out a more flexible career, organizations need to recognize that providing a workplace and a career path that offer flexibility is key to retaining staff. This recognition may become increasingly important as the emphasis on work-family balance may not only be important to women but also to a growing number of men, as well.

In summary, the success of a journey depends a lot on the external factors influencing the trip. Similarly, a career also is subject to the influences of a range of personal, social, and organizational factors and, therefore, does not occur in isolation. Individuals and organizations need to recognize this fact and view career as a journey that occurs in a dynamic and constantly changing environment.

REFERENCES

Adamson, S., Doherty, N., & Viney, C. (1998). The meaning of career revisited: Implications for theory and practice. *British Journal of Management, 9*, 251-259.

Allred, B., Snow, C., & Miles, R. (1996). Characteristics of managerial careers of the 21st century. *Academy of Management Executive, 10*(4), 17–27.

Armstrong-Stassen, M. (2008). Factors associated with job content plateauing among older workers. *Career Development International, 13*, 594-613.

Arthur, M., Inkson, K., & Pringle, J. (1999). *The new careers: Individual action and economic change.* London: Sage.

Arthur, M., Khapova, S., & Wilderom, C. (2005). Career success in a boundaryless career world. *Journal of Organizational Behavior, 26*, 177-202.

Arthur, M. & Rousseau, D. (1996). A career lexicon for the 21st century. *Academy of Management Executive, 10*(4), 28–39.

Bardwick, J. (1986). *The plateauing trap.* New York: Bantam Books.

Barnett, B., & Bradley, L. (2007). The impact of organizational support for career development on career satisfaction. *Career Development International, 12*, 617-636.

Baruch, Y. (2004). Transforming careers—From linear to multidirectional career paths: Organizational and individual perspectives. *Career Development International, 9*, 58-73.

Baugh, S. G., & Sullivan, S. E. (2009). Developmental relationships and the new workplace realities: A life span perspective on career development through mentoring. In S. G. Baugh & S. E. Sullivan (Eds.), *Research in careers: Vol. 1. Maintaining focus, energy, and options over the career* (pp. 27-50). Charlotte, NC: Information Age.

Bown-Wilson, D., & Parry, E. (2009). Career plateauing in older workers: Contextual and psychological drivers. In S. G. Baugh & S. E. Sullivan (Eds.), *Research in careers: Vol. 1. Maintaining focus, energy, and options over the career* (pp. 75-105). Charlotte, NC: Information Age.

Burke, R., Rothstein, M., & Bristor, J. (1995). Interpersonal networks of managerial and professional women and men: Descriptive characteristics. *Women in Management Review, 10*(1), 21-27.

Burke, R., & Vinnicombe, S. (2006). Supporting women's career advancement. *Women in Management Review, 21*(1), 7-9.

Cabrera, E. (2007). Opting out and opting in: Understanding the complexities of women's career transitions. *Career Development International, 12*, 218-237.

Cochran, L. (1990). Narrative as a paradigm for careers research. In R. Young & W. Borgen (Eds), *Methodological approaches to the study of careers* (pp. 85-102). New York: Praeger.

Cohen, A. (1991). Career stage as a moderator of the relationships between organizational commitment and its outcomes: A meta-analysis. *Journal of Occupational Psychology, 64*, 253-268.

Cohen, L., & Mallon, M. (2001). My brilliant career?: Using stories as a methodological tool in careers research. *International Studies of Management and Organization, 31*(3), 48–68.

Cross, C., & Linehan, M. (2006). Barriers to advancing female careers in the high-tech sector: Empirical evidence from Ireland. *Women in Management Review, 21*(1), 28-39.

Flick, U. (1998). *An introduction to qualitative research*. Thousand Oaks, CA: SAGE.

Gentry, W. A., Griggs, T. L., Deal, J. J., & Mondore, S. P. (2009). Generational differences in attitudes, beliefs, and preferences about development and learning at work. In S. G. Baugh & S. E. Sullivan (Eds.), *Research in careers: Vol. 1. Maintaining focus, energy, and options over the career* (pp. 51-74). Charlotte, NC: Information Age.

Gunz, H., & Heslin, P. (2005). Reconceptualising career success. *Journal of Organizational Behavior, 26*, 105-111.

Hall, D. (1996a). *Career development*. Boston: Boston University Press.

Hall, D. (1996b). Protean careers of the twenty-first century. *Academy of Management Executive, 10*(4), 8-16.

Heslin, P. (2005). Conceptualising and evaluating career success. *Journal of Organizational Behavior, 26*, 113-136.

Kanter, R. (1977). *Men and women of the corporation*. New York: Basic Books.

Keller, R. (2008). Make the most of mentoring. *Journal of Accountancy, 206*(2), 76-80.

Knabi, G. (1999). An investigation into the differential profile of predictors of objective and subjective career success. *Career Development International, 4*, 212–225.

Kram, K. (1985). *Mentoring at work*. Glenview, IL: Scott, Foresman & Co.

Larwood, L., & Gattiker, U. (1987). A comparison of the career paths used by successful women and men. In B. Gutek & L. Larwood (Eds.), *Women's career development* (pp. 129-156). Beverly Hills, CA: SAGE.

Levinson, D., Darrow, C., Klein, E., Levinson, J., & McKee, B. (1978). *The seasons of a man's life*. New York: Alfred Knopf.

Levinson, D., & Levinson, J. (1996). *The seasons of a woman's life*. New York: Alfred Knopf.

Lyness, K., & Thompson, D. (2000). Climbing the corporate ladder: Do female and male executives follow the same route? *Journal of Applied Psychology, 85*, 86–101.

Lynn, S., Cao, L., & Horn, B. (1996). The influence of career stage on the work attitudes of male and female accounting professionals. *Journal of Organizational Behavior, 17*, 135-149.

Mainiero, L. A., & Sullivan, S. E. (2005). Kaleidoscope careers: An alternative explanation for the opt-out revolution. *Academy of Management Executive*, *19*(1), 106-123.

Marshall, J. (1989). Re-visioning career concepts: A feminist invitation. In M. Arthur, D. Hall, & B. Lawrence (Eds.), *Handbook of career theory* (pp. 275-292). Cambridge, England: Cambridge University Press.

Marshall, J. (1995). *Women managers moving on: Exploring career and life choices*. London: Routledge.

McColl-Kennedy, J., & Dann, S. (2000). Success: What do women and men really think it means? *Asia Pacific Journal of Human Resources*, *38*(3), 29-45.

McDonald, P., Brown, K., & Bradley, L. (2005). Have traditional career paths given way to protean ones? Evidence from senior managers in the Australian public sector. *Career Development International*, *10*, 109-129.

Melamed, T. (1996). Career success: An assessment of a gender-specific model. *Journal of Occupational and Organizational Psychology*, *69*, 217-244.

Nash, L., & Stevenson, H. (2004). Success that lasts. *Harvard Business Review*, *82*(2), 102–109.

Ornstein, S., & Isabella, L. (1990). Age vs. stage models of career attitudes of women: A partial replication and extension. *Journal of Vocational Behavior*, *36*, 1-19.

Osipow, S. (1983). *Theories of career development*. Englewood Cliffs, NJ: Prentice-Hall.

Powell, G., & Mainiero, L. (1992). Cross-currents in the river of time: Conceptualizing the complexities of women's careers. *Journal of Management*, *18*, 215-237.

Pringle, J., & McCulloch-Dixon, K. (2003). Re-incarnating life in the careers of women. *Career Development International*, *8*, 291–300.

Richardson, C. (1996). Snakes and ladders? The differing career patterns of male and female accountants. *Women in Management Review*, *11*(4), 13–19.

Smith-Ruig, T. (2008). Making sense of careers through the lens of a path metaphor. *Career Development International*, *13*, 20-32.

Strauss, A., & Corbin, J. (1998). *Basics of qualitative research: Techniques and procedures for developing grounded theory*. Thousand Oaks, CA: SAGE.

Sullivan, S. E. (1999). The changing nature of careers: A review and research agenda. *Journal of Management*, *25*, 457-484.

Sullivan, S., & Mainiero, L. (2007). The changing nature of gender roles, alpha/beta careers and work-life issues: Theory-driven implications for human resource management. *Career Development International*, *12*, 238-263.

Super, D. (1957). *The psychology of careers*. New York: Harper and Row.

Super. D. (1984). A life-span, life-space approach to career development. In D. Brown & L. Brooks (Eds.), *Career choice and development* (pp. 197-261). San Francisco: Jossey-Bass.

Terjesen, S. (2005). Senior women managers' transition to entrepreneurship: Leveraging embedded career capital. *Career Development International*, *10*, 246-259.

Tharenou, P. (2009). Self-initiated international careers: Gender differences and career outcomes. In S. G. Baugh & S. E. Sullivan (Eds.), *Research in careers: Vol.*

1. Maintaining focus, energy, and options over the career (pp. 197-226). Charlotte, NC: Information Age.

Tharenou, P., Latimer, S., & Conroy, D. (1994). How do you make it to the top? An examination of influences on women's and men's managerial advancement. *Academy of Management Journal, 37,* 899–932.

Travers, C., & Pemberton, C. (2000). Think career global, but act local: Understanding networking as a culturally differentiated career skill. In M. Davidson & R. Burke (Eds.), *Women in management: Current research issues.* London: SAGE.

van Emmerik, H., Baugh, S. G., & Euwema, M. (2005). Who wants to be a mentor? An examination of attitudinal, instrumental, and social motivational components. *Career Development International, 10,* 310-324.

van Vianen, A., & Fischer, A. (2002). Illuminating the glass ceiling: The role of organizational culture preferences. *Journal of Occupational and Organizational Psychology, 75,* 315-338.

White, B., Cox, C., & Cooper, C. (1992). *Women's career development: A study of high flyers.* Oxford, England: Blackwell Business.

Wise, A., & Millward, L. (2005). The experiences of voluntary career change in 30-somethings and implications for guidance. *Career Development International, 10,* 400-417.

CHAPTER 8

SELF-INITIATED INTERNATIONAL CAREERS

Gender Differences and Career Outcomes

Phyllis Tharenou

International careers were once the province of company-assigned expatriates; now, however, professionals often initiate and finance their own expatriation in order to take advantage of lucrative work opportunities abroad, particularly in developed or mature economies which rely on foreigners to supplement a shortage of skilled workers (Cheng & Yang, 1998; Organisation for Economic Cooperation and Development [OECD], 2002, 2005), but also in developing or emerging economies (Docquier & Marfouk, 2004; Saxenian, 2002; OECD, 2008). Self-initiated expatriates generally choose to live and work abroad for work and career development as well as for cultural and personal experiences, relocating to a country of their own choosing, often with no definite time frame in mind (Harrison, Shaffer, & Bhaskar-Shrinivas, 2004; Myers & Pringle, 2005). By contrast, company-assigned expatriates are professionals deployed by their organization to complete a time-based task or organizational goal in a country of the company's choosing. Unlike company expatriates, self-initiated expatriates normally resign from their job and find work either before they leave their country or when they are abroad (e.g., Harrison et al., 2004; Inkson, Arthur, Pringle, & Barry, 1997; Lee, 2005; Myers &

Maintaining Focus, Energy, and Options Over the Career
pp. 197–226

Pringle, 2005; Richardson & Mallon, 2005; Suutari & Brewster, 2000; Vance, 2005). They also could be entrepreneurs seeking to set up ventures in their adopted countries or across their adopted and home countries (Saxenian, 2002, 2005). Self-initiated expatriates comprise the majority of expatriates (Doherty, Dickmann, & Mills, 2007; Hugo, Rudd, & Harris, 2003; OECD, 2002, 2005).

Company-assigned expatriation has traditionally been the province of men. In the United States, only about 20% of company expatriates are women (Cartus, 2007; GMAC Global Relocation Services, 2006, 2007), with the proportion usually lower in other countries (Tung, 2004), although there are some exceptions (e.g., United Kingdom [UK]: 28%, Forster, 1997; Finland: 27%, Jokinen, Brewster, & Suutari, 2008). Scholars paint a picture of an "expatriate glass ceiling" (Forster, 1999; Insch, McIntyre, & Napier, 2008) or a "glass border" (Linehan & Walsh, 1999) that prevents women from gaining company assignments. In stark contrast, studies of professionals of chiefly Western origin, especially from the United States and UK (Doherty et al., 2007), New Zealand (Inkson & Myers, 2003) and Australia (Tharenou, 2003), indicate that female professionals comprise about half of self-initiated expatriates. Finland is the exception: only 30% of self-expatriated Finns were women (Jokinen et al., 2008). Migration statistics gathered over several decades show that more than half the skilled migrants from Ireland, Australia (especially young adults), and the Philippines were women (Kofman, 2005). Suggesting the importance of self-initiated expatriation for women, in one Finnish study there were more than twice as many female self-initiated expatriates as female company-assigned expatriates (Suutari & Brewster, 2000) and, in another, a still considerable and similar percentage (Jokinen et al., 2008). Women may self-initiate expatriation as much as men as a way of taking advantage of international career opportunities that they cannot gain through company assignment.

Scholars show that professionals who self-initiate expatriation as opposed to being company-assigned are living "boundaryless" careers (Inkson et al., 1997; Jokinen et al., 2008; Myers & Inkson, 2003). In boundaryless career theory, individuals are self-directed and manage their own career rather than having it managed by an employer (Arthur & Rousseau, 1996; Mirvis & Hall, 1996). They are mobile across organizations rather than being bounded by them; they have an external (i.e., seeking networks, information) rather than an internal focus; they are motivated by intrinsic rather than extrinsic (i.e., career advancement) rewards; and they value freedom and growth more than hierarchical advancement (Arthur & Rousseau, 1996; Mirvis & Hall, 1996). An employee who has a boundaryless career orientation is likely to be proactive and leave firms, and perhaps countries, to seek opportunities in new firms and countries (c.f. Hall, 2004).

They may develop their own career by expatriating, then repatriating, then re-expatriating, so exploiting available networks, information, and opportunities. Women may exhibit boundaryless careers because career interruptions (e.g., due to family responsibilities) may compel them to change jobs and organizations or to initiate self-employment and entrepreneurial ventures. Gender stereotypes may also mean that women have to be proactive in managing their career; for example, changing organizations to be able to rise up the managerial hierarchy (Brett, Stroh, & Reilly, 1992; Tharenou, 2002a). This proactive approach may result in women self-initiating expatriation to manage their career (Fitzgerald & Howe-Walsh, 2008; Myers & Pringle, 2005).

In this chapter is a review of the literature on participation in international careers, especially that covering self-initiated expatriation, to explain why women are taking up self-initiated expatriation as a new option that may provide them with career opportunities they would not otherwise have (such as company assignments). I begin by contrasting company-assigned and self-initiated expatriates to clarify the difference between them, and then follow by examining gender differences in these two expatriation categories. Next, I then consider why professionals embark upon company-assigned or self-initiated expatriation and review gender differences to explain why women follow international careers not managed by organizations. Expatriates also repatriate and women may repatriate more frequently than men for reasons that suggest self-initiated expatriation is not always a successful or satisfactory career option for them. In the process of determining why female self-initiated expatriates repatriate, I examine why, in general, self-initiated and company-assigned expatriates repatriate, with a review of the gender differences informing the reasons. Women may also gain less from expatriation and repatriation than men; therefore, I examine the consequences of expatriation for career outcomes, again with an analysis of the gender differences affecting outcomes, and conclude with a look at re-expatriation. Finally, I summarize the relationship between gender and international careers.

TYPES OF INTERNATIONAL CAREERS

Company-Assigned Versus Self-Initiated Expatriates

The obvious difference between company-assigned expatriates and self-initiated expatriates is that the former are sent by their company on fixed-term assignments, whereas the latter organize and finance their own expatriation, generally for an unknown time period, and find their own work abroad. Professionals who initiate expatriation differ from company-assigned expatriates in ways that reflect the more exploratory nature of self-initiated expatriation. Compared with company-assigned expatriates, self-initiated expatriates are slightly younger; they are more often women, single, or have a partner who is employed or who was born in the host country; and they have fewer children or none at all (Doherty et al., 2007; Suutari & Brewster, 2000). They are, therefore, more likely to be in an "exploring life" stage with a career-oriented partner and are more likely to have married while abroad.

Consistent with their expatriating to seek work, self-initiated expatriates, by comparison with company-assigned expatriates, are more likely to work for foreign private and public sector organizations than for private companies based in their home country. They tend to have shorter organization tenure, are more often employed on temporary contracts rather than permanent ones, fill expert roles more than managerial roles, and are at lower managerial levels (Doherty et al., 2007; Jokinen et al., 2008; Suutari & Brewster, 2000). Self-initiated expatriates more often move to less challenging roles with lower salaries than the home-based position that they leave (e.g., Thang, MacLachlan, & Goda, 2002). By comparison, company expatriates move to comparable levels with more responsible roles (Doherty et al., 2007) and are more likely to be high flyers or rising stars. Moreover, self-initiated expatriates may expatriate not only to gain jobs, but also to pursue entrepreneurial ventures and to test business ideas in countries where opportunities abound and policies are welcoming (Jokinen et al., 2008; Saxenian, 2005). That is not to say that company expatriates do not have an entrepreneurial disposition, but entrepreneurship is not the focus of their international assignment (Doherty et al., 2007).

Despite self-initiated expatriates experiencing less favorable work status and conditions than their company counterparts (Suutari & Brewster, 2000), they have fewer plans to repatriate, are more willing to accept further international work and permanent stays abroad, and stay abroad longer (Doherty et al., 2007; Suutari & Brewster, 2000), perhaps contributing to a brain drain for their home country. If they do repatriate, they are likely to move to less challenging roles and to earn lower salaries than company expatriates who move to comparable or responsible roles and do not forego salary (Doherty et al., 2007). Hence, self-initiated expatriates have a riskier and more uncertain work environment, both abroad and on return, than do company expatriates.

Gender and Participation in, or Receptivity to, International Careers

Company-assigned expatriates are selected or approved by their company to move abroad to work, while self-initiated expatriates independently choose to expatriate. Sending an employee on an international posting is extremely costly (e.g., free accommodation of a high standard for the employee and family, schooling for children, yearly return trips home) (GMAC Global Relocation Services, 2008), which means that companies tend to minimize the number of employees they have abroad. Self-initiated expatriates, by contrast, are self-financing and larger numbers expatriate as compared to company-assigned expatriates. In order to access international career opportunities, which may otherwise not be available to them (Tung, 2004), women appear to self-initiate expatriation and, in general, do so in equal numbers to men.

Company-assigned expatriation. There are several reasons why most company-assigned expatriates are men. First, the positions are often senior management roles running subsidiaries abroad. Because women are less often managers and work at lower managerial levels than men (Tharenou, 1997), they may not be sufficiently represented in the applicant pools for selection for senior international positions (Altman & Shortland, 2008). Second, married women relocate for work less frequently than men because their partners are more often employed full time and have more substantial careers (Lyness & Thompson, 1997; Tharenou, 2008) and men are less inclined to relocate for their partners' careers than women (Feldman, 2001; Markham, 1987; Stroh, 1999). Therefore, fewer married women take international postings than married men. Third, women are less likely to be assigned abroad because of discriminatory practices based on unfounded male bias (Vance, Paik, & White, 2006); for example, male selectors believe that nationals in some host countries are prejudiced against female managers and that only men can be successful in a managerial role in those countries (Adler, 2002; Altman & Shortland, 2008; Tung, 2004), resulting in the selection of more men than women (Vance et al., 2006).

Yet, it cannot be claimed that there are fewer female company-assigned expatriates than male because women are less willing to expatriate. Most studies find that women are as willing to expatriate for work as men (Adler, 1984; Aryee, Chay, & Chew, 1996; Brett & Stroh, 1995; Lyness & Thompson, 1997; Stroh, Varma, & Valy-Durbin, 2000; Tharenou, 2003; Tung, 2004; Wan, Hui, & Tiang, 2002), although they may decline job offers to countries in which they would be accorded lower social status or where it is rare for women to be managers (Tung, 2004). Only a minority of studies has found that women are less willing to expatriate for work than men (Konopaske & Werner, 2005; Lowe, Downes, & Kroeck, 1999; Van der Velde, Bossink, & Jansen, 2005).

Women may expatriate to develop their career. Very little research has been conducted in this area. Results of a practitioner survey of company-assigned expatriates indicated that women more than men saw an international assignment as a way to enhance their resumé and make themselves more marketable (National Foreign Trade Council [NFTC], 2001). The top concern for women considering an assignment was its impact on their career development, while for men it was the impact of the assignment on their financial security.

Self-initiated expatriation. There is evidence that, like men, women translate their willingness to expatriate into self-initiated expatriation (Tharenou, 2008). Through self-selecting to expatriate, women are developing new career paths on their own initiative and are proactive in choosing to take advantage of opportunities abroad (Fitzgerald & Howe-Walsh, 2008). They may self-initiate expatriation as a career option because (a) companies do not assign them abroad as often as men; (b) they wish to leave the barriers to career advancement they encounter in the domestic workplace and try living in another country (Thang et al., 2002); (c) they see the value in developing their international experience; (d) they wish to take advantage of career opportunities in the global labor market; or (e) they accompany partners that are also seeking opportunities (Hearn, Jyrkinen, Piekkari, & Oinonen, 2008).

Women have also been shown to relocate domestically in order to advance, most often to leave behind barriers to their career development. And it pays off: women have realized more substantial promotions and increased rank than men as a result of relocating (Brett et al., 1992; Tharenou, 2002a). Further evidence suggests that professional women self-initiate expatriation more than men because they are not satisfied with their career progress at home (Suutari & Brewster, 2000; Thang et al., 2002), or to escape boredom, jobs, relationships, and a narrow life, unlike men, who most often do so for exploration and adventure (Myers & Pringle, 2005).

Nevertheless, there is little evidence to explain why women self-initiate expatriation as much as men and whether they do so as a way to develop international experience and advance their career. Are women using self-initiated expatriation as a new option for career development? The following research questions require examination:

1. Why do women self-initiate expatriation as much as men?
2. Why are women more often self-initiated expatriates than company-assigned expatriates?
3. Do women self-initiate expatriation to: (a) escape domestic barriers to career development and advancement, which appear to affect men less; (b) gain international experience because they cannot gain company international assignments to the same extent as men; (c) gain career advancement otherwise not available to them;

and/or (d) develop the global and international competencies that men are likely to gain through company assignments?

ANTECEDENTS TO PROFESSIONALS' BEGINNING INTERNATIONAL CAREERS

There is substantial evidence that explains why professionals participate in international careers (cf. Tharenou, 2006), although the distinction is rarely made between expatriation due to company assignment and that due to self-initiated expatriation.

Reasons Professionals Embark Upon an International Career

In the case of company expatriates, people who accept an international posting are often on a career fast track and are offered an assignment to run a subsidiary abroad and/or to develop their managerial and international competencies. Candidates are selected according to their technical skills, cross-cultural competence and adaptability, and willingness or motivation to expatriate (NFTC, 2001; PricewaterhouseCoopers, 2000; Stone, 1991; Stroh, Black, Mendenhall, & Gregersen, 2005). Partner employment and the ages of their children also influence who is considered (NFTC, 2001), since employees are more likely to accept an assignment when their partner does not have a career or when their children are not of high school age (GMAC Global Relocation Services, 2006, 2007; Tharenou, 2008).

Given that willingness to expatriate is a significant predictor of expatriation (Tharenou, 2008), it is important to understand why someone may be willing to move overseas. Tharenou (2006) reviewed the evidence and found four major factors: individual, organizational, family, and host country. With respect to individual attributes, professionals more willing to expatriate have positive attitudes toward and experiences with mobility: (a) they are more predisposed to moving, being more willing to relocate both generally and domestically and having a more positive attitude to new experiences; (b) they have greater personal agency for expatriation, as indicated by higher self-efficacy for working and living in a culture different from their own and a higher expectancy that expatriation will be instrumental in gaining them career benefits; and (c) they have more prior international or domestic relocation moves and experience. In relation to organizational factors, those more willing to expatriate are employed more often in companies with a strong international focus and with strong relocation support policies, especially for an expatriate's partner and family. With respect to family, professionals more willing to expatriate have fewer family responsibilities and a more supportive partner: (a) they are less likely to be married; (b) they are less likely to have an employed partner or a partner with a career; (c) they are more likely to have a partner who has positive attitudes toward and supports relocating in general and internationally; and (d) they are less likely to have children or children of high school age. The proposed host country also affects their willingness to relocate. Employees, especially women, are less willing to expatriate to culturally dissimilar countries or developing countries than to culturally similar countries or developed countries (see also Dupuis, Haines, & Saba, 2008). Surprisingly, the relationship between the explanatory factors and gender is rarely examined (cf. Tharenou, 2008).

The Role of Gender in Professionals' Embarking Upon an International Career

Before reviewing evidence for the role that gender differences play in participation in international careers, the underlying theory needs to be examined. The kaleidoscope career model can assist to explain when women participate in expatriation (Mainiero & Sullivan, 2005; Sullivan & Mainiero, 2008). The model suggests that the three parameters of challenge, balance, and authenticity (CBA) help to explain when gender differences influence career behavior. *Challenge* is engaging in activities that permit the individual to demonstrate responsibility, control, and autonomy while learning and growing. *Balance* is making decisions so that work and non-work aspects of life form a coherent whole. *Authenticity* involves being true to oneself during the resolution of personal development and work and non-work issues. Particular issues dominate at different points in one's life and usually one parameter takes center stage while the other parameters remain active but take on secondary roles. Women evaluate the choices and options visible through the lens of the kaleidoscope to determine the option that best suits their relationships, work constraints, and opportunities at that stage of their life.

Mainiero and Sullivan found that most women displayed a CBA career pattern (Mainiero & Sullivan, 2005; Sullivan & Mainiero, 2008): challenge was most important in early career, balance most important in mid-career, and authenticity most important in late career. Challenge, including ambition and advancement, tended to feature most prominently in early career, a time when balance and authenticity were often of secondary concern. A woman could decide to take a position that would offer more responsibility at the expense of flexibility, because challenge was more important to her. Women may expatriate when they are in early career and are single and childless, since the needs of others are not paramount at this time. In late early career and midcareer, balance increases in importance for most women, as marriage, child rearing and other responsibilities take over (Mainiero & Sullivan, 2005; Sullivan & Mainiero, 2008). Family responsibilities mean that family becomes a priority. Women's decisions and choices are strongly influenced by the needs of their children, partner, aging parents, and friends. These influences are assessed as part of the total career gestalt, and career ambitions may be adjusted to obtain a more flexible schedule. Hence, women may not expatriate for work reasons in late early career and mid-career when they have married and have children. Women may also stay abroad for their partner's career or they may repatriate if that benefits their partner's career. In late career, authenticity of leisure and business pursuits was central for most women (Mainiero & Sullivan, 2005; Sullivan & Mainiero, 2008). The desire for authenticity, being true to oneself, and making decisions that suit themselves dominated women's career and life decisions in late career.

By contrast, most men displayed a CAB career pattern (Mainiero & Sullivan, 2005; Sullivan & Mainiero, 2008). Challenge was most important in early careers (e.g., expatriating for career development); then in mid-career authenticity or concerns about the self were most important (e.g., staying abroad to satisfy career ambitions and aspirations rather than repatriating to reunite with and look after elderly parents and relatives); and in late career focusing on balance and spending time with family and others were most important (e.g., repatriating to retire and reunite with family at home).

Gender role theory also explains how family and career may differentially affect relocation for work by men and women. Gender role theory proposes that men and women are socialized to view relocation for work differently (Markham, 1987). Relocation supports married men's socialized role of family provider, in which work obligations have the highest priority. Married women, on the other hand, are socialized to view relocating for their career as inappropriate because it emphasizes the pursuit of personal advancement and threatens the traditional family roles of wife as caregiver and husband as provider (Markham, 1987). Women, therefore, feel pressured by society not to relocate and suffer role conflict and guilt when considering whether to relocate to advance their career, although single childless women, without partners to consider, do not feel the same social pressures and, therefore, have greater freedom to pursue work abroad (Tharenou, 2008). Married women, especially mothers, are expected to put family before work.

The research being reviewed, which was conducted chiefly with company-assigned expatriates, supports the explanation proposed by gender role theory that the gender differences in expatriation choices result from family versus career decisions (Dupuis et al., 2008; Hearn et al., 2008; Lyness & Thompson, 1997; Mercer, 2006a; NFTC, 2001; ORC Worldwide, 2007; Stroh et al., 2000; Tharenou, 2008; Tung, 2004).

Studies support family as presenting, by comparison with men, a greater barrier to women's choosing expatriation or being chosen by their company for expatriation (Hearn et al., 2008). Compared with male expatriates, female expatriates are more often single (half to three quarters of female expatriates are single versus a quarter of males), childless (about two thirds of female expatriates are childless versus about a third of males) (Mercer, 2006a; NFTC, 2001; ORC Worldwide, 2007) or have fewer children, are unaccompanied by a partner (Mercer, 2006a), or have a partner who works full-time (Hearn et al., 2008). Three quarters of women have a partner employed full time versus a quarter of men (Tung, 2004). The differences may be a result of the fact that female expatriates are younger than males. However, when male and female expatriates are matched (on age, education level, functional area, marital status, and management level), women still had fewer children than men (Tung, 2004). A fifth of female expatriates had children, whereas half of male expatriates did, consistent with children being a greater barrier to expatriation for mothers than for fathers.

It is not surprising, then, that studies show that having a family makes it difficult for a woman to consider an international career (Hearn et al., 2008). Women reported more restrictions to embarking on international assignments than men due to dual career (partner also with a career) and timing concerns (Lyness & Thompson, 1997). Both women and managers believed that having children was an obstacle to women considering an international assignment (Hearn et al., 2008; Stroh et al., 2000). As far as dual-earner couples are concerned, greater spousal willingness to relocate internationally was correlated with women reporting more readiness than men to accept an international assignment in culturally similar countries (Dupuis et al., 2008). Mothers were less willing than fathers to accept a posting in culturally dissimilar countries; yet when women were childless, they were more willing to accept an international assignment than childless men (Dupuis et al., 2008). The greater the proportion of the family income earned compared with their spouse, the more willing were men than women to accept an international assignment in both culturally similar and dissimilar countries (Dupuis et al., 2008). In the only inconsistent finding, having a spouse involved in a career was not related to women's or men's willingness to expatriate (Dupuis et al., 2008; Stroh et al., 2000). Having a family (a partner and/or children) was related to women being less able to translate their willingness to expatriate into search for an international job than men, the consequence being that women expatriated less often than men (Tharenou, 2008). Showing the important barrier that families are for women, women expatriated less often when they had partners and/or children than when they were childless singles, and women with families expatriated less often than men with families who, in turn, expatriated less often than unencumbered single childless males and females.

The inference from the results is that balance is an important consideration for expatriation when women are at the point in their life when they have family responsibilities. Overall, they do not make expatriation choices without considering their partner and children and the issue of balance is a central determining factor in their decision making (Mainiero & Sullivan, 2005). But when women are at the stage when they do not have family responsibilities, challenge can be their major focus and willingness to expatriate can translate into expatriation.

Despite family responsibilities proving to be a barrier to women engaging in international assignments, they are also barriers to men (Cartus, 2007). Hence, when they have family responsibilities, balance is also an important consideration in men's expatriation decisions (Mainiero & Sullivan, 2005). Human resource executives frequently identify dual-career issues as the reason employees (most of whom are in late early career or midcareer and are married men with children) refuse international assignments (Cartus, 2007; GMAC Global Relocation Services, 2006) and do not propose themselves as candidates (KPMG, 2006). Expatriation usually curtails a partner's employment and thus has a negative effect on the partner's career (Hearn et al., 2008). Partners—most of whom are women—often face insurmountable obstacles to gaining a job or practicing their chosen profession abroad because they (a) lack work visas, certification, or licensure; (b) have insufficient language skills; or (c) distrust local child care (Interchange Institute, 2004). In addition, moving to a foreign culture disrupts the education of high school age children (NFTC, 2001; PricewaterhouseCoopers, 2002, 2005); these studies are of chiefly male expatriates but the effect is also likely to occur for female expatriates. Having children of high school age was correlated with the reluctance of both women and men to accept international assignments (Van der Velde et al., 2005). Expatriates—mostly men—often left children at home to attend school (funded by their companies) because of concerns about safety and disruption to schooling (GMAC Global Relocation Services, 2006).Therefore, men also encounter family barriers to engaging in international assignments in late early career and midcareer.

Despite the evidence that family responsibilities reduce women's company-assigned and perhaps self-initiated expatriation more than men's, certain questions require research. These questions include:

1. Do family factors reduce women self-initiating expatriation as much as they reduce their participation in company-assigned expatriation?
2. Do career factors explain men's self-initiating expatriation as much as they account for their acceptance of international assignments for the company?
3. Does life stage interact with family and career to affect participation in self-initiated expatriation? Is the interaction affected by gender?

ANTECEDENTS OF PROFESSIONALS' REPATRIATION

Professionals not only self-initiate expatriation but also return home. Brain circulation helps reverse the brain drain through the repatriation of self-initiated expatriates, usually seeking new jobs in home-country organizations and also, on rare occasions, by establishing entrepreneurial ventures and new businesses at home (Myers & Inkson, 2003), especially when they repatriate to developing countries (Saxenian, 2005).

Making the decision to repatriate differs between company-assigned and self-initiated expatriates. Many company expatriates repatriate at the assignment's end through intracompany job transfer (GMAC Global Relocation Services, 2007, 2008). By contrast, most self-initiated expatriates must decide if they wish to repatriate and when. Unlike many company expatriates, they must resign their job and find a job at home prior to return, perhaps return unemployed and find a job once home, or establish a business at home and become self-employed (Dustmann & Kirchkamp, 2002; Inkson et al., 1997; Lidgard & Gilson, 2002; Suutari & Brewster, 2000). On rare occasions self-initiated expatriates transfer to jobs at home—like company expatriates—because their host-country employers have offices in their home country (Suutari & Brewster, 2000).

On occasion, company expatriates also need to decide whether to repatriate and when, rather than their repatriation occurring automatically at the end of the assignment's term. Company expatriates are increasingly being offered international assignments without the option of repatriation (GMAC Global Relocation Services, 2008) or a guarantee of a job on assignment completion (GMAC Global Relocation Services, 2007, 2008; ORC Worldwide, 2006; Tharenou, 2002b). Evidence indicates that fewer than half of North American expatriates are repatriated by intra-company transfer (Mercer, 2006b) and only about two thirds to three quarters of expatriates in countries other than the United States are transferred home (Mercer, 2006b). This means that at the end of their assignment, some company expatriates need to find a job with a new employer either abroad or at home (Suutari & Brewster, 2003) or, like self-initiated expatriates, to search for a job at home if they wish to repatriate. Therefore, for some company-assigned expatriates, the repatriation process is similar to that of self-initiated expatriates.

Why Company-Assigned Expatriates Repatriate

Little is known about why company-assigned expatriates choose to repatriate rather than stay abroad. Most of the evidence comes from studies that have examined why expatriates intend to quit assignments prematurely or intend to return early (Harrison et al., 2004). Only about five per cent of company expatriates return early (4.5% ORC Worldwide, 2007; 6%, GMAC Global Relocation Services, 2008). Expatriates most often intend to return early because of their own or their partner's failure to adjust to the culture abroad (Bhaskar-Shrinivas, Harrison, Shaffer, & Luk, 2005; Hechanova, Beehr, & Christiansen, 2003); job dissatisfaction (Bhaskar-Shrinivas et al., 2005; Hechanova et al., 2003); and personality issues linked to managing in a different culture (e.g., Shaffer, Harrison, Gregersen, Black, & Ferzandi, 2006). Human resource managers report that expatriates' early return is most often due to family concerns and infrequently due to other reasons such as taking another company job (GMAC Global Relocation Services, 2006, 2007).

There does not appear to be any evidence that premature return from international assignments is influenced by gender, although women have a slightly lower early return rate than men (3% vs. 5%; ORC Worldwide, 2007). Female expatriates may cope better than males during assignments (cf. Tung, 2004) and thus be less likely to return prematurely. A practitioner survey (ORC Worldwide, 2007) found that more female than male expatriates were aware of company work-life policy, reported that it made more of a difference to them personally, and took their full annual leave entitlement. Female expatriates reported less financial stress than males and noted that work intruded less into their home life. Their families temporarily returned home or traveled less often than the families of absent male expatriates, suggesting the family's better adjustment. However, female expatriates felt more overwhelmed by work than male expatriates and were more stressed, including by their partner's work being at a lower level than it would have been at home (ORC Worldwide, 2007). Overall, women may cope at least as well or perhaps better than men with family problems on assignment, suggesting they do not quit prematurely for family reasons.

Why Self-Initiated Expatriates Repatriate

Company-assigned expatriates usually have a set assignment length and know either when they are due to transfer home or, if they are not guaranteed repatriation, when they need to search for a new job. By contrast, self-initiated expatriates must decide not only whether they will repatriate, but also when they should do so. Some always intended to repatriate and, on leaving their home country, had a timeframe in mind and usually repatriated when the time came or somewhat later (Lidgard, 2001; Lidgard & Gilson, 2002; Myers & Inkson, 2003). However, many self-initiated expatriates do not intend to return. Some studies have calculated the percentages of expatriates who never intend to return, are undecided or uncertain about returning, or who are certain or likely to return. About a third of expatriates never intend to return and fewer than half of expatriates are certain or likely to return (Frank & Belair, 1999, 2000; Gill, 2005; Hansen, 2003; Hugo et al., 2003; Inkson et al., 2004; Mak, 1997). Although the proportion of skilled workers who repatriate is not known, it seems about half repatriate within 10 years (Frank & Bélair, 1999; Hansen, 2003) and that repatriation most often occurs in the first 3 years or perhaps 5 years abroad (Dustmann & Weiss, 2007). Expatriates from developing countries repatriate less often than those from developed countries (Dustmann & Weiss, 2007) and, due to United States career opportunities and working conditions, those from the United States repatriate more often than those from other countries (Hansen, 2003).

Anecdotal and descriptive evidence suggests that, generally, self-initiated expatriates do not repatriate because of problems or failure abroad; rather, they often leave successful careers and social lives to return (Gill, 2005; Hugo, 2006; Lidgard & Gilson, 2002). In deciding whether to return, they weigh the lifestyle and family ties at home against career development and financial opportunities abroad (Gill, 2005; Hugo, 2006). Their decisions are affected by the pull of the home country, how embedded they are in the host country, and dynamic factors such as shocks (e.g., family illness in the home country).

Push-pull theory proposes that expatriates repatriate because home-country factors pull or attract them back and host-country factors push or repel them away (Toren, 1976). Evidence shows that skilled workers repatriate because they are "pulled" or attracted home by family ties and the lifestyle, but not usually by career or financial benefits (Barrett & O'Connell, 2001; Frank & Bélair, 1999; Gill, 2005; Hugo et al., 2003; Inkson et al., 2004; Inkson & Myers, 2003; Ley & Kobayashi, 2005; Lidgard, 2001).

Juxtaposed against the pull of the home country is embeddedness in the host country. Adapting job embeddedness theory (Mitchell, Holtom, & Lee, 2001) to explain country rather than job turnover suggests that expatriates are less likely to repatriate if they have become embedded in their host country through the sacrifices they would have to make by repatriating, the links or connections they have made, and the fit they experience with the host country. Professionals may incur substantial career and financial sacrifices by repatriating. The greatest barriers self-initiated expatriates report to repatriation are the career and financial losses they would incur, along with future career and financial opportunities they would forego (Gill, 2005; Hugo et al., 2003; Inkson et al., 2004). Expatriates may also become embedded as a result of the relationships and friendships they have built up abroad and the feelings of compatibility they have with the host country. To leave would mean relinquishing the links and connections they have built up and the career and community fit they experience with the host country. Expatriates may have also become embedded through their partner. Expatriates who have a partner of host-country origin and/or a partner with a career abroad have less freedom than others to repatriate, due to the disruption that would be imposed on their partner's family ties and career. Compared with those of company expatriates, partners of self-initiated expatriates are more often employed full time, are of host-country or foreign origin (not home-country origin), and are men (GMAC Global Relocation Services, 2006, 2007; Suutari & Brewster, 2000). Hence, because partners of self-initiated expatriates are more likely to be embedded in their host country by career and family, self-initiated expatriates are less likely to consider repatriating. Skilled employees who have foreign born or employed partners are less likely to intend to repatriate than others (Gill, 2005; Hugo et al., 2003; Khoo, 2003; Ley & Kobayashi, 2005; Mak, 1997).

Expatriates may also be more embedded in host countries if their children are of high school age or were born there. Whereas company expatriates may leave their children at home (49%, GMAC Global Relocation Services, 2006), self-initiated expatriates, because they may marry host-country nationals, are more likely to have children born in the host county (Hugo et al., 2003). In these contexts, school and family links may increase expatriate embeddedness and reduce the likelihood of repatriation. Professionals whose children are of host-country origin or of school age are less likely to repatriate than others (Gill, 2005; Hugo, 2006; Hugo et al., 2003; Khoo & Mak, 2003; Ley & Kobayashi, 2005; Mak, 1997).

Apart from the substantive causes of repatriation—home-country pull and not being embedded in the host country—repatriation also may follow dynamic forces. Extrapolating the construct of shocks from the unfolding theory of job turnover (Mitchell & Lee, 2001) to explain country turnover, it can be argued that expatriates may experience events that lead them to appraise whether expatriation is meeting their goals and, if not, cause them to decide to repatriate. Self-initiated expatriates report that a family illness or death back home, becoming pregnant or having a child, and visa expiration would increase their intention to repatriate (Gill, 2005; Hugo et al., 2003; Inkson et al., 2004) and led to their repatriation (Inkson & Myers, 2003; Lidgard, 2001). Expatriates may also be compelled to appraise expatriation against their current goals following job offers from home (Gill, 2005) or job dissatisfaction abroad (Mak, 1997). The effect of gender on response to shocks has not been examined.

Thoughts of repatriation triggered by shocks may not result in return if professionals do not have a job to which to return. Expatriates who are not transferred home need to search for a job at home in order to assess the feasibility of return. When considering repatriation, professionals highlight the importance of obtaining information from their home country on employment and financial issues and of mobilizing social support and contacts (Gill, 2005; Hugo et al., 2003; Inkson et al., 2004). Furthermore, many claim that they would not repatriate unless they could obtain a good job or salary at least equivalent to what they have abroad (Hugo et al., 2003; Inkson et al., 2004).

Despite the evidence, comparative research is needed on self-initiated and company-assigned expatriates to explain why self-initiated expatriates repatriate. By comparing their reasons, more insight can be gained into how to reduce the brain drain. Using such information, strategies can be developed to address this issue. Home-country attraction, host-country embeddedness, and dynamic factors should all influence the repatriation of self-initiated expatriates more than they would company expatriates, because self-initiated expatriates must make a definite decision to return, while company expatriates tend to be transferred home. For company expatriates who have to choose to repatriate and find their own job, the causes of their return will be similar to those of self-initiated expatriates. Research questions that require answering are:

1. Do self-initiated expatriates repatriate rather than stay abroad for different or similar reasons to company expatriates who independently choose to return (e.g., those who do not have guaranteed repatriation or jobs on return)?

2. Are home-country pull, host-country embeddedness, and dynamic factors better able to explain self-initiated expatriates' repatriation than that of company-assigned repatriates?

Gender Differences in the
Causes of Professionals' Repatriation

Whether female professionals repatriate more or less frequently than males is unknown. One study of company-assigned expatriates found that more women had been guaranteed a position on successful completion of an international assignment than men (Tung, 2004). Based on frequency analyses, gender has been found to be unrelated to self-initiated expatriates' intentions to repatriate (Hugo et al., 2003; Khoo, 2003; Mak, 1997) and actual repatriation (Barrett & O'Connell, 2001; DeVoretz, Ma, & Zhang, 2003). However, the studies did not conduct significance tests to determine whether gender differences were an influencing factor (e.g., DeVoretz et al., 2003).

There may be gender differences that underlie the reasons for repatriation. The application of gender role theory (Markham, 1987) suggests that, when self-initiated expatriates have a partner or children of host-country origin or children of high school age, women will be less inclined to repatriate than men because they put the family caregiver role first. Men may be less inclined to repatriate than women when they would have to make career and financial sacrifices because they put the family provider role first. The literature supports gender role theory. Studies show that women's intentions to repatriate are more linked to family reasons than men's, which are more linked to career and finances. Women have the intention to repatriate less often than do men when they have a partner of host-country origin (as opposed to partners from the home country) and due to their partner's employment (Barrett & O'Connell, 2001; Hugo et al., 2003). However, they repatriate more than men because of family and children's needs (Barrett & O'Connell, 2001; Hugo et al., 2003; Lidgard, 1993). Women also have greater needs for affiliation than men (Boneva, Frieze, Ferligoj, Ferligoj, Pauknerova, & Orgocka, 1998) and needs for affiliation are positively related to intentions to repatriate (Inkson et al., 2004). Due to career and financial reasons, men less often intend to repatriate than women, but when they do repatriate it is more often for work and economic reasons (Barrett & O'Connell, 2001; Hugo et al., 2003; Lidgard, 1993; Ley & Kobayashi, 2005), supporting gender role theory that men make relocation decisions consistent with a family provider role.

It is possible that women may repatriate more than men due to their lower career advancement and development abroad. Women may have gained managerial jobs abroad less often than men, or gained jobs at lower managerial levels than men, as is generally the case for women (Tharenou, 1997), and thus have not become as embedded in the host country due to limited career and advancement options. A study of single

Japanese women working in Singapore who self-initiated expatriation found that, in response to career blocks abroad, they relocated within the country or to other countries to gain higher level, better paying jobs (Thang et al., 2002). Although expatriation opens up career opportunities for women, research is needed to investigate whether they gain fewer career opportunities than men, resulting in more frequent repatriation for that reason than men. Female company-assigned expatriates have been found to be offered less career development (fast-track programs, career counseling, career planning workshops) (Selmer & Leung, 2003) and report being less able to meet their career goals within the company (Selmer & Leung, 2002) than male expatriates. Lack of career advancement and development abroad, combined with the greater satisfaction of their affiliation needs at home, may lead women to repatriate more than men. However, several questions remain that need attention in future research:

1. Do female self-initiated expatriates repatriate more than males? If so, why? Do women have reasons different from men?

2. Are female expatriates more likely to be pulled home by family and be less embedded abroad by their career, and to be more responsive to dynamic factors (e.g., shocks) than males?

3. Do female self-initiated expatriates repatriate more often than males because of fewer career opportunities and less career advancement in host countries and/or due to being more responsive to family ties at home and higher affiliation needs?

4. Are women company-assigned expatriates less satisfied than men, especially with their job, causing them to repatriate more than men do?

CONSEQUENCES OF INTERNATIONAL CAREERS FOR PROFESSIONALS

A major reason that professionals accept international assignments or initiate expatriation is for future career advancement (Bolino, 2007. Expatriates believe that international experience will enhance their employability (Richardson & Mallon, 2005) and that international assignments will develop competencies they need to advance to leadership positions in multinational and global firms (Caligiuri, 2006; Tung, 2004). Career outcomes can be subjective, reflecting an individual's own sense of his or her career (e.g., competencies, satisfaction, intentions to quit) or objective, assessing publicly observable indicators (e.g., promotion, salary, rank).

Competencies

Company-assigned expatriates. International assignments are a critical way of developing global and cross-cultural competencies (Caligiuri, 2006; Thomas, Lazarova, & Inkson, 2005) and enable expatriates to build career capital—resources individuals accumulate that influence their career outcomes (DeFillipi & Arthur, 1994; Inkson & Arthur, 2001). According to the theory of career capital (DeFillipi & Arthur, 1994; Inkson & Arthur, 2001), people attain success in their career by developing three distinct, complementary types of competency: skills, knowledge, and expertise (knowing how); motivation, personal meaning, and identification (knowing why); and career-relevant relationships, personal connections, attachments, mutual obligations, and networks (knowing who). International assignments have been found to help develop competencies in: (a) general business understanding, broader management issues, and self-confidence (knowing how); (b) awareness and self-reflection and a global mindset (knowing why); and (c) networking opportunities (knowing who) (Dickmann & Harris, 2005). Company-assigned expatriates overwhelmingly reported that the international experience they gained resulted in personal and professional growth (see Lazarova & Cerdin's 2007 review).

Self-initiated expatriates. Although company-assigned expatriation is seen as a critical means for developing global and cross-cultural competencies, self-initiated expatriation is also useful in this regard (Inkson et al., 1997). On return, self-initiated expatriates pointed to their improved language skills (knowing how) and greater clarity of their work goals (knowing why), whereas company expatriates pointed to their greater ability to earn money (Doherty et al., 2007). Self-initiated expatriates especially commented on what they had learned and their improved skills and interpersonal and personal competencies (knowing how) (Inkson & Myers, 2003). Both men and women reported that they had developed self-confidence (knowing how), but men said they had developed more focused career aspirations (knowing why) and self-direction and technical skills (knowing how) (Myers & Pringle, 2005). Women reported higher interpersonal relations and communication skills (knowing how) and cumulative career experiences than men (knowing why). Women who self-initiated expatriation worked for the same employers abroad more than men did and stayed abroad longer, in effect gaining a de facto company expatriate experience (Myers & Pringle, 2005). As a result of self-initiated expatriation, women appear to develop competencies as least as well as men do.

Career Advancement

Company-assigned expatriates. It is unclear whether international assignments lead to career advancement (Bolino, 2007). Although company expatriation is believed to lead to future career opportunities, on return expatriates considered that international assignments are not sufficiently rewarded by advancement in the company (Thomas et al., 2005). Unlike the views held by organizational executives, repatriates did not see international assignments as critical for their career advancement (Dickmann & Harris, 2005). By contrast, in a further study, both expatriates and repatriates of a company perceived that international postings offered them more internal and external career opportunities than were available to domestic employees, despite expatriation having little or no impact on their actual career advancement compared with domestic employees of the company (Benson & Pattie, 2008). A qualitative review concluded that very few managers are promoted on return and many more are demoted (Stroh et al., 2005). By contrast, comparing conditions prior to expatriation with those post-return, Finnish repatriates gained increased status in the organizational hierarchy as well as an increase in salary and standard of living, and reported that the international assignment had had a positive impact on their career progress and would continue to do so in the future (Suutari & Brewster, 2003). The repatriates' expectations about career progress had been met—often more quickly than would be expected from company expatriation. In support, in a rare examination of objective measures of advancement, the only meta-analysis showed that individuals who had more international work experience were paid higher salaries and were promoted more often than those who did not (Ng, Eby, Sorensen, & Feldman, 2005).

Self-initiated expatriates. Studies support the view that repatriation provides self-initiated expatriates with a return on their investment. From a human capital theory perspective, when employees invest in the development of their own human capital by expatriating, repatriation should mean that they are rewarded for the international competencies they acquired, and for their consequently better job performance, with higher-level jobs and pay (cf. Barrett & O'Connell, 2001). Results from studies of self-initiated expatriates support human capital theory. United States scientists who repatriated were paid higher salaries than those who remained abroad (Hansen, 2003). Early-career Hong Kong (HK) graduates who repatriated gained higher salaries, top-income bracket status, and more promotions than the HK population in general, than HK stayers who never emigrated from HK, and than stayers in Canada who did not repatriate to HK (DeVoretz et al., 2003; DeVoretz & Zhang, 2004; Ley & Kobayashi, 2005). Some New Zealand repatriates gained a higher-level job and new opportunities due to their international experience (Inkson & Myers, 2003). However, others in the study repatriated to a similar job or organization without career advancement (Inkson & Myers, 2003), while other studies of New Zealanders showed that expatriates could not gain suitable work on return (Bedford & Lidgard, 1993). In sum, self-initiated expatriates gain career and income benefits from international experience when compared with nonrepatriates and stay-at-home nationals, supporting human capital theory that investment in developing skills and competencies provides a return in the form of higher salary and rank on repatriation.

But do women gain as great a return as men from self-initiated, self-financed expatriation? Male Irish professionals earned 10% more on return than men who stayed in Ireland, but comparable female expatriates were paid no more (Barrett & O'Connell, 2001). Of the men, those who self-initiated expatriation for labor-related reasons earned 15% more on return than those who went for adventure and to see the world, the adventurers on their return earning the same as men who stayed abroad (Barrett & O'Connell, 2001). Supporting human capital theory, investment in working abroad paid off on return, but only for achievement-oriented men. Research on gender differences, however, is rare. Research questions which need examination are:

1. Does company-assigned expatriation lead to career advancement and development and, if so, are the results better for men than women?
2. Does self-initiated expatriation lead to career advancement and development and, if so, is it better or worse than company-assigned expatriation?
3. Does self-initiated expatriation offer women better career development and advancement than staying in the home country or company-assigned expatriation?
4. Do female self-initiated expatriates gain less from expatriation and investment in international career capital than males in terms of career advancement and financial benefits, and what are the reasons for any such differences?

Satisfaction and Intentions to Turn Over

Company-assigned expatriates. In contrast to their positive views of their competency development and future career advancement, expatriates may be dissatisfied with their job or intend to leave their employer, especially on repatriation. They may not have been well looked after abroad by their employer and, when they return to their home country, do not get the promotion they had thought would be forthcoming and may leave as a consequence. Repatriates suffer reverse culture shock, rendering their re-entry and cultural reintegration problematic (Black, Gregersen, & Mendenhall, 1992; Stroh et al., 2005). Company-assigned expatriates may be dissatisfied if there are no jobs for them on their return or only jobs that they consider to have too little autonomy, responsibility, and significance (Black, Gregersen, & Mendenhall, 1999; Dickmann & Harris, 2005). Other causes of dissatisfaction on return include demotion and not being able to use their international experience and competencies (Black et al., 1999; Dickmann & Harris, 2005). Repatriates therefore decide to leave the company and often leave within two years (Black et al., 1999; GMAC Global Relocation Services, 2006, 2007; Suutari & Brewster, 2003).

Female company-assigned expatriates reported less satisfaction than males with both expatriation and repatriation (Tung, 2004) and fewer female than male expatriates reported pursuing a long-term career with their current employer (NFTC, 2001). Female company-assigned expatriates believed that they experienced more re-entry problems than males because they were pioneers (Linehan & Scullion, 2002). Hence, although the evidence is limited, women might be more dissatisfied than men with expatriation and repatriation.

Dissatisfaction is not the only reason for company-assigned expatriates leaving; they also leave because of external job offers and opportunities (GMAC Global Relocation Services, 2006, 2007; Lazarova & Cerdin, 2007). Despite leaving their organization while on assignment or after return, these expatriates expressed high satisfaction with their international experience and maintained a positive attitude toward the company during assignment, on repatriation, and subsequently (Suutari & Brewster, 2003). They left because of external job offers, including assignments in another country or new assignments in the same country with the same or a new employer.

Self-initiated expatriates. Anecdotal and descriptive evidence suggests that self-initiated expatriates have problems adjusting on return because of a lack of work opportunities, having to take lower level jobs than they had abroad, work not matching their interests or responsibility levels, dissatisfaction with working conditions, and poor fit with the lifestyle and culture of their home country (Bedford & Lidgard, 1993; Begley, Collings, & Scullion, 2008; Gill, 2005; Inkson & Myers, 2003; Myers & Pringle, 2005). Male and female repatriates report intending to re-expatriate for work opportunities (Bedford & Lidgard, 1993) and men to re-expatriate because of career disappointments on their return home (Myers & Pringle, 2005).

A small proportion of self-initiated repatriates intend to re-expatriate (Lidgard, 2001; Lidgard & Gilson, 2002) and do re-expatriate, often back to the original host country, but also to other countries (Bedford & Lidgard, 1993; Gill, 2005; Hugo, 2006; Inkson et al., 2004; Lidgard, 2001). The results support the brain circulation and boundaryless careers resulting from professionals expatriating, repatriating, and then re-expatriating, circulating their intellectual capital (Saxenian, 2005; Tung, 2008). Moreover, rather than undergoing this three-stage cycle, expatriate transnational entrepreneurs concurrently maintain business-related linkages with their home and adopted countries, at times living in both. Whether there are gender differences in the rate of re-expatriation or whether women participate in transnational entrepreneurship is unknown.

There is very little research on how gender influences the outcomes of expatriation and repatriation. Questions that need to be addressed include:

1. Are women more dissatisfied with company-assigned expatriation and repatriation than men? If so, does this greater dissatisfaction lead to higher company turnover for women than men?

2. Are there gender differences in the reasons for turnover of company-assigned and self-initiated expatriates?

3. Are more external job offers made to male than to female company-assigned and self-initiated expatriates and repatriates? Is there any difference in the rate of men and women accepting external job offers?

4. Do self-initiated expatriates re-expatriate more than company expatriates and why? Is it for career reasons caused by dissatisfaction with the work they obtained on repatriation? Are there gender differences involved in the reasons?

CONCLUSION

Professionals appear to use self-initiated expatriation as a way to advance their career and achieve their work aspirations in a lucrative global labor market that offers many opportunities. Unlike their participation in company-assigned expatriation, women participate in self-initiated expatriation as much as men. However, why they do so is not known. Women may be proactive, using self-initiated expatriation as a way to develop their career and gain advancement, opening up a world of opportunities not available to them through company assignments or in their home country. Research needs to examine whether women are using self-initiated expatriation as a new option to develop their career and how this alternative interacts with life stage and family.

Some career outcomes of expatriation, such as the development of competencies, are gained both by men and women, but others, such as satisfaction and objective career outcomes, may be less often attained by women. Whether women gain less advancement from expatriation than men requires additional research. It is also not known if self-initiated expatriation gains women greater career advancement than company assignments or why women may be more dissatisfied with company expatriation than men. Research is needed to determine whether self-initiated expatriation offers women more career advancement (e.g., rank, pay) or satisfaction than if they had remained in their home country (e.g., using research designs such as Barrett & O'Connell, 2001; DeVoretz et al., 2003) or had been company-assigned on international assignments (cf. Doherty et al., 2007; Jokinen et al., 2008).

A critical issue is determining what prompts expatriates to repatriate. Their different work and family circumstances mean that self-initiated expatriates will stay abroad more, and longer, than company-assigned expatriates. However, female self-initiated expatriates may repatriate more often than men in the same circumstances if they find fewer career opportunities and less career advancement abroad. Career advancement and development from self-initiated expatriation may not materialize for women and they may also repatriate for reasons different than men, including family and affiliation needs. The role that gender differences play in the reasons for professionals repatriating requires research.

Once repatriated, both company-assigned and self-initiated expatriates suffer problems with adjustment and career, although both leverage their investment in international career capital by accepting opportunities with other employers at home or abroad. Women may do so less than men. Research is needed to investigate whether women gain less from their investment in international career capital than men. There are many questions that require answering as to whether women's participation in self-initiated expatriation is merely an optimistic quest for career advancement and development or whether more of the same issues will arise for their career as in the domestic sphere, where comparable women gain less career advancement than men (Tharenou, 1997).

REFERENCES

Adler, N. (1984). Women do not want international careers. *Organizational Dynamics, 13*(2), 66-79.

Adler, N. (2002). Global managers: No longer men alone. *International Journal of Human Resource Management, 13*, 743-759.

Altman, Y., & Shortland, S. (2008). Women and international assignments: Taking stock—A 25- year review. *Human Resource Management, 47*, 199-216.

Arthur, M. B., & Rousseau, D. M. (1996). The boundaryless career as a new employment principle. In M. G. Arthur & D. M. Rousseau (Eds.), *The boundaryless career* (pp. 132-149). New York: Oxford University Press.

Aryee, S., Chay, Y., & Chew, J. (1996). An investigation of the willingness of employees to accept an expatriate assignment. *Journal of Organizational Behavior, 17*, 267-284.

Barrett, A., & O'Connell, P. J. (2001). Is there a wage premium for returning Irish migrants? *The Economic and Social Review, 32*, 1-22.

Bedford, R. D., & Lidgard, J. L. (1993). Home to work? The employment experiences of return migrants. In P. S. Morrison, (Ed.), *Labour, employment and work in New Zealand* (pp. 136-147). Wellington, New Zealand: Victoria University of Wellington Department of Geography.

Begley, A., Collings, D. G., & Scullion, H. (2008). The cross-cultural adjustment experiences of self-initiated repatriates to the Republic of Ireland labour market. *Employee Relations, 30*, 264-282.

Benson, G. S., & Pattie, M. (2008). Is expatriation good for my career? The impact of expatriate assignments on perceived and actual career outcomes. *International Journal of Human Resource Management 19*, 1636-1653.

Bhaskar-Shrinivas, P., Harrison, D. A., Shaffer, M. A., & Luk, D. (2005). Input-based and time-based models of international adjustment: Meta-analytic evidence and theoretical extensions. *Academy of Management Journal, 48*, 257-280.

Black, J. S., Gregersen, H. B., & Mendenhall, M. E. (1992). *Global assignments*. San Francisco: Jossey-Bass.

Black, J. S., Gregersen, H. B., & Mendenhall, M. E. (1999). *Global assignments*. San Francisco: Jossey-Bass.

Bolino, M. C. (2007). Expatriate assignments and intra-organizational career success: Implications for individuals and organizations. *Journal of International Business Studies, 38*, 819-835.

Boneva, B., Frieze, I., Ferligoj, E. H., Ferligoj, A., Pauknerova, D., & Orgocka, A. (1998). Achievement, power, and affiliation motives as clues to (e)migration desires: A four-country comparison. *European Psychologist, 3*, 247-254.

Brett, J. M., & Stroh, L. K. (1995). Willingness to expatriate. *Human Resource Management, 34*, 405-424.

Brett, J. M., Stroh, L. K., & Reilly, A. H. (1992). Job transfer. In C. Cooper & I. Robertson (Eds.), *International review of industrial and organizational psychology* (pp. 323-362). New York: Wiley.

Caligiuri, P. M. (2006). Developing global leaders. *Human Resource Management Review, 16*, 219-228.

Cartus. (2007). *Emerging trends in global mobility*. Chicago: Cartus Corporation.

Cheng, L., & Yang, P. Q. (1998). Global interaction, global inequality, and migration of the highly trained to the United States. *The International Migration Review, 32*, 626-653.

DeFillipi, R. J., & Arthur, M. B. (1994). The boundaryless career: A competency-based perspective. *Journal of Organizational Behavior, 15*, 307-324.

DeVoretz, D., Ma, J., & Zhang, K. (2003). Triangular human capital flows. In J. G. Reitz (Ed.), *Host societies and the reception of immigrants* (pp. 469-492). La Jolla CA: Center for Comparative Immigration Studies, University of California, San Diego.

DeVoretz, D., & Zhang, K. (2004). Citizenship, passports and the brain exchange triangle. *Journal of Comparative Policy Analysis, 6*, 199-212.

Dickmann, M., & Harris, H. (2005). Developing career capital for global careers: The role of international assignments. *Journal of World Business, 40*, 399-408.

Docquier, F., & Marfouk, A. (2004). *Measuring the international mobility of skilled workers* (1990-2000): Release 1.0. World Bank Policy Research Working Paper No. 3381. Retrieved March 6, 2009, from http://ssrn.com/abstract=625258

Doherty, N., Dickmann, M., & Mills, T. (2007). *Are you a hero or a heroine? An exploration of the expatriation journey.* Bedfordshire, United Kingdom: Cranfield University School of Management.

Dupuis, M. J., Haines, V. Y., & Saba, T. (2008). Gender, family ties, and international mobility. *International Journal of Human Resource Management, 19*, 274-295.

Dustmann, C., & Kirchkamp, O. (2002). The optimal migration duration and activity choice after re-migration. *Journal of Development Economics, 67*, 351-372.

Dustmann, C., & Weiss, Y. (2007). Return migration: Empirical evidence from the UK. *British Journal of Industrial Relations, 45*, 236-256.

Feldman, D. C. (2001). Domestic and international relocation for work. In C. L. Cooper & I. T. Robertson (Eds.), *International review of industrial and organizational psychology* (pp. 215-244). New York: Wiley.

Fitzgerald, C., & Howe-Walsh, L. (2008). Self-initiated expatriates: An interpretive phenomenological analysis of professional female expatriates. *International Journal of Business and Management, 3*(10), 156-174.

Forster, N. (1997). The persistent myth of high expatriate failure rates: A reappraisal. *The International Journal of Human Resource Management, 8*, 414-433.

Forster, N. (1999). Another glass ceiling? The experience of women professionals and managers of international assignments. *Gender, Work, and Organizations, 6*, 79-90.

Frank, J., & Bélair, E. (1999). *South of the border.* Hull, Quebec, Canada: Minister of Public Works and Government Services.

Frank, J., & Bélair, E. (2000, Spring). Stateward bound. *Statistics Canada, 56*, 23-26.

Gill, B. (2005). Homeward bound: Return mobility for Italian scientists. *Innovation, 18*, 319-341.

GMAC Global Relocation Services. (2006). *Global relocation trends 2005 survey report.* Woodridge, IL: Author.

GMAC Global Relocation Services. (2007). *Global relocation trends 2006 survey report.* Woodridge, IL: Author.

GMAC Global Relocation Services. (2008). *Global relocation trends 2007 survey report.* Woodridge, IL: Authors.

Hall, D. T. (2004). The protean career. *Journal of Vocational Behavior, 65*, 1-13.

Hansen, W. (Ed.). (2003). A web-based E-survey on international mobility of scientists and engineers. In *Brain drain: Emigration flows for qualified scientists.* Retrieved March 17, 2006, from http://www.merit.unimaas.nl/braindrain/

Harrison, D. A., Shaffer, M. A., & Bhaskar-Shrinivas, P. (2004). Going places: Roads more and less traveled in research on expatriate experiences. *Research in Personnel and Human Resources Management, 23*, 199-247.

Hearn, J., Jyrkinen, M., Piekkari, R., & Oinonen, E. (2008). "Women home and away": Transnational managerial work and gender relations. *Journal of Business Ethics, 83*, 41-54.

Hechanova, R., Beehr, T.A., & Christiansen, D.E. (2003). Antecedents and consequences of employees' adjustment to overseas assignment: A meta-analytic review. *Applied Psychology: An International Review, 52*, 213-236.

Hugo, G. (2006). An Australian diaspora. *International Migration, 44*, 105-133.

Hugo, G., Rudd, D., & Harris, K. (2003). *Australia's diaspora: Its size, nature and policy implications.* Melbourne, Australia: CEDA.

Inkson, K., & Arthur, M. B. (2001). How to be a successful career capitalist. *Organizational Dynamics, 30*, 48-61.

Inkson, K., Arthur, M. B., Pringle, J., & Barry, S. (1997). Expatriate assignment versus overseas experience. *Journal of World Business, 32*, 351-368.

Inkson, K., Carr, S. C., Edwards, M., Hooks, J., Jackson, D., Thorn, K., et al. (2004). From brain drain to talent flow: Views of Kiwi expatriates. *University of Auckland Business Review, 6*(2), 29-39.

Inkson, K., & Myers, B. (2003). 'The big OE': Self-directed travel and career development. *Career Development International, 8*, 170-181.

Insch, G. S., McIntyre, N., & Napier, N. K. (2008). The expatriate glass ceiling: The second layer of glass. *Journal of Business Ethics, 83*, 19-28.

Interchange Institute. (2004). *Many expatriates, many voices.* Newark, NJ: Prudential Financial.

Jokinen, T., Brewster, C., & Suutari, V. (2008). Career capital during international work experiences: Contrasting self-initiated expatriate experiences and assigned expatriation. *International Journal of Human Resource Management, 19*, 979-998.

Khoo, S. E. (2003). Sponsorship of relatives for migration and immigrant settlement intention. *International Migration, 41*, 177-199.

Khoo, S. E., & Mak, A. (2003). Career and family factors in intention for permanent settlement in Australia. In M. W. Charney, B. S. A. Yeoh, & T. C. Kiong (Eds.), *Chinese migrants abroad* (pp. 181-203). Singapore: Singapore University Press.

Kofman, E. (2005). Gender and skilled migrants. *Geoforum, 36*, 149-154.

Konopaske, R., & Werner, S. (2005). US managers' willingness to accept a global assignment. *International Journal of Human Resource Management, 16*, 1159-1175.

KPMG. (2006). *Global assignment policies and practices survey 2004.* New York: Author.

Lazarova, M. B., & Cerdin, J. L. (2007). Revisiting repatriation concerns: Organizational support versus career and contextual influences. *Journal of International Business Studies, 38,* 404-429.

Lee, C. H. (2005). A study of underemployment among self-initiated expatriates. *Journal of World Business, 40,* 172-177.

Ley, D., & Kobayashi, A. (2005). Back to Hong Kong: Return migration or transnational sojourn? *Global Networks, 5,* 111-127.

Lidgard, J. (1993). Neglected international migrants: A study of returning New Zealanders. *New Zealand Population Review, 19*(3&4), 94-124.

Lidgard, J. (2001). Return migration of New Zealanders: A profile of returnees in 2000. *New Zealand Journal of Geography, 104,* 10-17.

Lidgard, J., & Gilson, C. (2002). Return migration of New Zealanders: Shuttle and circular migrants. *New Zealand Population Review, 28*(1), 99-128.

Linehan, M., & Scullion, H. (2002). Repatriation of European female corporate executives: An empirical study. *International Journal of Human Resource Management, 11,* 254-267.

Linehan, M., & Walsh, J. S. (1999). Senior female international managers: Breaking the glass border. *Women in Management Review, 14,* 264-272.

Lowe, K. B., Downes, M., & Kroeck, K. (1999). The impact of gender and location on the willingness to accept overseas assignments. *International Journal of Human Resource Management, 10,* 223-234.

Lyness, K. S., & Thompson, D. E. (1997). Above the glass ceiling? A comparison of matched samples of female and male executives. *Journal of Applied Psychology, 82,* 359-375.

Mak, A. S. (1997). Skilled Hong Kong immigrants' intention to repatriate. *Asia and Pacific Migration Journal, 6*(2), 169-184.

Mainiero, L. A., & Sullivan, S. E. (2005). Kaleidoscope careers: An alternate explanation for the opt-out revolution. *Academy of Management Executive, 19*(1), 106-123.

Markham, W. T. (1987). Sex, relocation, and occupational advancement. In A. Stromberg, L. Larwood, & B. A. Gutek (Eds.), *Women and work* (pp. 207-232). Beverly Hills, CA: SAGE.

Mercer. (2006a). *More females sent on international assignments than ever before.* London: Author.

Mercer. (2006b). *International assignments survey 2005/2006.* Geneva, Switzerland: Author.

Mirvis, P. H., & Hall, D. T. (1996). Psychological success and the boundaryless career. In M. B. Arthur & D. M. Rousseau (Eds.), *The boundaryless career* (pp. 237-255). New York: Oxford University Press.

Mitchell, T. R., Holtom, B. C., & Lee, T. W. (2001). How to keep your best employees. *Academy of Management Executive, 15*(4), 96-108.

Mitchell, T. R., & Lee, T. W. (2001). The unfolding model of voluntary turnover and job embeddedness. *Research in Organizational Behavior, 23,* 189-246.

Myers, B., & Inkson, K. (2003). The big OE: How it works and what it can do for New Zealand. *University of Auckland Business Review, 5*(1), 44-54.

Myers, B., & Pringle, J. K. (2005). Self-initiated foreign experience as accelerated development: Influences of gender. *Journal of World Business, 40,* 421-431.

National Foreign Trade Council. (2001). *Maximizing your expatriate investment.* New York: CIGNA.

Ng, T. W. H., Eby, L. T., Sorensen, K. L., & Feldman, D. C. (2005). Predictors of objective and subjective career success. *Personnel Psychology, 58*, 367-408.

OECD. (2002). *International mobility of the highly skilled.* Paris: Author.

OECD. (2005). *Trends in international migration.* Paris: Author.

OECD. (2008). *The global competition for talent: Mobility of the highly skilled.* Paris: Author.

ORC Worldwide. (2006). *2006 worldwide survey of international assignment policies and practices.* New York: Industrial Relations Counselors.

ORC Worldwide. (2007). *2007 expatriate work-life balance survey.* New York: Industrial Relations Counselors.

PricewaterhouseCoopers. (2000). *Managing a virtual world: Key trends 2000/2001.* London: Author.

PricewaterhouseCoopers. (2002). *Managing mobility matters.* London: Author.

PricewaterhouseCoopers. (2005). *Understanding and avoiding the barriers to international mobility.* London: Author.

Richardson, J., & Mallon, M. (2005). Career interrupted: The case of the self-directed expatriate. *Journal of World Business, 40,* 409-420.

Saxenian, A. (2002). Transnational communities and the evolution of global production networks: The cases of Taiwan, China, and India. *Industry and Innovation, 9*(3), 183-202.

Saxenian, A. (2005). From brain drain to brain circulation. *Studies in Comparative International Development, 40*(2), 35-61.

Selmer, J., & Leung, A. S. M. (2002). Career management issues of female business expatriates. *Career Development International, 7,* 348-358.

Selmer, J., & Leung, A. S. M. (2003). Are corporate career development activities less available to female than to male expatriates? *Journal of Business Ethics, 43,* 125-136.

Shaffer, M. A., Harrison, D. A., Gregersen, H., Black, H. S., & Ferzandi, L. A. (2006). You can take it with you. *Journal of Applied Psychology, 91,* 109-125.

Stone, R. M. (1991). Expatriate selection and failure. *Human Resource Planning, 14*(1), 9-18.

Stroh, L. K. (1999). Does relocation still benefit corporations or employees? An overview of the literature. *Human Resource Management Review, 9,* 279-308.

Stroh, L. K., Black, J. S., Mendenhall, M. E., & Gregersen, H. B. (2005). *Global assignments.* Mahwah, NJ: Erlbaum.

Stroh, L. K., Varma, A., & Valy-Durbin, S. J. (2000). Why are women left at home: Are they unwilling to go on international assignments? *Journal of World Business, 35,* 241-255.

Sullivan, S. E., & Mainiero, L. (2008). Using the kaleidoscope career model to understand the changing pattern of women's careers. *Advances in Developing Human Resources, 10,* 32-49.

Suutari, V., & Brewster, C. (2000). Making their own way: International experience through self-initiated foreign assignments. *Journal of World Business, 35,* 417-436.

Suutari, V., & Brewster, C. (2003). Repatriation: Empirical evidence from a longitudinal study of careers and expectations among Finnish expatriates. *International Journal of Human Resource Management, 14,* 1132-1151.

Thang, L. L., MacLachlan, E., & Goda, M. (2002). Expatriates on the margins—A study of Japanese women working in Singapore. *Geoforum, 33*(4), 539-551.

Tharenou, P. (1997). Managerial career advancement. In C. Cooper & I. T. Robertson (Eds.), *International review of industrial and organizational psychology* (pp. 39-93). New York: Wiley.

Tharenou, P. (2002a). Gender differences in explanations for relocating or changing organizations for advancement. In R. J. Burke & D. Nelson (Eds.), *Advancing women's careers* (pp. 97-115). Malden, MA: Blackwell.

Tharenou, P. (2002b). *The global executive: How Australian international and multinational organizations staff leadership roles performing international work.* Melbourne, Australia: Monash University.

Tharenou, P. (2003). The initial development of receptivity to working abroad: Self-initiated international work opportunities in young graduate employees. *Journal of Occupational and Organizational Psychology, 76,* 489-515.

Tharenou, P. (2006). International careers. In J. H. Greenhaus & G. A. Callahan (Eds.), *Encyclopedia of career development* (pp. 398-404). New York: SAGE.

Tharenou, P. (2008). Disruptive decisions to leave home: Gender and family differences in expatriation choices. *Organizational Behavior and Human Decision Processes, 105,* 183-200.

Thomas, D. C., Lazarova, M. B., & Inkson, K. (2005). Global careers: New phenomenon or new perspective. *Journal of World Business, 40,* 340-347.

Toren, N. (1976). Return to Zion. *Social Forces, 54,* 546-558.

Tung, R. L. (2004). Female expatriates: The model global manager. *Organizational Dynamics, 33*(3), 243-253.

Tung, R. L. (2008). Brain circulation, diaspora, and international competitiveness. *European Management Journal, 26,* 298-304.

Van der Velde, M. E. G., Bossink, C. J. H., & Jansen, P. G. W. (2005). Gender differences in the determinants of the willingness to accept an international assignment. *Journal of Vocational Behavior, 66,* 81-103.

Vance, C. M. (2005). The personal quest for building global competence. *Journal of World Business, 40,* 374-385.

Vance, C. M., Paik, Y., & White, J. A. (2006). Tracking bias against the selection of female expatriates. *Thunderbird International Business Review, 48,* 823-842.

Wan, D., Hui, T. K., & Tiang, L. (2002). Factors affecting Singaporeans' acceptance of international postings. *Personnel Review, 32,* 711-732.

ABOUT THE AUTHORS

Gary A. Adams (PhD, Central Michigan University) is a professor at the University of Wisconsin, Oshkosh. His research interests include older workers and occupational health. He has published two edited books, several book chapters, and over 25 articles in journals such as *Personnel Psychology, Journal of Applied Psychology, Journal of Occupational Health Psychology, Journal of Organizational Behavior,* and *Educational and Psychological Measurement.* He has made over 50 professional presentations at national conferences. Dr. Adams has also served as a consultant on over 50 projects with a variety of private organizations such as the Eaton Corporation, Affinity Health Systems, Kimberly Clark, and Alto Dairy, as well as public sector organizations such as the Department of Defense and the National Center for Post-Traumatic Stress Disorder.

S. Gayle Baugh (PhD, University of Cincinnati) is an associate professor at the University of West Florida and a multiple winner of the university's Dyson Research Award and the Hopkins Award as well as earning the Gabor Award for Faculty Excellence. Her research interests include mentoring, career theory, and leader-member exchange. Gayle has published in journals including *Journal of Vocational Behavior, Career Development International, Journal of Business Ethics, Group and Organization Management, Journal of Applied Social Psychology,* and *Journal of Social Behavior and Personality.* Gayle served as the division chair of the Academy of Management's Gender and Diversity in Organizations Division. She has also won the division's prestigious Sage/Janet Chusmir Service Award. In addition, she has been involved for a number of years with the Careers Division in a number of roles and has served on the board for the Southern Management Association, and is a past president of the Southwest Academy of Management. She is a member of several editorial boards including *Journal of Management*, *Career Development International*, *Journal of Business and Psychology*, and *Journal of Managerial Psychology*.

Terry A. Beehr (PhD, The University of Michigan) is a professor in the Department of Psychology at Central Michigan University and a faculty member in the PhD program in industrial and organizational psychology there. He previously held appointments at the Institute for Social Research (Ann Arbor) and Illinois State University. He has conducted research on employee retirement decisions, occupational health psychology and stress, leadership, and careers. He is a fellow in the Society for Industrial and Organizational Psychology and the Association for Psychological Science.

Dianne Bown-Wilson (MA, Cranfield University) is currently undertaking PhD research at Cranfield School of Management into the motivational drivers for career progression or lack of progression in older managers and how these drivers differ by gender. After receiving her bachelor's degree in psychology from Victoria University in Wellington, New Zealand (in the 1970s), she moved to the United Kingdom where she developed a successful career in senior marketing and management roles across many different types and sizes of private and public sector organizations. She holds the Chartered Institute of Marketing (CIM) Post-graduate Diploma and CIM "Chartered Marketer" status. In 2000 she set up her own management consultancy, extending this in 2003 to cover advisory services relating to the employment of older workers. She is also a trained executive coach and mentor. Dianne is co-author of a book, *Marketing, Management and Motivation: Successful Business Development for Professional Services Firms*, published by the UK Law Society. She has also written several other nonacademic books and numerous articles for practitioner and consumer journals.

Jennifer J. Deal (PhD, Ohio State University) is a senior research scientist at the Center for Creative Leadership (CCL) in San Diego, California, and the manager of CCL's World Leadership Survey and the Emerging Leaders Research Project. In 2002 Jennifer coauthored *Success for the New Global Manager* (Jossey-Bass/Wiley Publishers) and she has published in peer reviewed journals on a wide range of subjects, including generational issues, executive selection, cultural adaptability, global management, and women in management. Her second book, *Retiring the Generation Gap* (Jossey-Bass/Wiley Publishers), was published in 2007. An internationally recognized expert on generational differences, she has spoken on the topic on six continents (North and South America, Europe, Asia, Africa, and Australia), and she looks forward to speaking to Antarctic penguins about their generational issues in the near future.

Daniel C. Feldman (PhD, Yale University) is Synovus Chair of Servant Leadership at the University of Georgia, where he also serves as associate dean for research and international programs in the Terry College of Business. He has served as editor-in-chief of *Journal of Management* and as chair of the Careers Division of the Academy of Management. Daniel has published over 150 articles related to careers in organizations on such topics as early career indecision, socialization, job embeddedness, layoffs, career plateaus, transfers and promotions, expatriation, and early retirement.

William A. (Bill) Gentry (PhD, University of Georgia) is currently a senior research associate at the Center for Creative Leadership (CCL), coordinator of internships and postdocs at CCL, and also an adjunct assistant professor in the leadership studies doctoral program at North Carolina A&T State University. His research interests are in multisource (360) research, survey development and analysis, leadership and leadership development across cultures, managerial derailment, and in the area of organizational politics and political skill in the workplace. Bill received his MS and his PhD in applied psychology from the University of Georgia and was also a postdoctoral fellow at CCL. Before coming to CCL, Bill was an organizational effectiveness specialist at United Parcel Service. He has published in such journals as the *Journal of Applied Psychology, Journal of Vocational Behavior, Journal of Leadership Studies, Leadership Quarterly,* and the *European Journal of Work and Organizational Psychology.* He is a past contributor to businessweek.com on the nonverbal behaviors of candidates in the 2008 presidential and vice presidential debates, and his research on workplace political skill and derailment was featured in more than 40 internet and newspaper outlets.

Tracy Lambert Griggs (PhD, University of Georgia) is an assistant professor in the Department of Psychology at Winthrop University in Rock Hill, South Carolina. She received her masters and doctoral degrees in applied psychology from the University of Georgia. Her research interests include performance management, career management, job loss, re-employment, networking, work family-conflict, work issues for minority and under-represented populations and issues in teaching and pedagogy. Her research has been published in peer-reviewed journals such as the *Journal of Applied Psychology, Journal of Career Development,* and *Academic Exchange Quarterly.* She has also co-authored several book chapters. Tracy is a member of the

American Psychological Association, the Society for Industrial Organizational Psychology, the Academy of Management, and the Society for the Teaching of Psychology.

Scott P. Mondore (PhD, University of Georgia) is currently a managing partner with Strategic Management Decisions (SMD). Before cofounding SMD, he served as east region president for Morehead Associates, a survey and human capital analytics company. Prior to joining Morehead, Scott worked as a corporate strategy director and talent management director at Maersk, Inc. He also worked as an employee relations manager at UPS, focusing on employee assessment and measurement as well as working as a consultant to large and small organizations in both the private and public sector. Scott has over 10 years of experience in the areas of strategy, talent management, measurement, customer experience, and organizational development. He has internal management and consulting experience across a variety of industries, including transportation, healthcare, manufacturing, utilities, and hospitality. He has published several articles on various topics, including employee turnover, employee safety, coaching, litigation, and leadership. Scott is also an adjunct professor of psychology at the University of Georgia and Fairleigh Dickinson University.

Emma Parry (PhD, Cranfield University) is a senior research fellow at Cranfield School of Management. Her research interests include managing an aging workforce, generational diversity, the use of technology in HR, and HRM in the voluntary sector. She has conducted a considerable amount of research looking at the aging workforce including age and recruitment, total rewards for an aging workforce, and "The Impact of Generational Diversity on People Management" for the Chartered Institute of Personnel and Development. Emma is also a member of the "5C" academic collaboration examining career success and career transitions across cultures and generations. Outside of this area, Emma has undertaken a wide range of research in both the public and private sectors, including work for UK National Health Service and the Ministry of Defence. She also manages Cranet, an international network of business schools that conducts a comparative survey of HRM policies and practices in as many as 40 countries. Emma is the author of numerous publications and conference papers, including several in the area of managing an aging workforce.

Sally J. Power (PhD, University of Minnesota) is a professor of management and department chair at the University of St. Thomas in St. Paul, Minnesota where she teaches the MBA course "Careers in the 21st Century." Her research interests include business ethics, the Myers-Briggs Type Indicator, the Herrmann Brain Dominance Instrument, career theory, and midcareer issues. She has published in journals including the *Journal of Business Ethics, Journal of Psychological Type, Teaching Business Ethics,* and *Counseling Psychologist.* She has made numerous presentations at conferences including the Academy of Management, National Career Development Association, Midwest Academy of Management, and Southwest Academy of Management. Sally is author of the *Midcareer Success Guide: Planning for the Second Half of Your Working Life* (Praeger, 2006) and earned a significant contribution recognition from *The Counseling Psychologist* (March 2003).

Kenneth S. Shultz (PhD, Wayne State University) is a professor of industrial and organizational psychology in the Psychology Department at California State University, San Bernardino. He has published two books, most recently an edited book (with Gary Adams) titled, *Aging and Work in the 21st Century* by Lawrence Erlbaum Associates (now Psychology Press). He has also published a half dozen book chapters on various aging and work issues and more than 30 articles on various topics, including mid- and late-career issues, bridge employment, and retirement. He is currently coauthoring a book (with Mo Wang and Deborah Olson) titled, *Mid and Later Career Issues: Psycho-Social Dynamics and Perspectives*, due to be published in 2010 by Psychology Press.

Theresa F. Smith-Ruig (PhD, University of New England) is a lecturer in the School of Business, Economics & Public Policy at the University of New England, Armidale, New South Wales, Australia. She teaches at both the undergraduate and postgraduate level in the areas of human resource management. Her research interests are in the areas of career development and diversity management (with a particular focus on people with a disability). Theresa has published numerous conference papers, journal articles and book chapters, including in *Career Development International, British Journal of Management, Equal Opportunities International*, and the *Journal of Management and Organization.* Theresa has held roles in the banking sector in Australia, as well as numerous management and board directorships of non-profit organizations in the disability sector. Theresa is one of a handful of vision-impaired university academics in Australia.

Sherry E. Sullivan (PhD, Ohio State University) is the research director of the Reed Center for Careers and Diversity and director of the Small Business Institute at Bowling Green State University. She is coauthor (with Lisa Mainiero) of *The Opt-Out Revolt: Why People Are Leaving Companies to Create Kaleidoscope Careers* (2006) and coeditor (with Yehuda Baruch and

Haze Schepmyer) of *Winning Reviews: A Guide for Evaluating Scholarly Writing* (2006). She has published extensively in journals including *Journal of Management, Journal of Applied Psychology, Journal of Vocational Behavior, Group and Organization Management, Career Development International, Academy of Management Executive,* and *Journal of International Business Studies.* She has served as chair of the Academy of Management's (AOM's) Careers Division, on AOM's Gender and Diversity in Organizations (GDO) Board, on the Board of Southern Management Association (SMA), as Treasurer and a Track Chair for Midwest Academy, as Secretary and Track Chair for the Southwest Academy, and as VP and Secretary of the International Division of the United States Association of Small Business and Entrepreneurship. Sherry is the recipient of GDO's Sage/Janet Chusmir Service Award and Southwest Academy's Outstanding Educator Award, as well as being a Fellow of the SMA.

Phyllis Tharenou (PhD, University of Queensland) is a professor of organizational behavior in the Division of Business at the University of South Australia, currently on leave of absence as the executive director of Social, Behavioral and Economic Sciences at the Australian Research Council, an agency of the Australian Federal Government. Her current research interests are in receptivity to international work abroad and at home, self-initiated international careers and repatriation, and gender differences in receptivity to international careers and career advancement. She has published in the areas of managerial career advancement, gender differences in career advancement, training and development, international careers, absenteeism, and employee self-esteem in journals such as in the *Academy of Management Journal, Journal of Applied Psychology, Journal of Occupational and Organizational Psychology, Journal of Organizational Behavior, Journal of Vocational Behavior, Organizational Behavior and Human Decision Processes,* and *International Review of Industrial and Organizational Psychology.*

Ryan M. Vogel (BA, Wilfrid Laurier University) is currently a doctoral student in the Department of Management at the University of Georgia, Terry College of Business. He ran several entrepreneurial ventures before returning to graduate school. His current research interests include person-environment fit, abusive supervision, and role breadth.

Mo Wang (PhD, Bowling Green State University) is an assistant professor in the Department of Psychology at the University of Maryland, College Park. He majored in both industrial-organizational psychology and developmental psychology, with a minor in quantitative methods. His research interests include four broad areas of investigation: (a) older worker employment and retirement, (b) expatriate management and global/

cross-cultural HR practice, (c) application of advanced quantitative methodology, and (d) occupational health psychology. He has received the Academy of Management HR Division Scholarly Achievement Award (2008) and the European Commission's Erasmus Mundus Scholarship Award for Work, Organizational, and Personnel Psychology (2009). Dr. Wang has published his work in prestigious academic journals, such as *Journal of Applied Psychology, Personnel Psychology, Organizational Science, Organizational Research Methods, Psychology and Aging,* and *Journals of Gerontology*. He also serves on the editorial boards of *Journal of Applied Psychology, Journal of Management,* and *Journal of Business and Psychology*. He has been contracted by several Fortune 500 companies and government agencies to provide consulting services in both English and Chinese.

Printed in the United States
153580LV00002B/1/P

9 781593 119577